MY SCOTLAND

MY SCOTLAND

BY
WILLIAM POWER

EDINBURGH
THE PORPOISE PRESS

FIRST PUBLISHED IN 1934
BY THE PORPOISE PRESS
133A GEORGE STREET, EDINBURGH
LONDON: FABER AND FABER LIMITED
24 RUSSELL SQUARE, W.C.1
PRINTED IN SCOTLAND
BY J. AND J. GRAY, EDINBURGH

CONTENTS

THIS book is based to some extent on articles that have appeared during the last few years in the *Daily Record*, the *Glasgow Evening News*, and *The Scots Observer*, and for permission to make use of these I have to thank the proprietors.

W. P.

A GREAT INHERITANCE

GLASGOW'S Buchanan Street is one of the few thoroughfares in Britain, outside London, that have a more than local renown. It runs north from Argyle Street, and its upper portion climbs the ridge of the inner city. Its lower part is cosily handsome, a brief abstract of Bond Street, Lombard Street, and Pall Mall. Its pavements are haunted by the ghosts of merchant princes. The County patronize its shops, and lunch at its club.

But as you ascend the hill, you pass out of the enclave of handsomeness, and enter the broad belt of solidified gloom. At the top of the hill, where the street bends slightly leftward, you have a dim vision of a further height, crowned with dark tenements and queer industrial constructions. In front of you, a few feet above the street level, is a not much glorified shed, flanked by a goods yard, and leading under black, high bridges into a mephitic tunnel. That is Buchanan Street Station, the gateway to Perth and the North, to Callander and Oban and the Hebrides.

It was a quaintly poetic idea to erect this humble portal to paradise in the most horrifically dismal quarter of the city. Buchanan Street Station is symbolic of social history. It was amid such surroundings, the creation of the Moloch of nineteenth-century industrialism, that most of us who were brought up in Glasgow found ourselves imprisoned, shut out by miles of dreary smoky streets from the clean green earth and the horizon stars. It was from amid such surroundings that we had to fight our way out into our own country, into Scotland. The exodus from Cowcaddens—the discovery of Scotland by the youth of Glasgow—is now in full swing. It is the most portentous social phenomenon in the Scotland of our day.

The Clyde coast we late-Victorians knew, of course, and some of us had even spent holidays in South Argyll and on the Ayrshire coast. But these places were, so to speak, in our own terrain. They were a playground extension of westward-facing Glasgow. We had still to link them up with the rest of Scotland.

For ever memorable are the first journeys from Buchanan Street to the North. Through the chemical inferno of St. Rollox we passed, and out into the purgatory of the dull and smudged country to the northeast. The name "Bannockburn" caught the eye. Our pulses quickened. Stirling Castle, the Abbey Craig, the Ochils, the links of Forth, the Grampians. This was Scotland. Our Scotland.

But at Perth we had a reminder of another Scotland, of which we were to have many reminders thereafter. It was the Scotland of the Sportsman's Guide, of shooting-boxes and comic ghillies, of dogs and gun-cases, of Bond Street kilts and the Inverness Gathering; the Scotland to which all the best people in London went "down" at the socially appointed period. That was all funny enough, but the point of the joke became rather blunted when one realized that the Scotland of Mayfair and the sporting-estate agent had eaten up most of the real Scotland. There was not going to be much of it left for the Scots.

A Great Inheritance

My first two or three experiences of the Highlands so saddened and disgusted me that for many years I avoided that half or more of Scotland. The unequalled beauty and grandeur of the scenery only deepened the shame of wholesale surrender to the sporting system. No other race in Europe would have borne it. My wrath was roused by the paunchy fools who strutted in kilts and cairngorm jewellery on the platform at Highland gatherings and prated about bens and glens and heroes. The whole thing was a ghastly and a cruel mockery, and my sense of it was sharpened by visits to countries where the people had clung to the land and had their rights in it confirmed by the State, and where sport was made to subserve the interests of cultivators.

Since the war there has come an awakening and a new hope for Scotland. People like myself no longer find themselves isolated or peculiar. Their views and aims are shared by the vast majority of the younger men in Scotland. They have discovered Scotland, and are going to make it their own country. The Scotland of the future will be Scotland of the Scots.

And so I am now able, with a mind at ease, to enter into my own mental inheritance, and enjoy my Scotland. It is a Scotland of the past, and also a Scotland of the future. The one has no meaning without the other. I see no glory in a Scotland dead and done with as a nation. We entomb heroes, and cover their graves with flowers. We cannot do that with a nation. The nation goes on.

My Scotland of the past is not primarily that of the Jacobites, of Mary Stuart and Knox, the Mortons and

Bothwells, and all the picturesque ruffians who were tearing their defeated country to pieces. My Scotland is that of the patriots and makars and nation-builders; of Columba and Kenneth MacAlpine, Alexander III, Wallace and Bruce, James I and James IV, the Woods and Bartons, Barbour and Dunbar, Henryson and Gavin Douglas, Buchanan and Napier, the Covenanting visionaries and the Darien adventurers, the Gaelic bards from Ossian to Ban Macintyre, Adam Smith and James Watt, Reid and Hume, Ramsay and Burns, Scott and Galt and Hogg, Lord Cockburn and Thomas Muir, Raeburn and Thomson of Duddingston, Henry Bell and the Napiers, the brothers Adam, the brothers Chambers, Chalmers and the Cairds, the Geikies and Dr. W. S. Bruce; not forgetting George Drummond and Patrick Colquhoun, remakers respectively of Edinburgh and Glasgow, and Lord Provost Stewart of Glasgow, who fought down ignorance and vested interests and brought the water of Loch Katrine into the city in 1859.

With the fame and achievements of Scots like these, and of their successors in our own day; with the memories of the countless leal-hearted, kindly, and capable folk of my own race that I have known, in every country-side from Maidenkirk to John o' Groat's; and with my own dreams and plannings for the Scotland that is yet to be, my map of Scotland is filled and humanized. As I close my eyes at night, it shines up out of the darkness, like a brave piper with waving plaid and ribbons flying, sounding a heartsome rallying tune against the Atlantic gale.

As I gaze on this queerly shaped map of my own

country, with all its main features running so persistently from south-west to north-east, as if channelled by the prevailing wind, its detail begins to unfold before me. I see the bare green southern uplands, from Loch Ryan across to St. Abb's; the central plain, with its smouldering cities and towns and black-countries, where, in about one-sixth of Scotland, over two-thirds of the population are huddled; the coastal extension of the plain, to Aberdeen, Inverness, and beyond; the vast confusion of rugged mountain-land that is the Highlands, so strangely divided by the tremendous straight "fault" of the Great Glen; the inner and the outer Hebrides, the Orcades and Ultima Thule, whose inclusion as an "inset" conceals the enormous total length of Scotland, and the fact that our domain includes one of the stormiest reaches of the Atlantic.

Exercising the only perfectly developed sense I possess, that of country, I proceed to a mental survey of my Scotland from south to north. As I come out on the flat waste around Gretna, I am tangibly conscious of all the country to west and north-east. My mind goes over the sweet-scented moorland to Carlyle's Craigenputtock, to Dalry, New Galloway, Loch Dee, and the Dungeon amid the dark Merricks, and on by Cairnsmuir and the Cruives of Cree to the shores of Loch Ryan and Luce Bay. Or it goes up Liddesdale or Annandale to the head of the Tweed basin, to lone St. Mary's silent lake, and Ettrick Kirk and Tushielaw, and round the Eildons to broomy Bemersyde, and down by Kelso to Flodden Field and Berwick.

But the road my mind best loves to travel is up

Nithsdale, past Lincluden Abbey, and Ellisland, the Poet's choice, and Penpont of the preachers, and the lovely valley of the Cairn, and grandiose Drumlanrig, with its once beautiful gardens, and sweet little Durisdeer with its delightfully incongruous Inigo Jones church, nestling up in a fold of the fells, and Kirkbride, "where the Lord's redeemed anes lie". On the right is the gloomy Enterkin Pass, leading over the Lowthers to Leadhills and Wanlockhead, "God's Treasure-house in Scotland".

And now we are in Ayrshire, a great green tableland, rolling down to the shining sea-sands, and the towers and masts of Troon and Ayr. Here, high above the Lugar, is Bozzy's Auchinleck, a Graeco-Italian villa in the hyperborean wilds; and there, on the brow of that hill, is the field where Burns turned up the daisy and the mouse's nest, and saw stretched down before him his whole beloved county. Half-way to the coast is the queerest village you ever saw: a line of high stark houses running up a steep bare hill, with a pretty river at the foot. That is Barbie, a village that lives for ever in the apocalyptic vision of a great prose-poet. As illustrious as Germany's three B.'s of music are Ayrshire's four B.'s—Bruce, Boswell, Burns, and Douglas Brown.

And now the mind goes over the bleak hills into Clydesdale, and round Tinto to the Falls and orchards and the haunts of Wallace Wight, and that forgotten gem of Lowland scenery, Cadzow, lost amid the grime of the Lanarkshire black-country. On the right the hills lower to the grim bitten plateau of south-central Scotland, along whose northern slopes run the Roman

Wall, the Forth and Clyde Canal, and the Edinburgh and Glasgow Railway.

Here the mind becomes conscious, on the one hand, of Edinburgh and the Pentlands, Rullion Green and Swanston Cottage, Roslin and the Moorfoots, Tantallon and the broad Forth, and the red-tiled roofs and red roses of the mellow shores of Fife; on the other hand, of the Firth of Clyde, Argyll's Bowling Green, Arran, Ailsa Craig, and the Road to the Isles by Crinan. But our road lies downward, between the Kilsyth Hills and the Ochils, into the Plain of Stirling. There, on that Rock, within the palace which Cochrane may have carved and where Dunbar sang, the palace of the Jameses, lies the real heart of Scotland.

And so the picture unfolds itself northward. It is singularly clear at the junction of the Highland line, north of Perth. In front is a wooded bluff, the last surge of the Grampians. To the right of it stretches the almost flat farmland of Angus and Mearns, the land of the Picts, running far north-east, past the silver towers of Aberdeen, to the Bullers of Buchan, the well-tilled fields of the Aberdeenshire farmers, and the rich Laich of Moray. To the left opens the enchanted land of Drumalbain. There, by Tummel and Loch Rannoch, lies another Road to the Isles, a wondrous road, lovely everywhere, but loveliest, perhaps, to one who in a September sunset walks down from Kinloch Rannoch by Tummel Bridge and the Queen's View to Pitlochry.

Hereabouts, as a rule, sleep comes, and only in my dreams do I go on by Strathspey to the Cairngorms, and over the Larig Ghru into Deeside, and back by

Glenfeshie to Strathspey, and on by Culloden to
Inverness and Strathoykell, and down by Loch Ness,
where the strains of "Crodh Chaillean" once rang
from the white cottages on the high meadows above
the waterfalls; and on by the Prince Charlie country,
or by Loch Maree and Gairloch, to the haunted peaks
of Skye, and the Atlantic shores of the Outer Isles,
immortally described in Neil Munro's *Children of
Tempest*.

Or I retrace my seven-league steps to Glasgow, and
go north-west by Loch Lomond, tasting the miraculous, swift transition from the tenements and torn
posters and fish-and-chip shops of Clydeside to the
wildwood slopes of the "bonnie banks". At Tarbet,
a pleasing agony of choice assails. I can go over by
Glencroe to Inveraray, and on to Loch Awe, and
round through the fantastically tumbled seaward
Land of Lorn to the Falls of Lora, and Deirdre's
Benderloch, and ghostly Appin and Duror; and from
Oban I can go out to Mull and Ulva, Staffa and Iona,
perhaps the most grandly interesting region in western
Europe. Or from Tarbet I can go up Glen Falloch
and over by Tyndrum and the Moor of Rannoch to
Glencoe. If a choice is forced, I decide for the western
route.

The nearer the western ocean the better, is a good
rule in Highland travel. The only exceptions are the
Cairngorms and Glen Cannich and Glen Affric.
Miraculous is the heightening of beauty as one goes
west into Morar and Moidart. The crescendo is towards the north-west. That man is little to be envied
who does not shout with admiration when he comes

over from Clunie into Glen Shiel, or who is not awed
to silence by the first sight of Loch Torridon, Loch
Hourn, Loch Erriboll, or the Coolins, or those in-
credibly shaped, incredibly hued mountains, Canisp,
Coulbeg, An Stack, Ben More Assynt, or astounding
Suilven.

There are no words in which to describe that scenery
of north-west Scotland, with its sudden depths and
heights, its dreamlike shapes, its wooded chasms and
awesome waterfalls, its contrasts between savage mountains of naked rock and lush straths ablaze with flowers,
its enormous vistas, over great sills and ledges, out to
island upon island in the enchanted sea. Nothing like
it have I seen in any other land. I question if anything like it exists elsewhere. For here is the tumbled
and broken debris of some of the oldest and hardest
rocks in the world, twice or thrice crushed by super-
incumbent sheets of ice thousands of feet thick, and
heaved high at last, to be eroded and chiselled by
water, frost, and storm, in a fashion so defiant of geological conformity that beds of ancient rivers are found
on some of the topmost peaks.

The play of that astonishing scenery upon the
human mind is faintly traceable in some of the old
poems and legends and melodies of the Gael, and in
certain of the intriguing subtleties of the Gaelic temperament. But, for generations, almost the only crea-
tures that have been subjected to its influence have
been deer and grouse, shooting-tenants and gamekeepers. Its effect upon responsive modern minds is
still untried. Even painters have walked wide of it.
The general impression it conveys is like that of the

later music of Beethoven. It holds secrets too profound, too subtle, too terribly beautiful for mere language or mere paint. It has dimensions unknown to
poet or artist. Its influence will not be unfelt by the
Scots who are visiting the north-west in ever-increasing
numbers, or who may settle in its rich straths. It will
express itself in a manifold and indirect manner, in a
deepening and enriching of the whole spiritual nature.
It is the grandest part of my Scotland, and the one
from which I was longest excluded. I possess it as one
may possess the kingdom of heaven; as something
which, while it is within one, retains for ever that
sacred quality of the "wholly other", reminding us
that not in this state of existence can we articulate,
still less realize, the deepest aspirations of our being.

CHAPTER I

RIVERS, FIRTHS, AND PORTS

§ i

WILLIAM DRUMMOND of Hawthornden, the scholarly recluse whose ivory tower above the Midlothian Esk was invaded by that blustering, pedantic, gossiping, strong-fisted, brick-laying, play-building Scoto-English Bobadil, Ben Jonson, was moved, by the visit of King James I and VI to his native kingdom, to write a panegyrical poem entitled *Forth Feasting*.

Drummond is not among the poets who write with their "eye on the object". He was an erudite eclectic. *Forth Feasting* owes its title to Marino's *Tebro Festante*; much of the poem is a paraphrase of a similar poem by Ronsard, and there are suggestions of Pindar and other classic poets, as well as the inevitable mythological "machinery".

Drummond was an exile of the Renaissance, in a country that had refused to "receive" it. Flodden and the Calvinistic theocracy (which he disowned) lay between him and William Dunbar, cutting the line of Scots literary history, and rendering futile, for national purposes, his garnerings in classic, Italian, and French fields. He was like a honey-bee whose hive has been destroyed.

Drayton, in *Polyolbion*, has sung the rivers of England; Spenser, in the *Faerie Queene*, the rivers of Ireland.

My Scotland

But for this convention, it is unlikely that **Drummond's** Forth would have made mention of his brother-streams in Scotland. The laird of Hawthornden made several journeys in England and on the Continent, but his knowledge of Scotland did not extend much beyond the Lothians. Forth's selection of Scots waterways is rather arbitrary:—

> Whate'er beneath Albania's hills do run,
> Which see the rising or the setting sun,
> Which drink stern Grampius' mists, or Ochells' snows:
> Stone-rolling Taye, Tine tortoise-like that flows,
> The pearly Don, the Deas, the fertile Spay,
> Wild Neverne which doth see our longest day,
> Nesse smoking-sulphure, Leave with mountains crowned,
> Strange Loumond for his floating isles renowned:
> The Irish Rian, Ken, the silver Aire,
> The snaky Dun, the Ore with rushy hair,
> The crystall-streaming Nid, loud-bellowing Clyd,
> Tweed which no more our kingdoms shall divide:
> Rank-swelling Annan, Lid with curled streams,
> The Eskes, the Solway where they lose their names. . . .

"Neverne" is the Sutherlandshire Naver, "Leave" the Dunbartonshire Leven, "Ore" the Galloway Urr; the other names are easily recognized.

Why the smooth Tay should be described as "stone-rolling", the amber Don as "pearly", the Spey as "fertile", the Ness as "smoking-sulphur", or the Doon as "snaky", I cannot imagine. Drummond, I expect, was going by hearsay, or primitive maps, and his descriptions are mostly a "nice derangement of epitaphs"—though he seems to have heard of the Falls of Clyde.

Drummond has brought lochs into the picture, but

Irish "Rian" is an inadequate representative of that noble Scots family. He seems to have gone on the "intelligent foreigner's" principle of picking out a river or two in each geographical group.

But why mention Urr and miss out Cree? And why name so many rivers in the south-west and omit noble streams like North Esk, Deveron, Findhorn, Beauly, Oykell, and so forth?

A modern Scots poet would be sorely embarrassed by our wealth of riverine beauty and associations. Besides all the streams mentioned, he would have to admit the claims of Clackmannan Devon, of Fife Eden, of Ugie and Gamrie, of Nairn, Conan, Brora, Lochy, Spean, Coe, Awe, Add, Aray, Echaig, and many more. And there are tributaries as illustrious as any main streams: Teith, Earn, Garry, Tummel, Tilt, Feugh, Bogie, Glass, Massan; the minor streams of Burns-land; Clydesdale's Cart, Kelvin, Luggie, Avon, Nethan, Douglas; Endrick and Blane; and the legend-haunted Teviot, Leader, Ettrick, Yarrow, Manor, Moffat, Bladnoch, and so forth.

A river is merely the ditch or drain of a country-side. But in regions like Western Germany, the Thames Valley, Devonshire, Wales, Lakeland, and all Scotland, rivers are, so to speak, the arteries and veins of history and romance.

In Scotland there is not a tiny burn but has its song literature, its own private scenery, and its channel in the hearts of those who have lived and loved on its banks. Much of the spell of Burns is due to his harmonies of love magic and river magic.

The Border streams have a place in European lyric

poetry beside the famous little rivers of Greece. The elemental romance of our own Clyde has been over-shadowed by shipbuilding, dimmed by collieries, and occulted by "doon-the-water"-ism; yet Clyde has a place in legend and history, and is celebrated in one of the most poignant of ballads, *The Drowned Lovers*, which contains an immortal cry from the secret depths of the Scots heart:—

> O roaring Clyde, ye roar ower loud,
>   Your streams seem wondrous strang!
> Make me your wrack as I come back,
>   But spare me as I gang.

And there is a stream perhaps more illustrious than any—unknown, possibly, to Drummond—the Stirling-shire Carron, whose industrial history is a signi-ficant pendant to a wealth of prehistoric, Roman, Arthurian, Norman-Celtic, and Jacobite associations.

In the window of an Edinburgh shop, I saw a picture of Glen Affric, with the river leaping from pool to pool amid boulders and high rocks crowned with wild-wood, against a background of pine forest and rugged mountains.

Instantly the city vanished. I was aware of nothing but my desire to be standing at the point from which that picture was taken. Happy the birds who dwelt in those branches or flittered from rock to rock, wetting their wings in that water; fortunate the fish that played in those amber pools, or leaped those foaming linns!

Why had I seen so little of those wonderful rivers beyond the Great Glen? What did my heirship of all the ages amount to, if I was not able to transport myself at will to the heart of Glen Affric and the slopes of Mam Soul?

History, politics, economics, and progress, so called, seemed merely a vast conspiracy to keep us from following our heart's desire, and being where we longed to be.

Affric is beautiful above all rivers, but every river has a beauty of its own. My dreams of all the rivers I have seen have made me wish that I could write a book on the rivers of Europe. The most of vital history would come into it.

The Scot has a special interest in the subject, for the Celtic race to which he belongs has named nearly all the rivers of Europe. The names express the primitive poetry with which rivers irrigate our matter-of-fact age.

Strangely various are the careers of the great rivers. The Rhine has a wild birth, and a romantic youth and middle age, but it sinks into flat prose towards the end. Less romantic in its origin, the Danube flows through three capitals, and then passes into a weirdly mournful solitude.

The Seine that winds solemnly amid the sombre forest bluffs of Normandy does not seem the river that reflected the stir and glitter of Paris.

Mountain solitude, pastoral beauty unsung, neglected and despoiled grandeur, orchard and sylvan loveliness yielding to smudge and blight, Glasgow and the shipyards, Rhine-like beauty and oil-containers, Greenock and the glorious mountain-circled Firth—such are the unparalleled vicissitudes of the Clyde.

I am haunted by the wraith of the beautiful main theme of Smetana's *Ultava*, which I heard played by the Reid Orchestra in Edinburgh.

The air was comparatively simple, and it was several times repeated; yet it eludes me—mainly because it has merged with the beautiful idea which inspired it, and which it inimitably conveys—namely, the movement of a noble river, the Moldau, flowing through a beautiful and historic country. Bohemia is the country of one great river, the Moldau, just as Poland is the country of the Vistula, and the old Germany was the Rhineland.

The Danube flows through the heart of several countries, but by the magic of music it has become chiefly associated with Austria. In Johann Strauss's famous waltz the spirit of the Danube and of Vienna has diffused itself throughout the world. Other Austrian composers have deepened the spell; and Vienna has become the dream-city of the European peoples.

Ireland is very nearly the country of the Shannon; and the heart of Scotland is the basin of the Tay.

The Masters of the World were without this central inspiration. It was typical of their unexplained power that lordship over Nile and Euphrates, Danube and Rhine, Rhone and Tagus, Seine and Thames, was wielded from the banks of "the puny Tiber", one of the least inspiring of streams.

A river like Tay or Clyde or Tweed is itself a great symphonic poem, expressing even more moods and phases than are summed up in Matthew Arnold's fine poem on the River of Life, or in the closing lines of his *Sohrab and Rustum*.

The beautiful and busy serenity of large rivers, with their harmony of Nature and man, has never been better depicted than by the old English water-colourists. But the word "river" has also suggestions of raving madness and of suicidal gloom; and what a river may hold of wild terror was brought home to me one winter evening when I wandered down through an orchard towards the flooded Clyde, just below the weir at Stonebyres.

I came on it almost unexpectedly, in a semi-darkness deepened by a black high cliff opposite, and the trees overhead. It was not like water, or anything else. It was a dreadful grey terror, leaping out from the darkness on the right, lashing and rearing and whirling against the wall of black rock, and plunging into a misty void on the left, from whose depths there echoed a perpetual deep thunder.

The person who sees in such a spectacle only a waste of hydro-electric power may be a useful citizen. But he is not the person for whom poets and composers write. And he is not the person for whom the rivers of the world were made.

§ ii

Leith, Middlesbrough, Hull, Garston, Mostyn, Cardiff, Swansea, Newport (Mon.), Goole, Water-ford. Such was the order in which the ports of the British Isles came into my ken.

The order of the Continental and Mediterranean

ports was as arbitrary: Caen, Stettin, Danzig, Stockholm, Kronstadt, Rotterdam, Antwerp, Barcelona, Oran, Genoa, Naples, Patras, Odessa, Galatz. Over the ocean were Newport News, Baltimore, Callao, Los Angeles, 'Frisco, and Portland (Oregon).

And Queenstown and Dunkirk, "for orders".

The catalogue shows the haphazard fashion in which a sailor, or a sailor's son, obtains his knowledge of the world. But the order mattered little. For when I made acquaintance with a few of these ports, and with others, I found that they had strong family resemblances.

Always there was the flashing beam of a lighthouse, like a flaming sword turning in the darkness, and reflected in waves sullenly subsiding; the ringing of the engine bells, and the checking of speed as the pilot came aboard; the resumption of full speed in calming water; whistlings and boomings, and the rattle of rudder chains; forlorn lights of vague low shores, and of vessels looming past; full speed, quarter speed, dead slow; and always the sucking, churning and flowing of strange currents.

And always, next morning, the same smell of dirty water; the familiar set-out of quays, sheds, cranes, trucks, pug-engines, masts, and funnels; the same pathetic eagerness of dock labourers; the journey townward through a labyrinth of railways and bridges, dreary warehouses, slummy streets, and a dusty no-man's-land.

Why docks and quays should be so difficult of access is as hard to explain as the dreariness of the harbour zone. One would think mankind were afraid of the

siren lure of the sea, and tried to cut themselves off
from it by a belt of devastation.

In the inner town, all the spick-and-span apparatus
of civilization. In dockland, pigs' feet and hand-me-
downs, litter and decay, the standards of the kraal.

The contrast perpetuates the tradition of a time
when the "common sailor" was a desperado and an
outcast, the hero of sentimental songs, the victim of
crimps and other harpies, and the special care of the
police.

That tradition did not obtain in old Carthage,
Venice, or Genoa, where argosies anchored before the
palaces of merchant princes, and the jetties were
marble steps. It is being departed from in many
modern seaports, where dockland is included in
municipal improvement schemes.

In massing her finest buildings on the river front,
Liverpool has acknowledged the value of maritime
life as an element in the city noble and picturesque.
She has crowned and adorned her chief activity, and
"married the sea".

When the reformer, John Durie, returned from
exile, he was welcomed at Leith by the whole able-
bodied population of Edinburgh, who marched in
procession up to the city, singing "Now Israel may
say".

That incident gives the suggestion of a modern
Edinburgh with "magic casements opening on the
foam".

Some of us may live to behold an Edinburgh beautiful and romantic to the water's edge, and a Glasgow
that has found the sea and touched the Highlands.

My Scotland

Though I was born in Glasgow and have spent most
of my life there, my earliest maritime memories are
of Leith. At a tender age I voyaged thence to France,
the Baltic, and East of England ports. I have a recollection of the stout little tramp steamers on which
I sailed, of their personnel and cuisine, and the shrinking misery with which I looked out over the grey
North Sea. Particularly do I remember a stout, red-
bearded chief engineer, Mr. Huskie, who counselled
me to sup my porridge and read the works of Robert
Burns. As we approached the Bass Rock he sang, for
my special behoof, "Gae fetch to me a pint o' wine",
and got me to join in the refrain. But of Leith and its
docks I retained no impression.

Yet the Leith docks are rather impressive. They
project boldly into Neptune's domain. The inner-
most steamer sticks her bows up into the Water of
Leith, alongside hotels and ship-chandlers'; the ships
in the outer dock lie clear of the coast-line, with open
water visible on three sides; and at the end of the
breakwater one is right out in the main track of
storms.

Here, when the wind is in the east, there is no
speculation as to the "weather outside". You bump
into it at once, and get your full money's-worth of a
life on the ocean wave.

Leith docks are a marine promenade, and they have
a Continental flavour that is lacking in the West; but
I doubt if they have the romantic attraction for boys
that Glasgow's harbour had in my young days. Somehow the remoteness of Glasgow from the sea lent "a
certain strangeness" to the maritime life of the Clyde.

Rivers, Firths, and Ports

From central thoroughfares that knew nothing of ships or foreign parts, one passed in a few minutes to a "forest of masts" and a grove of funnels, facing outward to New York, Rio, and far Cathay, and linked by the river with perilous seas in faerie lands forlorn. Glasgow harbour was a city of dreams within a city of realities. It was like *Sindbad the Sailor* bound into the middle of *The Wealth of Nations*.

Bridge Wharf had its cherished associations, but these were of a poignant nature if the holidays were newly over. We looked for something remote from the sphere of our sorrow. We found it, to start with, in the old *Fire King* or *Fire Queen*, quaint-looking London traffickers with high bows and funnels well astern.

Farther down were the Dublin boats, the *Duke of Leinster* or the *Duke of Connaught*, big sturdy boats with black funnels behind enormous paddle-boxes. They were survivors of the old type of paddle-boats that crossed the Atlantic and the Indian Ocean. One had often wondered how they did it, with their low-powered engines, their paddles clawing wildly at the steep sides of enormous combers, and the wind pushing up into their clumsy paddle-boxes. But the iron *Dukes* seemed fit for anything.

It was refreshing, not long ago, to meet a man who remembered the old *Waldensian*, one of the fiddle-bowed vessels of the Allan Line. We had talk of other old-time craft: the *State of Nebraska*, which held the blue ribbon of the Clyde till the *State of California* came along; *Ethiopia* and *Devonia*, fine boats in their day, though they gave their passengers a more inti-

21

mate acquaintance with the Atlantic than modern seafarers would relish; and that remarkable steel box, the old *Furnessia*, which used to spend a fortnight in safe but clumsy gambollings with the Atlantic billows.

In the Kingston Dock there were the Cornish sloops and schooners, bringing china clay; in the Queen's Dock were the liners for India, Burma and China, with their coolie life, and beside them the strangers from Spain, Sweden, and Hungary, and the sailing-ships of the Loch and Shire Lines, with an occasional French sailing-ship, giant of her class, carrying nickel-ore from the Pacific.

At the General Terminus Quay was a miscellaneous array of "tramps" loading coal. Some of those vessels were of a smallness now inconceivable. One of them, on which a relative of mine made a voyage as chief engineer to South Africa, did not look bigger than a tug-boat. The increase in the size of vessels has diminished the interest of dock life. The Clyde was livelier when funnels and skippers were more numerous. It must have been livelier still when steamers were still rare and cargoes were divided among hundreds of sailing-ships, many of them captained by part-owners, who held princely state in their beautiful cabins.

"Any for Sawmill Road?" Such was the cry of the gallant crew of *Clutha No. 3* as she swept down the river towards her turning-point at Whiteinch. It is sad to have to explain that the *Cluthas* were little twin-screw passenger boats that used to ply in Glasgow harbour. Once, in a westerly gale, we were battened down off Highland Lane. The *Clutha* pitched dreadfully, and began to ship seas, or sewers, rather. It was dirty weather, literally. Through the port-holes the trembling passengers had a vision of filthy water in violent commotion. It was like a storm in a slop-pail. Black billows and grey foam obscured the heavens. One could hardly have believed that water so thick could be lashed to such a fury.

Dismally overhead sounded the tackety boots of the crew, making all fast. The *Dunara Castle* went by, but our skipper disdained assistance. The black squad in the shipyards ceased riveting to gaze at our poor devoted bark. Amid the drumly spray we discerned Sawmill Road. No landing there to-day. On we plunged and staggered, growing dirtier and dirtier, till at last there was a welcome hail—"Whiteinch!" I made the return journey overland, by tramway car, wondering if my tale of the storm would head off my boss from the subject of my long absence from the office.

A voyage at lunch-time is no longer possible in Glasgow. It is a pity—and I do not like to see a quay shed turned into a garage. To be hurled on wheels is good enough. To float is far better.

An interesting corner of the Kelvingrove Galleries is the one devoted to prints and models of early steamships. There is an engaging ugliness about the earliest specimens, with their tall straight funnels, serrated at the top, behind the high paddle-boxes. The steamer as a separate model, with artistic lines of her own, was long in developing. The first steamers were inelegant mongrels.

The *Comet* and the *Industry* were sailing smacks with funnels and paddles stuck on. Coasting steamers like the ill-fated *Orion* were hideous composites of trading schooners and primitive locomotives. Stiff, short, and high, they looked as if they were stuck in the water, uncertain which was ahead or astern.

Probably it is a Glasgow and Liverpool steam-packet, of a century ago, of which the poop saloon-cabin is shown in a fine old Glasgow engraving at Kelvingrove.

At a table in the foreground, two elderly Glasgow merchants are discussing business over the papers and refreshments. On the right is a funny little domestic group with huge poke-bonnets and redundant drawers. On the left a whiskered young dandy is languidly reclining on the set-in sofa that runs round the cabin. In rear, beside the stair, a steward is mixing a cocktail at the bar. The scene is curiously old—and curiously modern. For long the first-class portion of a steamer was invariably in the poop.

The lines of the full-rigged sailing-ship forced a certain gracefulness upon the early ocean steamers, which began to ply in the late 'thirties of last century. In their design the artistry of Clyde technicians found ideal scope. New forms developed rapidly, and, by the time I was conscious of such things, ocean grey-hounds of the most beautiful models, like the *Alaska* and the *City of Rome*, were ferrying the Atlantic.

Clyde artistry, also, was shown in the development from the ugly *Comet* and *Industry* to the long, thin, raking river-steamers, as swift as they were beautiful, that were built in large numbers at the beginning of the 'sixties. Most of them disappeared from the Clyde to become blockade-runners in America. The river-steamers that were left, like the *Balmoral* and *Vesta*, were small and by no means beautiful.

The new *Jeanie Deans* recalls her old namesake, swiftest and neatest of a motley Clyde flotilla that included *Guinevere*, *Lancelot*, *Elaine*, *Viceroy*, *Sultana*, *Hero*, *Vivid*, *Adela*, *Ivanhoe*, *Meg Merrilees*, *Shandon*, *Marquis of Bute*, *Scotia*, *Benmore*, *Edinburgh Castle*, and *Lord of the Isles*. Round these lovely names fond memories cling, but none of the old river-steamers was half so beautiful as the new cruising vessels like the *Duchess of Hamilton*. She is the perfection of compact and graceful strength; as beautiful as a Bengal tiger, or a sailing-ship in full sail in a spanking trade wind.

In striking contrast with such a miracle of technical artistry—matched by the Clyde-built mail-boats that needle daily and nightly the storms of the Irish Sea, the North Sea, and the English Channel—were the lumbering old tramp steamers like the long-vanished *Alrune*, in which, as a small boy, I voyaged with my father and mother to Danzig.

It was in a stormy September, and a north-west gale caught us as we were floundering light in the North Sea. A tongue of water hissed down the dark cabin stair beside me; a door banged; and my father, in streaming oilskins, caught me up, bedclothes and all, and carried me up to the chart-house below the bridge.

In the leaden dawn, as the boat heeled over, I looked down through the port-hole at the dreadful dish-water of the North Sea, and felt sick with terror —till my father looked in, and the steward, and the first mate, and the chief engineer, to see how the boy was getting on, and I felt ashamed to be afraid in the company of all those fine brave men.

§ iii

Edinburgh turns her back on the Forth. Despite the annexation of Leith, the Scottish capital remains an inland city. The shoreward roads from Cramond down to Joppa have a back-yard aspect. The villa suburb of Trinity stops short of the water's edge. "Sea view" has no allurement here. Leith, though augustly historic, is more sourly grim than Motherwell. It is not the beauty of the Firth that draws crowds to Portobello sands.

All this is passing strange to the Glasgow man, whose keenest regret concerning his own city is that it was not built somewhere below Erskine Ferry.

From Arthur's Seat, the Forth seems a great river, widening towards the east. In city vistas the green hills of Fife look pleasantly near. They have sunk far down by the time one has reached Newhaven. All one sees is a drumly section of the North Sea, with a smallish steamer thrashing dourly out into the void.

The Glasgow man sighs as he thinks of the crescent of mountains and lochs and seaside towns, over from the Cloch; the deep blue water between; the liners, pleasure-steamers, coasters, herring-boats, puffers, and yachts.

Even on a fine day, with a north-west wind, the

Forth has a grey and gurlie look. Even in mist and
rain, the Clyde has charm. The Forth in driving rain
gives one a grue.

Of the clouds of glory trailed across those grey
waters by legionaries, saints, vikings, kings, queens,
prelates, statesmen, legates, soldiers, admirals, reformers, pirates, explorers, the Forth bears never a
trace.

In old days the East Coast was harried by Scandinavian pirates. The Scots clung to their inland howes
and glens, leaving fishing and sea-trade to Flemish,
Dutch, and Danish settlers. Burns inherited the
Pictish tradition; there is as little of the sea in his
poems as in those of Ramsay or Fergusson. The Newhaven fishwife in Edinburgh was like a trader from a
foreign land.

Compared with the Thames, the Humber, and the
dreadful Tyne, the Firth of Forth is beautiful. Its
upper reaches are sheltered by the Ochils, and have
glimpses of the Highland hills. Its Fife coast is picturesque at some points. On its shores are old towns
beloved by artists. There are the famous islands of
Inchcolm, Inchkeith, the May, and the Bass Rock.
But these are not big or high enough to link up Fife
and the Lothians.

The Clyde has scenic unity; the Forth has not. The
Firth of Forth is a dividing feature. In old days, as
the Scottish Sea, it guarded the citadel of the Scots
kingdom at Dunfermline from the English forces that
overran Lothian. It is less an estuary than a pro-
trusion of the North Sea.

In an easterly gale, the steep waves of the North

27

Sea sweep under the Forth Bridge. At such times small craft cannot venture out. A swift tide hinders yachting. Fogs and drizzles are common in winter. In summer there are the haars. The coasts are seldom quite clear.

The Forth does not invite pleasure-sailing. The crowds at the watering-places bathe but do not boat. To sail out of Leith is to cut yourself adrift from Scotland. The waves seem alien. They taste of the Skagerrack.

But here before me, in the fleeting sunshine of the West, lies a broad inland sea, flecked with the white sails of yachts and furrowed by pleasure-steamers. Motor-boats and lugsails and rowing-boats cross it fearlessly; yet the water beneath them is deeper than in the North Sea, and it deepens further in the fjords that stretch far up amid the rugged Highland hills.

The hills that encircle this sheltered sea take on myriad hues as the moist sunlight and the cloud-shadows float across them. Along their base are villas and cottages amid shrubs and trees. At night there is a crescent of lights, broken where the shores are wild and remote, and concentrating at one point in the red glow of a big pier.

There was a sunset last autumn that brought the whole population out to gaze. Vast wings of greenish feathery plumes, tinged with rose, spread out over the heavens. The wings slowly rose and faded, and the sky took on a green light that shone along the crests of the whole range of hills, where white patches of mist were sinking into the hollows. Then, gradually, sky and sea were suffused with wine-red, with the hills black between, and the town and hills that faced the glory were like carvings of gold and amethyst and coral, sunk in a translucent sea.

This wonderful stretch of deep, wide, mountain-circled water extends south for sixty miles. Off the south point of the most beautiful mountain-island in the world, it feels the swing of the Atlantic rollers that travel round the north of Ireland; and the most majestic rock-islet in Europe marks the point where the firth gives place to the open sea.

There is a River Clyde, a fact of which one is unconscious on the Firth. It rises in the southern uplands, and æons ago it was thrust eastward at Tinto, and flowed into the Tweed. But one night the Clyde had a vision; and by next morning, more or less, it had cut a way for itself to the north-west, and was thundering over Bonnington, Corra, and Stonebyres, and hurrying down to reinforce some little streams that flowed into a western system of ice-trenched canyons, now half-filled with sea-water.

This thoughtful action of the Clyde made the existence of Glasgow possible, and it was prophetic of the action of Glasgow in deepening the Clyde and opening up, towards the west, the coal and iron fields of Clydesdale.

A huge centre of trade and of coal and iron industry developed in an inland valley, but towards the mountains and the ocean. The seaward trade of that area passes right amid this lovely system of firth, lochs, sounds, mountains, and islands. Before my window go Atlantic liners, and great merchant vessels for

India, China, South America, South Africa, and Australia.

At other big ports, one creeps out of dock into the open sea; or crawls half-blindly, amid hootings and shoutings, down a long reach of dirty water between low misty shores, whose disappearance and the quickening of the propeller are the only signs that one has reached the sea.

But here, after Glasgow harbour is cleared, the humblest tramp has a day of glorious cruising ere land is cleared. The most disgruntled engineer, coming up on deck off Gourock, may look north to a white strand and white houses at the foot of a big glen, and exclaim, "Yon's Arranteenie!"

CHAPTER II

CITIES AND TOWNS

§ i

So long as my acquaintance with Edinburgh was confined to an occasional visit, I was able to write about the city with fluent confidence. But now that I have lived in it for over a year, I am conscious of my ignorance. Edinburgh as an urban entity seems to have faded from my vision, just as an organism seen under the microscope loses total shape and becomes a mere assemblage of unrelated parts. Nothing so cramps one's style as knowledge.

Edinburgh's history has almost faded out so far as I am concerned. The architectural reminders of it are fewer than I had supposed. The closes in which famous people lived and notable events happened are mostly surrounded by dull modern buildings. The Royal Mile has been denuded of most of its picturesque features, without being redeemed from the slumminess into which the Old Town declined after the gentry had moved out. Apart from the public buildings, the greater part of Old Edinburgh has a gaunt, bleak, or shabby look, where it is not absolutely frowsy. Elsewhere, there is little that carries the mind back to the days of the Scottish nation.

Edinburgh came late into the centre of Scottish history. It has its St. Margaret's Chapel, and its legend of David I and Holyrood. But it is not much associated with Wallace, Bruce, or the early Stuarts. It did not become a real capital till after the assassination of James I. The period thence to Flodden is the most glorious in Scottish annals. It was the period of the makars, of fine architecture, of illustrious foreign visitors, of Scottish military glory in France, of the Scottish Navy. But Edinburgh, somehow, did not gather up into herself the lustre of that age, and she cares so little about it that Scottish history and literature have no place in her university.

It was the disaster at Flodden that roused Edinburgh to self-consciousness. Of her old national monuments, the one that appeals most to me is the Flodden borestane at Boroughmuir, where the Scottish army mustered for doom. What happened in the two centuries thereafter bulks largely in the city's annals. But its lively colours are those of fever and decay. Morton and Albany, Mary and Knox, theocrats and prelatists, Covenanters and Royalists, Montrose and Argyll, Carstares and Dundee, are portents of a nation in wild disintegration. The Scottish nation began to go out of sight not long after Flodden. Edinburgh was never very actively conscious of it, except in the hectic years of Darien. The '45 was a shadow play on a stage empty, swept, and garnished. The literary period that followed seemed to promise an all-round national revival, but the French wars swept Scotland away on a stream of imperialism, and the Scott Monument stands between Edinburgh and a history that has become mere literary romance and the garnishing of guide books.

Cities and Towns

The Old Town of Edinburgh, about the time of Burns's visit, with its microcosmic streets rising vertically from the Rock ridge to dizzy heights, was the most fascinating architectural fantasy in Europe. Its builders left an impress that the dull-minded Victorian Age could not entirely efface. In ideal contrast were the massive classical buildings spaciously ranged in Georgian days along the evenly horizontal ridge on the opposite side of the deep northern valley. That line, the pillars on the Calton Hill at the east end, and the deepening of the smoky valley beneath the Calton Crag, formed a superb set-off to the Old Town, the Castle Rock, and the astonishing massif of Arthur's Seat.

The result of congenially bold building on a uniquely bold site is a wildly varied beauty that defies description and analysis. Shakespeare did not describe Cleopatra. Why should one try to describe Edinburgh? The city as a whole, seen from the Arboretum; the Castle Rock from the centre of Princes Street, in glistering July sunshine, or against a livid thunderstorm; the Castle from over the Meadows, rising like a warm-grey dream from the pearly haze of summer dawn; the westward vista of George Street, closed by the dome, on a wild rainy evening; the lights of Princes Street, at shut of eve, from the top of the Mound; finest of all, perhaps, the view from Calton Hill against a stormy sunset in late autumn, with the lights of Princes Street running straight out to the towered west, the grey-white smoke lying between the dark lines of buildings, and the Old Town heaving high like the forepart of a great ship, rising upon the first huge billow of an advancing tempest: no other city holds visions like these.

In pathetic contrast is the long water-front of Edinburgh, a middenish stretch, with outcrops of picturesqueness at Cramond and Newhaven. The country to east and west is tame, and the suburbs comfortably banal. The south is different. The Grange, Blackford Hill, and the Braids form a striking scenic unit. On the Pentlands, looking into the city, one can taste the solitude of Border hills. The canyon of the Esk between Roslin and Polton has a sombre grandeur. The long glen of the Water of Leith, below the Pentland slopes, is rich in sylvan beauty. And the whole country, for twenty miles round, is starred with demesnes familiar in history, legend, literature, and song. It is Scotland's Attica.

What kind of people should inhabit this city and this region? They should be bold, strong, intelligent, gay, artistic, rich-minded, masterful, enterprising, romantic, and passionately Scottish. Their society should have the same pronounced character, the same variety and also the same unity, as their scenery.

Bold and strong and masterful they are when they are roused to action; keener on vigorous forms of sport than any other people in Europe; intelligent and well educated, particularly in professional matters; enterprising in organization for social welfare; a kindly and efficient folk; romantic on occasion, in a retrospective way; loyal supporters of their churches; and remarkably interested in mostly all subjects that have nothing to do with literature, the arts, or modern Scotland. Socially, they are ranged in strata, cliques, and coteries that have few dealings with one another. There is no Edinburgh society; and the stranger who has lived in the city for a year has nothing on his palate that he can identify as an Edinburgh savour, whether of the upper class, the middle class, or *hoi polloi*.

Yet the stranger likes and admires the Edinburgh people, and has found them kindly and sympathetic; and he is disturbed by this strong taste of nothing in particular, for which his own palate cannot be entirely to blame. Dilution and diffusion must be the causes. Edinburgh is neither a Scottish city-in-itself, like Glasgow, nor a real Scottish capital; nor, as yet, a purely English city. Edinburgh hangs in a neutral region, where purpose and culture wither. The diluting element is English. Edina sends the brightest of her sons out to run the Empire, and brings in many Englishmen to run her own concerns. She keeps her eye respectfully on London. Most of her young advocates speak and comport themselves precisely like English products of the public school. The fine Lothian accent that Stevenson was so proud of is dying.

These are partial and superficial impressions. Certain notable experiences suggest that fundamentally they may be all wrong. That only deepens one's bewilderment. The real fact seems to be that Edinburgh is just beginning to pass out of a long phase in which her metropolitan leadership of Scotland was almost deliberately renounced, and in which she desperately imagined she could find her account in becoming a northern district of London. In becoming conscious of the living Scotland, and of a history that goes back beyond the wranglings of Marians and Knoxians, she is finding her true self, and obeying the suggestions of her unique urban scenery.

§ ii

Novelists and poets who have dealt with modern Edinburgh have been baffled, even the most brilliant of them, by the lack of a general social savour, and have had to concentrate on the delineation of isolated classes and coteries. In Glasgow the difficulty has been all the other way. "Here's richness." The local savour is so strong, so varied, so all-permeative, that the writer finds his powers of characterization and diction inadequate to the rendering of it; and he finds it so easy to bring all kinds of Glasgow people into his picture that he is apt to make his canvas much too big. Even to-day, in spite of rationalization and the English dilution, the inhabitants of Glasgow remain to a very large extent Jock Tamson's bairns.

In the Middle Ages the people of Glasgow were vassals of the Church and the nobles. They banded together for self-protection. The establishment of the university brought the usual hostility between Gown and Town. Down to the time of the tobacco lords in the eighteenth century, the merchants who counted were largely scions of old landed families; the crafts-men were plebeians, most of them natives of the city. Jealousies between them led to Royal regulation of their respective organizations at the beginning of the seventeenth century. Both the Merchants' House and the Trades' House, however, had a share in civic administration. Glasgow was the meeting-place of the General Assembly that renounced prelacy. The whole community were virtually solid in Covenanting sympathy, and the Whig tradition declared itself in strong opposition to the Jacobites.

Glasgow was always democratic, in the American sense; and, after the downfall of the tobacco lords in 1777, the merchants ceased to be in any way aristocratic. Meanwhile, there had been a remarkable *rapprochement* between city and university. Adam Smith acquired the material for *The Wealth of Nations* from the traders of Glasgow, who in 1783 established the first Chamber of Commerce in Britain. It was in the old College that James Watt perfected the steam-engine. The university put brains behind the movement for the deepening of the Clyde, the establishment of technical industries, and the opening up of coal and iron fields. From lectures voluntarily given by Glasgow professors to working men arose the Technical College.

Irish immigration, over-rapid development of trade and industry, and the spirit of anti-social greed made Glasgow in the first half of last century a hell of slums, smoke, poverty, and disease. But the spirit of communal self-help declared itself in the bringing of water from Loch Katrine, the formation of a city improvement trust, and the rebuilding of the university on Gilmorehill. The great evangelistic movements of the 'thirties and the 'seventies seemed to intensify the smug God-and-Mammonism that was one of the city's objectionable features, but the working of the leaven resulted at length in a reinforcement of benevolent and remedial agencies.

My Scotland

Even in the darkest trough of the industrial era, Glasgow never lost the sense of communal solidarity. It shines out in *Glasgow Past and Present*, the finest of the many volumes that make up the remarkable literature of "Glasgow books". Glasgow's wealthiest families might creep farther and farther away from the city, till they disappeared over the horizon to Edinburgh, the "County", or the hunting shires of England; but Glasgow always remained Glasgow.

Glasgow, Scotland's Genoa, with her Westland Whig tradition, and with her trading interests over the western main, had tended to turn her back on the rest of Scotland. She was confirmed in this attitude by the jibes of Lockhart, Aytoun, and other smart young Tory snobs. But it was in Glasgow, not in Edinburgh, that Lockhart found the subject of his immortal character-sketch, *Captain Paton's Lament*. By the middle of last century, however, Glasgow had become un-Scottish to the point of adopting London slang and aping London ways. The comedians admired by her young men were London favourites, like the famous Lloyd. Only in a few of the free-and-easies did Scots song and the Doric survive.

Then came a curious awakening, exemplified by songs like "Ta Clerk in ta Offish". It seems to have arisen somehow out of the clash of Highland, Irish, and native elements; and one cannot forget the "Turnimspike" of the previous century. In Glasgow the "Scotch comic" emerged, attaining almost at once a height of genius in J. C. Macdonald, first of a Glasgow line that includes Neil Kenyon, Sir Harry Lauder, Tommy Lorne, Will Fyffe, and George West. The

"South-Side Pantomime" became an annual feast of local humours, jests, and locutions. The Glasgow "genius" expressed itself also in cleverly written and illustrated weeklies like *Quiz* and *The Bailie*. Then came J. J. Bell's *Wee MacGreegor* and Neil Munro's *Erchie*, and the Scottish Historical Exhibition of 1911, which led to the founding of the Chair of Scottish History and Literature in Glasgow.

The interest of this remarkable little history, to which there is nothing corresponding in Edinburgh, is that, so far as one can see, it was the real beginning of what is called the Scottish literary renaissance, if not, indeed, of the Scottish national movement, which had its focus in Glasgow. In becoming humorously conscious, Glasgow had roused Scotland to consciousness. In Glasgow itself there were the city novels of William Black and Frederick Niven. To-day Glasgow is represented in Scots literature by some of our best dramatists and novelists. A curious paradox is that the city of Dunbar and Scott has a Chair of Celtic, but not even a lectureship in Scottish History and Literature, whereas the purely Celtic city of Glasgow has only a lectureship in Celtic.

Glasgow is usually thought of as an ugly city. Its centre contains some handsome buildings, but they are too closely massed; the outlying tenement quarters are dull and dreary beyond description; the slum districts are ghastly; and everywhere there is evidence of the lack of aesthetic control. A city can scarcely be beautiful unless it wants to be beautiful. The visitor who is introduced to Glasgow by way of St. Rollox, Parkhead, or Polmadie gets an impression of unrelieved horribleness which he finds it hard to remove.

Yet Kelvingrove Park is a magnificent piece of urban scenery; and everywhere, but particularly along the docks, there are glimpses that make one less forlorn. An Italian landscape artist who came to Scotland not long ago in search of subjects, discovered that Glasgow was far richer in material than Edinburgh. Edina is too much of a made-up picture in herself for the artist's purpose: he can add little to it, and there is nothing he can find out for himself. In the fortuitous groupings of a great riverine city like Glasgow, with its infinitely varied life and its changeful western atmosphere, the artist finds marvellous gleams of beauty, unexpected and unadvertised, and touched with a wistful nobility, a spiritual pathos. In Edinburgh I have seen little that I should hope or wish to make spiritually my own by drawing or painting it; but in Glasgow's Port Dundas I could find twenty good subjects.

Glasgow in 1901 is the title of a well-known book by James Bone and A. H. Charteris, with drawings by Muirhead Bone. The year, that of the great Glasgow Exhibition, was well chosen. Then, or very shortly thereafter, Glasgow reached the height of its prosperity, and the apogee of its career as a self-centred city, facing out to the Seven Seas, and little regardful of its Scottish hinterland. In the days of economic depression since the war, Glasgow, with over a third of its population dependent on some form of public aid, has faced round to Scotland. In the heyday of its prosperity it was a famous art centre, buying Corots and Monticellis and

Marises and Boudins, and producing the Glasgow
School, the most notable group of Scots painters since
Raeburn and Wilkie.

Thus did the technical genius of Glasgow flower into
art. Painters require wealthy patrons. They exist no
longer, or their spare cash is being expended on rural
dwellings and motor cars. But Glasgow has become
a literary centre, with writers like Principal Rait, Professor Macneile Dixon, Professor Mackie, John Brandane, James Bridie, George Blake, Robins Millar,
William Jeffrey, Campbell Nairne, the Reids, Robert
Craig, G. P. Insh, Adam Kennedy, and many others.
No longer do her literary lads o' pairts slip away to
London as a matter of course. They are bound by
cords of affection to their own city, where, also, the
newspapers afford them a journalistic basis. They are
strongly nation-conscious, and the increasing inter-
relations of Glasgow and Edinburgh writers have
helped to bring the two cities nearer each other for
Scottish purposes. It is no longer quite true that the
shortest route between Edinburgh and Glasgow is via
London.

My fancy has played with the idea of a successive
interchange of populations between Edinburgh and
Glasgow. The effect on both cities would be salutary.
The Glasgow deportees would come back resolved to
re-plan and rebuild their own city, clean its atmosphere, and make the Kilpatricks a public park. They
would not lose their native savour, and they would
make Edinburgh exchange its own strong taste of
nothing in particular for the flavour of a Lothian town
and a Scottish capital. It would be something to the

purpose if there were late trains between the cities, and if Edinburgh took its rightful place in the first division of the Association football league.

§ iii

The traditional estrangement of Edinburgh and Glasgow is not surprising. Geographically, they are cut off from each other by something more impassable than a mountain range or an ocean strait. The journey "through" is swift and comfortable, but a great part of it is amid a scenic void that has the effect of a lapse into unconsciousness in the middle acts of a play.

Half an hour ago I was distinctly in the land of Jock Howieson, where red-tiled farms look down to the Forth and up to the Pentlands. Now I feel the touch of Glasgow and the West. But of what lay between, I have no clear mental picture.

It is like a queer enchantment. Something of the kind must have befallen Thomas the Rhymer when he passed to and from the realm of Faerie. Something not unlike it happens in Hogg's *Confessions of a Fanatic* and in Cazotte's *Diable Amoureux*.

The void is longest and deepest on the old Caledonian line. It begins on the Glasgow side of Shotts, and extends almost to Midcalder. Breich, Addiewell, Fauldhouse suggest nothing but a dreadful prolixity of dark, sodden, moorland slopes, with a few pit-heads, miners' rows, and stunted trees. In heavy rain it is worse than the wilderness traversed by Milton's Fiend or Browning's Childe Roland.

Cities and Towns

The old Edinburgh and Glasgow route is beautiful in places, with heartsome outlooks on hill and mountain, and it follows a track known to history since Roman days. Yet in some ways it is the most elusive route of all.

There is a hiatus even between Edinburgh and Linlithgow. On the other side, confusion begins east of Lenzie. Dullatur, with its citified terrace, does not relate itself clearly to Castlecary (home of Hector Macneil's "Mary") or to Bonnybridge. Buses ply between Glasgow and Falkirk, but their route I do not mentally "see".

As for the country between Linlithgow and Falkirk, that is a blank in my Scotland. From Polmont one goes down to beautiful Bo'ness, and from Manuel (there was a Byzantine Emperor of the name) one penetrates to Slamannan, deep in the prehistoric province of Manann.

To me these names are as mystic as Ctesiphon, Ecbatana, or Balkh. Yet there was once a public school, Blairlodge, near Polmont.

There is an old two-story house at the edge of a field on the north side of the Edinburgh and Glasgow line. I have noticed it since I was a child, yet I cannot fix its position: so little impression does the route make on the mind.

The ugliness, or featurelessness, or topographical indefiniteness of the country between our great Scots cities has had an unfortunate effect on our history. Had the country been picturesquely beautiful, there would have been an extension of "dormitories" from both ends; Edinburgh and Glasgow would have met

43

on golf courses and tennis courts, and exchanged ideas and influences.

There would have been no imagined division of interests. There would have been a fruitful unity of Scottish purpose.

The spectacle of the sister cities avoiding each other's gaze, and looking fixedly to London, is ludicrous—and tragic. Is the dreariness of the country between them a cause or an effect of the estrangement?

Anyhow, I vote we bring our will to bear on the matter, and beautify and humanize that mystic mid-region. Let us afforest the Shotts-Fauldhouse wilderness, restore Linlithgow Palace, and build a swagger hydro, with a super golf-course, at Polmont. It is time we broke the divisive spell of Merlin, the old wizard of Manann.

§ iv

Edinburgh is the only large British city in which ideal use has been made of an ideal site. Glasgow's not very favourable site suggests to an architect a row of handsome buildings along the river, with broad boulevards and squares, opening on the north side into broad avenues leading up to the "drumlins", or clay hills, which would have gardens on their slopes, and churches, public buildings, and fine terraces on their crests. Such a plan was beyond the imagination of nineteenth-century Glasgow. But Glasgow did better than Dundee.

From the slopes of Dundee Law one looks east to the sandy narrows and the North Sea, south over the water to the green hills of Fife, and west up the fertile

Carse of Gowrie and the lake-like widening of the Tay to the Perthshire mountains. Over this majestic site the Dundonians of last century haphazardly distributed jute mills, offices, warehouses, churches, mean tenements, trim terraces, and cottages of gentility. At the centre was an ancient graveyard, the Howff, flanked by newspaper offices.

There had been a medieval city, with many fine old churches, monasteries, and mansions, but all of these were swept away to make room for the products of crude industrialism. Dundee, when I knew it first, had the look of a village that had swollen into a slummy manufacturing town.

Yet there was something rather cosy about the centre of Dundee. Reform Street was like a junior Buchanan Street. Even in those days, Dundee was famous for its restaurants. The esplanade and the docks, with the ferries and the grand sweep of the Tay Bridge, made up for the meanness of the inner city. Dundee was a good place to live in, provided one could live out of it, in the west end or towards the Sidlaws, or over in Newport, or down in Broughty of the palaces, a Pollokshields *sur mer*.

Dundee, like Glasgow, was a real community, the centre of the universe for its inhabitants. It is said that the editor of one of its newspapers, many years ago, instructed his assistant to the following effect: "Crowns and thrones may perish, kingdoms rise and wane, and you may safely take no notice. But if a Dundee man tears the seat of his trousers at the Cape of Good Hope, for Heaven's sake give it a half-column!"

Perhaps it was the influence of Thomas Hood, who

45

spent part of his youth with relatives in the city, or of the Rev. George Gilfillan, that famous discoverer of literary swans who turned out geese, that made Dundee a famous centre of journalism. There was a time when nearly every big newspaper in Britain was edited by men who had been trained in Dundee. That distinction was afterwards shared by Aberdeen. Dundee's most typical intellectual product was the *People's Friend*. It is balanced to-day by the *Scots Magazine*, which combines a high literary standard with popular appeal.

With a staple industry that employed women mainly, so that in many houses the wife was the bread-winner and the husband the housekeeper, Dundee was the despair of the eugenist and the sociologist. Conditions have improved of late, but the effect of labour-saving machinery in the mills will make the problem of unemployment more acute than ever.

A new Dundee is emerging, clean, handsome, and well planned. It is being built out of the well-invested savings made in days of prosperity. Dundee's well-off citizens have developed a social sense. The city is organizing for the future. Its College is becoming the most important part of St. Andrews University. When its theatre reopens, and it shares with Edinburgh and Glasgow the support of the Scottish Orchestra, Dundee will have become a real city.

§ v

If the Granite City were disposed by a master-planner over the site of Dundee, all the world would come to see it. It would be of cities *a per se*. The site between the mouths of Dee and Don is not imposing. Only from the sea or from the beach can one have anything like a *coup d'œil* of Aberdeen.

Aberdeen is a miniature Edinburgh. Union Street is a blend of Princes Street and George Street. The railway runs across the city at the bottom of a dell, overlooked by a fine art gallery. But Edinburgh has no modern building so imposing as Marischal College. The beach is a decided improvement on Portobello. Old Aberdeen, with the lantern-towered King's College, St. Machar's Cathedral, and the mellow houses of the Chanonry, all beautifully clustered near the Brig o' Balgownie, is unique in Britain. It is a precious relic of the old Scotland.

Aberdeen has come to depend almost entirely upon fish and education. Her "supporters" might be a haddie and a professor. The combination is appropriate, since fish is a brain food, and trawling is a virile accompaniment to scholarship. The fish market and the dispatch of the fish train are great sights, finely set off by the astonishing collection of old books in the gallery of the general market.

But there is also Aberdeen county, the most notable region in Scotland, comprising the best cultivated farmlands in Britain, and some of the grandest mountain and river scenery in the west of Europe. It is about half an hour's journey by bus from Aberdeen to Banchory, and a few minutes' walk thence over the Dee and up to the Brig of Feugh, where a splendid Highland river, amber-coloured in spate, races loudly down over boulders amid pine forests from the Grampians. Beyond, and within easy reach nowadays, are Lochnagar, the linns of Muick and Dee, Ben Macdhui and the Larig Ghru.

No wonder that I, reared far within the dark industrial ergastula of Glasgow, was filled with amazement when I first beheld Edinburgh, Dundee, and, particularly, Aberdeen. This was not life real and earnest. This was not soul-discipline. To live and work and earn your living within sight of ocean, forest, and mountain, with the heather almost at your door, was semi-holidaying. It was an evasion of one's teind to hell.

The Aberdeen story is a quaint ironic bluff, invented by the Aberdonians themselves. Scots literature was born in Aberdeen. Barbour's *Bruce* is the literary fruit and expression of Bannockburn and the Arbroath declaration. Aberdeen thrift was the necessary sacrifice to freedom and the things of the spirit. It was the defence against economic servitude. Note how Aberdeen escaped the Babylonian doom of the factory system. Her sons could reap the harvest of earth and sea, and cultivate literature on a little oatmeal, seasoned with an occasional haddie. They have been careerists in the noble sense, ambitious of distinction in arms, administration, science, literature, journalism, art, divinity, and scholarship. They chose professions in which danger, strain, or intense toil was certain and the monetary rewards inconsiderable. I have yet to hear of an Aberdonian of any mental account who went into a business because of the money that could be made in it. The building of the city in granite is symbolic. Aberdeen has always chosen the hard and noble way.

Aberdeen, even more than Edinburgh, has been the brain-centre of Scotland. She has been our citadel against industrialism and mass-production. If she has tended to look past Scotland to London and the regions beyond, it is not because of Balmorality and the shooting tenant, but simply because a spiritless and provincialized Scotland could not give scope for the highest aptitudes. The real test of the Scottish Nation will be its ability to make the right use of Aberdeen.

§ vi

Perth is famous for dye-works, whisky, and office ink. There are also the Perth Sales. At Perth the Scottish nobles committed the dastardly crime that evidenced their determination not to let Scotland live. There was a queer echo of it in the Gowrie Conspiracy. At Perth, under the eyes of Knox, the destruction of "Popish images" began; and Perth has vied with Dundee in the obliteration of historic architecture. In the railway age, before the advent of "the car", Perth station was the gateway to the "Scotland" of Mayfair and the Sportsman's Guide. I retain a dim vision of gun-cases and leashed dogs, robust women in smart tweeds and with high-pitched Belvoir voices, and large men in fore-and-aft caps, loud jackets, and brand-new kilts, hurrying out of the refreshment-room and screwing the stoppers on to their flasks as they glanced at the clock-dial indicators and made their way to the Highland Railway train, with its green-painted straight-sided carriages and its handsomely verdant engine. The Glorious Twelfth.

Such a record is scarcely good enough for a city that lies at the head of navigation on Scotland's noblest river, at the meeting-point of Lowland and Highland, near the fork of the roads for Aberdeen and Inverness. Perth was the preordained capital of Scotland. At Scone, on the Stone of Destiny, the Scottish Nation came into existence. It was a Celtic nation. Bannockburn, as Mr. Evan Barron has shown, was a Gaelic victory. But the age-long struggle, hard to define, between Celtic and Norman polities had already begun. Scotland failed to retain the loyalty of the people to whom she owed her Christian civilization and her very existence. She harried them into barbarism. The atrocious gladiatorial combat on the North Inch of Perth was a confession of failure. It wrote the doom of Perth. The city that should have been the crucible of Scotland's races and cultures became merely a "mark" of Normanism against "the wild Highland-man".

So, as Chaucer would have put it, "there is no more to say." Perth's sense of the destiny she has missed has been signalized now and then by conventions of various sorts, and by sporadic publishing enterprises. The national sentiment is stronger there than in Dundee or even Edinburgh. When Scotland reads aright the index of industrial unemployment, and colonizes the now empty North-West, the centrality of Perth may reassert itself. Perth may even become, some day, the focus of a new Scottish culture, in which

the Gaelic, Norse, and Teutonic elements will at last
be harmoniously blended.

§ vii

Were I a multi-millionaire, I should be in little
doubt as to what to do with my money. The
greater part I would devote to the establishment of a
colonizing scheme on co-operative lines in Argyll
and Inverness-shire, with the proviso that Gaelic
should be taught in all the schools and used in all
lessons. With the remainder I would found a Gaelic
University, with colleges at Inverness, Oban, Dunoon,
and Portree, and a summer-school on Iona.

Inverness and Dunoon are regarded by some Gaels
as hopeless. That would be my reason for making them
strong centres of Gaelic instruction. It would afford
me stern joy to counter the anti-Gaelicism of education
committees.

MacGonagall would probably have described Inverness as a town "most beautiful to be seen"; but, apart
from the river and the islands, there is little of real
beauty about it. So far, both in Scotland and Ireland,
the Gael's notion of a town is a composition of castle,
jail, and tenement slum, with no paint. Drogheda is
the archetype: it is an ideal setting for an execution.
Clach-na-Cudain had not attained that height of
development when it was Anglified. The Gaelic touch
is in the rather sour acceptance of dull Victorian monu-
mentalism, which has become duller with age. The
seaward fringe is dismal. The suburbs are pleasant
but undistinguished. The Castle Hill imposes a certain

beauty. But it is on the abode of the dead that beauty is lavished. Tomnahurich is the most wonderful of Scottish cemeteries.

In Inverness, when I first saw it, two human streams were visible: the bright stream of touristism, bound for the north and west; and the dull undertow of semi-loaferism, the dregs of the sporting system, of which Inverness was the centre and the sink-hole. A healthy element was supplied by the railway works. These are virtually gone. Yet the spirit of the town has improved. The Highland bus services are not used mainly by visitors, but by the people themselves. They are making Inverness their real capital, and are beginning to enjoy their own country.

That a leading solicitor in Inverness should become Provost, learn Gaelic, write a manual of Scottish self-government, and identify the cause of the Gael with that of Scotland, would have seemed incredible to the Inverness of forty years ago. Sir Alexander Mac-Ewen typifies the new Inverness, the town of Evan Barron, the historian; of Neil Gunn, the novelist; of Dr. D. J. Macleod, who has introduced modern Scots Gaelic to Europe; and of others who are making Inverness not only the capital of the Highlands but a centre of national and international culture. In their persons a Gaelic University already exists. They are not conspicuous at the Inverness Gathering.

When I think of Oban, I see the MacCaig Coliseum on the hill. In forbidding its completion, the law showed its usual lack of imagination. We shall never know what a MacGillivray might have made of those statues of the MacCaigs that were to have filled the niches. Apart from Dunollie Castle, which it well balances, the MacCaig ruin is the only architectural feature of interest in Oban. A brightly neutral sea-front masks the huddle of banal structures thrown down amid the seaward bluffs of this strangely twisted Land of Lorn.

When hydro-electric development in the Highlands was talked of, one had visions of electrified farms and crofts, and of interestingly varied industries in pretty, brightly lit towns. But it seems that the powers of the firmament and the mountains have been harnessed only for one purpose. The Highlands are to go on making aluminium for ever and ever. That is rather a dull prospect, and one is not reconciled to it by the townships that have sprung up. Fort William, as it persists in calling itself, is like a smokeless Wishaw; and it is remarkable how the grandest natural features fail to neutralize the ugliness of an industrial town. The Parthenon in Motherwell would be of no avail, but a coal-pit, a jam factory, and a chemical work would wash out the Mer de Glace, and make Mont Blanc look like a bing.

It is the more remarkable, therefore, that in the district around and between Oban and Fort William there has been a spontaneous movement to revive Gaelic culture. Here and there one comes upon a little school where a young woman teacher—dark and Celtiberian mostly, and of crofter parentage—is doing her best, without any official encouragement, to keep alive the language and the spirit of her race. These are the true heroines of Gaeldom, against whom the MacGradgrinds shall not prevail.

53

Another heartsome feature is the forestry holding, where the new agrarianism is rooting itself in a setting that affords economic balance and appeals to the imagination of the Gael. When I was told by daughters of the house on these holdings that they had no wish to return to the city, and that papers, radio, and an occasional bus jaunt to Oban gave them as much of the outside world as they wanted, I felt that a great tide was beginning to turn.

Little towns in the far north put up dramatic teams that carry off the first prizes at big festivals. Stornoway, which has a famous academy, is to have a combined theatre and cinema-house, with up-to-date equipment, restaurant, lounges, and so forth. What does Stornoway require of Glasgow or London? What would Inverness and Oban require, if they applied themselves to self-development? They would find an absorbing interest, and refute the racial theorists, if they made the Gaelic genius express itself in planning and architecture.

§ viii

East and West mirror each other curiously in central Scotland. The Ochils, with Dollar Glen, Rumbling Bridge, and the Devon linns, are balanced by the Campsies, with Campsie Glen, Finnich Glen, the Pot of Gartness and the Loup of Fintry; Loch Leven by the Lake of Menteith, both associated with Mary Stuart; the Lothian Esk by the Clydesdale Avon; the Water of Leith by the Cart; Edinburgh Castle Rock by Dunbarton Rock; the Bass Rock by Ailsa Craig. The balance of towns has been disturbed by corn, coal, and trade. Dalkeith and Hamilton, ducal towns inhabited largely by miners, are singularly like each other. But even an amalgam of Dunfermline and Kirkcaldy would scarcely reproduce Paisley.

Paisley, which was a creation of the Celtic Church and of the family of feudal "in-comers" afterwards known to history as the Stuarts, commemorates a notable fact which was forgotten when the Anglo-Saxon superstition was foisted upon Scotland over a century ago.

The Scottish kingdom, reversing historical tradition, was formed in the West, and spread by conquest to the East and South-East. Its successive early stages were Kintyre, Crinan, Lorn, Inverness, and Scone. Thereafter it hovered between Dunfermline, Edinburgh, Perth, and Stirling. In the dire struggle after the death of Alexander III, it fell back upon the West. Wallace was the Knight of Elderslie, a mile or two west of Paisley. Bruce, Comyn, and Baliol were west-country nobles, inheriting the powers of Celtic ancestors. Bruce found his main support in the Gaelic west and north.

The great Renfrew and Paisley family who were High Stewards of Scotland, and who obtained the crown by marriage, were not Norman, but Breton, hailing from Dol. The point is not without interest in relation to the character of the Stuarts; for the Bretons, the southern Celts, are dark, passionate, and artistic. The Stuarts were of the same race as the Strathclyde Britons who were their vassals around Paisley. The Norman feudalism for which they stood was challenged by the Gallo-Norse Somerled, who met his death at Renfrew.

Thus Paisley Abbey, the Lamp of Renfrewshire, now gloriously restored, stands even more authentically for Scots history than the Abbey and Palace of Dunfermline. The pity is that, in the great period of the Jameses, the West was neglected by the Court and its cultured circle. The nemesis was the sour anti-Royalism, anti-aestheticism, almost anti-Scottishness, that displayed itself in the West from Langside onward. The West had become dull and morose. Paisley on the eve of the Age of Reason burned six poor wretches on a charge of bewitching Christian Shaw of Bargarran, who afterwards introduced the manufacture of thread into Paisley.

Then came the age of the weavers, supplying packmen and Glasgow oversea traders. Paisley became famous for her muslins, gauzes, and shawls. The weavers were a hungry and a brainy folk, reading and composing at their looms, bird-nesting and ornithologizing when trade was slack, and discussing the affairs of the universe at their meetings. They wrote many of the poems included in *The Harp* of *Renfrewshire*. Tannahill, Alexander Wilson, John Wilson ("Christopher North"), and Motherwell were the best-known of a long line of Paisley poets.

One evening, many years ago, as I was walking into Paisley from Renfrew, I resolved to test the legend of Paisley poets. I stopped the first man I met, an elderly, decent-looking workman, and began a conversation that led round to the question, Was he a poet? He was, and his bent was Biblical. I remarked that the

Raising of Lazarus was a likely subject. He had written a poem on it, and would send me a copy! I believe he sent it, but of its quality I remember nothing.

For all these reasons, and because of the Coats Church, the museum and art gallery (where there is a remarkable picture of Paisley notables by James E. Christie, a Paisley man), and the mellow old buildings about the observatory, I have spent many a wet Saturday afternoon in Paisley, and have dragged down to it many people who were surprised to find that thread-making was not Paisley's sole distinction.

Old historic distinction shines out through the industrial drabness of Paisley. It has a core of characteristic handsomeness; even its thread-mills are handsome; and improvement is opening out a stately beauty. Paisley must never allow Glasgow to swallow her up. She has a destiny of her own to fulfil, as Scotland's Düsseldorf.

§ ix

The narrow main street is busy with "through" traffic, and crowded for the time of day. Most of the men are walking slowly, with hands in pockets; their lack-lustre eyes do not seem to light on anything in particular. Groups of them are standing in front of a massively dull church that looks down into a gloomy square, through which one has a glimpse of grey-blue water. They seem to be waiting for something that never comes, and of which they have given up hope.

The square and the narrow main street are over-

shadowed by a solidly ornate town-house, with arch-
ways and piazza and a handsome tower, soaring high
above the town roofs, and forming a landmark for many
miles round. In contrast to this monument of civic
opulence, many of the houses in the street are old and
mean, with small windows, decaying grey stone, and
triangular cornices.

On the right, frowsy streets run up steeply, showing
vistas of an upper quarter, a walled and bastioned
public park, and vividly green hills. As one continues
eastward, a stillness falls, where noise and bustle ought
to reign. Only three funnels are visible in the repairing-
slips, the stocks are empty, the cranes and gantries idle,
the yards and foundries shut and deserted.

At a corner is a huge bar, relic of pre-war prosperity
and war-time activity, with elaborate fittings and an
imposing array of picturesquely labelled bottles on
mirrored shelves. The three customers at the long
counter are contenting themselves with "half pints".

Nearly opposite is a fairly large dock. A low line of
buildings on one side of it, comprising a public-house
and marine stores, is labelled "West India Breast".
The Indies, East or West, are unknown to the two or
three puffers and old paddle-tugs that occupy the
dock. On the quays men are sitting or lying about
reading, or not reading, newspapers.

But what is this large monumental edifice of mellow
greyish-brown stone and pre-Victorian majesty, with
fluted columns massive as those of the temple at
Segesta, and frowning Doric entablature? It is the
Custom House. Smaller than the famous one at
Dublin, and less tomb-like than the one at Liverpool,

it is an average sample of the imposingly classic structures that the British Government erected throughout these islands in Georgian days, when the New Town of Edinburgh was being built.

Involuntarily I doffed my hat as I went up the broad steps. I felt that a lustration would have been in keeping. But this was only a minor office of some kind, with one clerk in a big room and a staircase that led to a blank door. The main entrance, classically small, was in front. I went through a narthex, or something of that sort, and found myself in a big central hall with a glass dome and a broad staircase with iron railings. High up in the yellow-painted walls were arched niches, meant, perhaps, to be filled by statues of lamp-bearing deities, or of eminent Commissioners or Collectors.

The whereabouts of the various officials and offices were indicated in large white letters on a blackboard. The Receiver of Wreck might have had a thrilling tale to tell, but I didn't feel bold enough to approach him.

There was a Long Room—long in all dimensions—in which a few clerks could be discerned, enjoying the fine view of the firth through the high windows. The Still Life effect was relieved by the passage of a young man, with papers in his hand, from one room to another. I might have asked him what lay behind the numerous arched doors marked "Private", giving the place the air of Bluebeard's castle; but I suppose his lips were sealed.

What specially intrigued me was a large arched double door marked "King's Warehouse". I sniffed at it, but there was no aroma of anything dutiable.

Perhaps it contained doubloons and pieces-of-eight of the late Captain Kidd.

Reverently I went forth from this hall of mystery and mausoleum of defunct commerce. A fitting adjunct to it was a coeval building close by. Beside one of its ancient doors was a long list of shipping lines represented within. Forcing open the door, I had a weird glimpse of a plastered steam-pipe, an antique heater, and a narrow stair. Ghosts are about the only things I am not afraid of—but my nerves gave way. I walked off quickly, past frowsy old buildings, poor struggling shops, an old marine hotel, and up across the main street to the public park on the flat-topped ridge.

On the seats and on the grass were men, mostly middle-aged or elderly, reading and rereading papers, or smoking. The view below them of the town, the bright firth, and the blue Highland hills, was magnificent; but to them its very brightness in the June sunshine was a mockery. Only a few of the factory chimneys were smoking; the shipyard region was silent.

At the other end of the town were broad avenues lined with trees, and the gardens of handsome villas, representing mainly what bankers call "old money", money no longer circulating at the local industrial end. Farther along the shore the holiday crowds were parading, bathing, motoring, hiking, rowing, shopping, eating ice-cream; splendid pleasure steamers, crowded, with bands playing, were dashing to and fro on the sparkling Firth. All was gay. Nobody wondered where the money was coming from.

And in the public park of the old town, those men

were wandering about like forgotten ghosts on the banks of Styx—wandering round and round the handsome granite war-memorial. "Their name liveth for evermore." And are they not to be envied who are spared this sight of their native town, and of the land for which they died?

CHAPTER III

STORM, SUN, AND SHOWER

§ i

WHEN, after spending half a lifetime in a big commercial city, with only holiday glimpses of rusticity, I went to live in the country, I made some surprising discoveries.

I found that the sun shone in winter as well as in summer, and that Nature, in our country, is never really fast asleep: autumn and spring overlap. I found that hares, hedgehogs, weasels, moles, foxes were not confined to school story-books, or to the sportsman's "Scotland", but could be seen in or near my own garden. I saw the hovering of hawks, the muster of the swallows for migration, the low flight of the heron with wide wings extended; on a dark spring night I heard from my window the honk-honk of the wild geese far overhead.

I realized the beauty of snow in sunshine, cold blue in the hollows, rose-sparkled on the dazzling crests. Sunsets I had witnessed, but blood-red winter dawns were a revelation. The constellations swam bright into my ken; Orion blazed above my garden; I could count the stars of the Pleiades, and distinguish the cleavages of the Milky Way; moonrise and lunar rainbows were new wonders, and for the first time I saw stars big and luminous low down on the horizon.

Storm, Sun, and Shower

On a glorious night I stood alone under the stars on a hill-top and solemnly cursed the industrial system, the Manchester School, landlordism, tenements, and everything that had conspired to shut out me and most of my fellow-Scots from our natural heritage—depriving us of the very language of the soul. If we were not all blind atheists and crapulous degenerates, it was not the fault of those who had killed trees and grass and flowers, blotted out colour, and obscured the stars.

But the survival of wild Nature within sight of the smoke-pall of Glasgow was not the most wonderful of my discoveries. Johannes Agricola had survived. Ringan Gilhaize or Cuddie Headrigg would have been a foreigner amongst us denaturalized incomers. He would have been at home amongst the farmer-folk of the district. They retained their old speech and customs, their old exclusiveness, and for aught I know, their old superstitions. They married among themselves. Every farm-house was a citadel of the old Scotland, a museum-piece in its internal arrangement and furnishing, with a life remoter than that of the castle from the life of the bungalows. At farm-dances one even beheld the gala costume of pre-Reformation days.

This sturdy consolidation of agrarian primitiveness in face of industrialism and housing schemes and far-flung factories presages a long continuance of mankind on this planet. It is an assertion of the principle of life, which is largely characteristic "difference". Having survived Presbyterian theocracy's application of the patent roller invented by the ecclesiastical Lenin, John Calvin, it has not much to fear from industrialism.

The Glasgow area is not peculiar in this respect. In the shadow of Edinburgh Castle one may find survivals of the life described in Fergusson's *Farmer's Ingle*. The Berlin day-trippers to the Havel pass amongst peasant folk as staunchly primitive as the Bavarian mountaineers or the Mecklenburg farmers. Within the English home counties one can find remnants of a rusticity almost medieval. A huge metropolis cannot urbanize the agricultural life in its neighbourhood; it can only destroy it.

It is said that the Scots county in which the greatest number of old Scots words and phrases survives is Lanarkshire. A city like Glasgow tends to preserve rustic life in its neighbourhood, by fostering a spirit of unconscious resistance, providing a market for small "mixed" farms, and repelling the residential element.

It is in the remoter and more beautiful counties, used largely as pleasances and playgrounds by the wealthy, that rustic regionalism has been undermined. The agrarian life of the Borders has never been allowed to recover from the blow dealt it by English marauding armies in the sixteenth century. It has worn so thin that another decade may see its extinction. In Perthshire there is little trace of real Gaelicism or real Scottishness. In such counties, also, sport and the residential estate have obscured the economic or "subsistence" aspect of land work, and there is nothing to counter the deceptive glamour of Londonism.

In the West and North Highlands, the same influences have been at work, with deadlier effect. The result is reflected in the novels of our younger writers. Finding no substantial body of native material that could be used in a "normal" fashion, and being too honest to invent it, they have voiced their indignation in a satiric realism that has offended those good people who hold that the principle of a novelist should be "Let's pretend".

To assert that the strength of racial and regional characteristics in Scotland makes hay of nationalism is erroneous. The fact is that their weakness makes a national movement necessary and difficult. The only parts of Scotland where they survive strongly are Clydesdale, Wigtown, Aberdeenshire, the Outer Hebrides, Orkney, and Shetland.

The essence of nationality is microcosmic diversity. It was the sense of the decline of that diversity in Scotland—the grinding down of racial and regional characteristics into something as dull and colourless as boulder clay—that largely inspired the national movement.

§ ii

The starry heavens, and the moral law in the heart of man, seemed to Kant the most impressive things in the universe. The sky on a clear moonless night in early winter is the first thing in nature that strikes a city-bred man who has gone to live on the open uplands.

The majestic spread of the Plough, the gem-like brilliance of Orion, the glittering swarm of the Pleiades, move him to admiration. He had only read of the Milky Way: now he beholds it, a mighty fountain-arch of luminous dust, stretching overhead across the sky, breaking into two streams as it falls. He is puzzled by bright lights close down to the very horizon, where in the city there is only a sulphurous dimness. They are stars!

In time he notices the difference between the hard sparkle of the stars on a still, frosty night, their blown and washed appearance in a north-west gale, and their liquid softness in clear, moist spells, "when stars are weeping". And he recalls Rousseau's inspired word for the secular stellar movement—"deploying"—and, in a kind of awed despair, murmurs, "The heavens declare the glory of God; and the firmament sheweth His handywork."

Sunset is an expansion of a wonder already glimpsed, but a vast, blood-red dawn over slopes of snow, cold purple, with rose sparkles, is a revelation.

On a bright mild morning in April, after a week of tepid smirr succeeding frost, he looks out over the valley to the huge stretch of meadow and moorland that for months has been tawny and dull. This morning it is like the plains and hills of heaven, a shimmering expanse of light green and silver, miles on miles, with beacons of shining gold.

A constant wonder is the winter wind. In the city it merely whistles, shrieks and bellows. Out on the forest ridge between valley and upland, its note is infinitely varied.

Last night the fading moon was greasy. Today, despite the clear air, the light almost failed, so thick was the blanket of drizzling cloud. The rooks have flown over early to their winter dormitory in the valley. The weather-wise remark that they are glad they have not to cross the Irish Sea tonight.

Storm, Sun, and Shower

The evening darkness is thick and almost hot. Through its clammy folds comes a faint breathing, then a whistling and moaning, then a booming. Doors and window-frames creak. There is a pause of indecisive sighings and strainings. Then a moment of complete calm. The advance-guard has completed its reconnaissance, and fallen back on the main army.

Straining ears through the blackness, one hears, far down in the south-west valley, a sound like muffled thunder, or great distant waters fighting their way through choked canyons. The sound changes to a noise like Attila's cavalry debouching on the plain of Chalons. The viewless horsemen of the blast have broken cover, on a front of a hundred miles. They are thundering and bellowing up the slope. With a shriek and a yell they strike the house. The battle is let loose.

Nature cowers and quivers. The birds cling faster to the branches, and push their heads farther under their wings. The night-birds are silent. Bunnies dig deeper into their burrows. Tonight the weasels fast. The kennel-dog jumps out, gives a frightened bark and howl, and, with tail down, rushes back into his lodging and buries himself in the straw.

The gale rises and rises. The world lies prostrate. The whistling is constant and despairing. Fastenings of all kinds rattle. The surroundings of the house are disquietingly vocal. The chimneys boom. At the climaxes of the gale, other sounds are drowned by a thunderous drumming and roaring. The big guns are in action. One feels the slates lift, all at once. The south-wester has his fangs in us. He is shaking us

as a dog shakes a rat. The general sensation is as if
the house were suspended in the midst of the main
fall of Niagara. Is the whole house really lifting? It
can hardly resist that terrific aerial pressure.

Listening again, one can hear the successive cohorts
of the storm galloping up at the charge. When they
have passed, one can hear them thundering away up
into the north-east. Distant crashes and bangings
bespeak the work of the hooves. The noise of heavy
trains, throbbing up the incline or rattling down, is
only intermittently audible; their whistlings are
twisted and spun away.

The air, because of the sub-tropical latitudes from
which the gale blows, and the rapid movement of the
particles, is curiously warm. Thunder-and-lightning
is very rare with a south-west gale; but millions of
electrical discharges—invisible lightnings—create an
absorbed luminosity, making darkness visible, and
suffusing the eyes with a woolly mist. On such a night,
a wanderer in broken country would be stunned and
overwhelmed, and would be in danger of coming to
grief in an old quarry or a swollen stream.

Through all this tumultuous orchestration there
runs a rich solemn music. Whenever the drums and
tubas ease off, one hears the voluminous but muted
theme given out by the strings and wood-winds of the
forest. It is a beautiful rushing sound, like a multitude of flooded streams washing along in beds of vary-
ing composition and declivity. In the heart of pine-
woods scarcely a draught is felt, and the rushing and
whishing and tossing and surging overhead are like
the noise of a great impetuous river, flowing over an

enchanted cave. One thinks of the Rheingold—and of the nursery rhymes of infancy—"Hush-a-bye, baby, on the tree-top".

The noise and the electric tension make sleep impossible. One's thoughts follow the gale, across moorland and farmland, and the streaming and empty streets of towns, where the lights flicker and glisten and the chimney-cowls whirl and scream; and over the hills and far away, down white-whipped estuaries to the boiling cauldron of the open sea, where steamers with sparks flying from their funnels plunge and smother in acres of ghostly foam, mingling with the breaking crests of the inexorable combers that tear it up as the horns of a mad bull might tear a web of lawn.

It is there, on a night like this, that the high hearts of our race are steeled and tested. On those obstinately wallowing boxes of metal are the flower of mankind. They do not undervalue their adversary. Have you noticed the quiet contempt with which a sailor regards a landlubber who sighs for a snoring breeze, and the white waves heaving high? I shouldn't be ashamed to confess to an old salt that I was "thankful to be at home on a night like this".

§ iii

Among the best posters I have seen is an unpretentiously coloured one advertising some fishing concern. It represents trawlers out on the fishing grounds. The weather they are experiencing is not abnormal, yet the sight of those gallant little craft, poised slantwise on the crests of mountainous waves, or half hidden in the troughs, with their decks awash, is awesome to the landsman.

The picture helped to make one realize the significance of certain episodes during spells of stormy weather. There was the dash of a trawler from the island of Unst, through terrific seas and currents, to get a man to hospital for an urgent operation. He could not be got below, and had to be laid aft at the engine-room, with tarpaulins round him, and a nurse in attendance.

There was the trawler that raced from Rockall to Campbeltown, in heavy weather, to get medical aid for a man who had been badly injured in a storm. There was the fifteen hours' battle of a Kerry lifeboat to reach a vessel in distress. There were the buffetings, accidents, wrecks, rescues, disasters, on various parts of the storm-vexed winter seas off North-West Europe. There was the repair of an exterior valve far below the water-line of an Italian liner in mid-ocean. There was the tragic burning of *L'Atlantique*.

All that is merely topical matter, of passing interest. It can be matched during most winters. Increased size and power of cargo vessels, and the installation of radio, may have reduced the incidence of mishap, but there is no absolute guarantee against disaster.

"Danger?" said a grizzled Norwegian skipper with whom I was discussing this matter. "There is always danger at sea. It is to meet it that we are trained."

The sea laughs as grimly at man and his works as

in the days of *Childe Harold*. There is not a seaman who may not at any moment be called upon to display the highest powers of courage, resourcefulness, and endurance of which a human being is capable.

On the smaller craft, especially on trawlers, the demand is constant. To say that the fishing industry is a perpetual school of heroism is merely to state a simple fact.

A learned professor has stated that the biggest wave known is only 60 feet high and 560 feet long. That is enough to be going on with. Those who want waves bigger than a Glasgow tenement are hard to please.

To come on deck and find that your ship, which looked big and steady off the Cumbraes, is now a minor and maltreated object in an animated hill country, is an alarming experience. It is not a mere case of climbing and descending. Those big fellows are like elephants or giant anacondas; they are swift travellers. That is why a boat is banged and buffeted when she is moving against them, and in danger of being pooped when she is travelling in their direction.

Down goes her head, with a long, sickening plunge, while you cling to the rails and feel the shudder caused by a racing propeller. A steep hill of water is advancing. She rises to it, but it boils up over her fo'c'sle, and pours a waterfall down on the main deck. She shakes herself, shoots up over the crest, and plunges down the other slope into the next trough, amid a hissing acre of dazzling foam that seems to throw the billows out of step. But the next big fellow is ready ahead. Bad steering, or a trifle more speed

71

than fits the various factors that converge in impact, would bring a whole wave on board, and an immediate repetition of the dose might founder the ship.

To watch the play of a big sea with a fine modern vessel, and let your mind roam back to the days of Columbus, Vasco da Gama, the vikings, Hanno, and Ulysses, is to realize the part the sea has played in history. Ulysses had cause for fright in a norther in the deep Aegean. Those Phoenicians and Greeks who weathered the mistral and got through the Pillars of Hercules were no effeminate amateurs. The Carthaginians who reached Britain and rounded Africa were first-rate heroes.

All men, of whatever race or colour, who bluffed the eternal sea were he-men in a real sense. The point of their achievement has been seized by modern novelists and dramatists who, in reconstructing history, have brought out the contrast between those old sailors and the people they had often to serve. Luxury and vice might ruin courts and demoralize cities; consuls and captains might be corrupted; rot might invade armies. But the sailor was never affected. For him there was no decline and fall. In battling with the implacable unremitting ocean, and keeping his ship afloat, he preserved his manhood and self-respect. He carried the corn, gold, silks, slaves, menageries, traitors, libertines, and male and female intriguers, that were ruining his country: but him they did not ruin.

To him the whole ruck and truck was merely passengers and cargo, to be handled carefully and safely delivered. Faithful to his trust, his manly job, and the code of his profession, like Britain's "army of mercenaries", he "saved the sum of things for pay".

And meanwhile, on plains and valleys swept by armies degenerating into barbarian hordes, his opposite number on land, the peasant-cultivator, was doing his best to keep himself and the rest of the world alive. Those two knew little of each other. The sailor sneered good-humouredly at the "hayseed", and the peasant feared and suspected the deep-tanned creature with the strange oaths and the gold ear-rings. But each was doing the world's essential work and a man's job. Together, they countered the efforts of clever degenerates, and criminal lunatics in high places, to destroy civilization. They brought manhood and integrity through.

§ iv

Forth from Calais, at dawn of night, when sunset
    summer on autumn shone,
Fared the steamer, alert and loud, through seas
    whence only the sun had gone. . . .
Whence came change?—What anguish awoke in the
    dark? . . .
Three glad hours, and it seemed not an hour of
    supreme and supernal joy,
Filled full with delight that revives in remembrance
    a sea-bird's heart in a boy.
And an end was made of it: only remembrance
    endures of the glad loud strife;
And a sense that a rapture so royal may come not
    again in the pangs of life.

SWINBURNE, *A Channel Passage.*

My Scotland

I understand exactly what Stevenson meant when he said that it is better to travel than to arrive. A journey always excites me, and I am always disappointed when it is over. Rothesay—in spring—is the only place I have come across of which the charm does not evaporate in a few days. There must be a tinker strain in me, for my idea of perfect felicity is to wander, like the youth in Müller's poem,

> Downward, and ever onward,
> And ever the brook beside;

and the words that sing in my head are "Over the hills and far away". It is not that I expect to find happiness in some distant vale, for I know that my burdensome self goes on as advance luggage, and will be delivered to me without fail as soon as I make my halt. But I am rid of it so long as I am in motion. The world resolves itself into a travelling theatre, a wonderful dioramic film. I would rather be wheelbarrowed through the Chartreuse than spend a week in the swellest hotel at Aix-les-Bains.

For many people, travel seems to be rather a bore. They are not interested in the speed of the train, the rivers that flash below them, or the hills that slowly rise and fall on the horizon. When they have read their story magazine or comic weekly they go to sleep. When they go to Paris or Switzerland or the Riviera, the middle portion of their journey seems to them a dreary blank, and the Channel passage a kind of temporary death.

The transit from England to France is perennially

amazing. Among the passengers at Victoria you pick out a German Jew, an Egyptian, a French governess, a Breton sailor, a Swiss waiter. If it is the night train, and a south-west gale is blowing, you begin to be apprehensive about the crossing. What will all those people look like in three hours? "O, blindness to the future, kindly given!"

The Calais crossing is the most dramatic. When you have got on board you gaze up at Shakespeare's white cliffs (which are like a clean edition of Tennant's soap-waste heap at St. Rollox), and round at the noblemen and ambassadors and millionaires and spies and crooks and vamps and dupes and also-rans that crowd the deck. All the ingredients of an Edgar Wallace or Sax Rohmer shocker are effervescing here. The boat seems unimpressed. She is a strong, shapely construction, Clyde-built of course—Denny's best, and only the men who built her know what's inside her, for she seems to consist mainly of locked doors, and one can discover nothing that corresponds to the roomy saloon of a Clyde steamer.

The Glasgow man misses the melodious outburst of pipe and tabor that accompanies the first beat of the paddles of a Clyde steamer. It is a sound associated with blue water, green hills, and a fresh breeze laden with the odour of ham and eggs, or steak and onions.

The sun shines brightly, though it's certainly a bit —why, it's raining! No, that is the spray thrown up by the great speed of the vessel. The Glasgow man sniffs the caller breeze and goes out to come his viking on the neb of the boat. She rolls slightly—gathers speed—and hits a big wave a wild skelp. The top of the wave breaks off, leaps into the iridescent air, and souses down on the Glasgow man. He clutches a rail, holds his breath, and, drenched to the skin, retreats into the shelter of the covered lee-deck.

Nobody notices him. The passengers, in two rows, are huddled up on seats or deck-chairs, trying to keep up conversation. The boat gives a heavy roll, a sudden pitch, and a vicious twist. There is a crash of breaking glass, the passengers are thrown on the deck, women shriek, and a lady faints and is carried downstairs on the shoulders of two sailors, strong men who are amiably silent in two languages.

Wealth and poverty, virtue and wickedness, are blent and blotted out in the misery of sea-sickness. The works of nature and of art are undone. Green has become the fashionable complexion. Vamps and respectable matrons roll and groan together on the floor of the ladies' cabin. Dreadful sounds proceed from the private cabins into which the opulent have locked themselves. Even brandy is rejected with loathing. Making a cautious tour of the boat, the Glasgow man discovers that only five passengers besides himself have escaped sickness. Three of them are Scots.

And still the wonderful steamer drives ahead. Calais lighthouse and church rise above the steep green waves. We are going to be up to time. Three cheers for Denny! The telegraph bell rings, and from the ridge of the last wave we shoot into calm water. The long quay wall is manned by blue-clad gesticulating Gauls. They leap on board and seize hold of the baggage. Reeling with sickness, the passengers are pushed forward to undergo the barbarous ordeal of the *douane*. The infantile toot of the big engine scarcely prepares us for the rapidity with which, a few minutes later, the long train is travelling amid the well-cultivated farmlands of north-east France. Soap and water and combs and vanity bags and tea (the best tea in the world is that served on the Calais-to-Paris express) have reconverted mere suffering humanity into ambassadors, vamps, and respectable also-rans. We draw aloof from each other, and remember to "be British".

All this is not a bit like Swinburne. He writes as if he had been the only passenger. One feels like that on a fine night on the Newhaven-Dieppe crossing. The lit boat is strangely silent; one hears nothing but the swish and surge of the waves along her side. The turning swords of the great lighthouses flash over the dark water. The constellations swing rhythmically amid the cordage. Midway, a large lit liner crosses our bows. We are crossing the main avenue of the world's maritime commerce, and of the world's history. This way came William the Conqueror, and Drake, and Nelson, and the fleets and armies of the Great War. But the waves reck as little of it all as the stars they brokenly reflect. . . . The night breeze is blowing from France. The grey dawn will reveal the cliffs and casino of Dieppe. When the sun is warm we shall be having rolls and *café au lait* in a French café, and forgetting the shrivelled-up cates and dusty dearness of London in contemplation of the butter, cream, peaches, apricots, and artichokes spread out in the street market. And beyond are the rich fields and dainty valleys and broad streams and lonely forests and famous towns and churches of big, beautiful France.

CHAPTER IV

TRAVEL AND RETURN

§ i

BEHOLDING the sadness of the wise, one may wonder why Solomon chose wisdom as a divine gift. Wisdom itself would elect rather for courage and patience.

For the latter of these qualities, there is constant occasion. At the counter of a busy post office in the late afternoon, for example, when, with a train to catch, you have to get a money order, dispatch a parcel, and buy stamps.

A man before you has handed over a requisition for remittances to a dozen places in Britain, and three or four abroad. You try to think of the happiness he is diffusing, and to admire the calligraphy of the clerk.

At the parcels counter, the clerk is weighing an endless succession of packages handed up by a boy, who seems to be conjuring them out of his cap. Behind him is a girl festooned with parcels. You feel like Macbeth at the supper-table: "What! Will the line stretch out to the crack o' doom?" If this is trade depression, what would a boom be like?

At the stamp counter, collectors are buying sheets of stamps, of denominations you never heard of. What they are going to do with them you can't imagine. Sheaves of bank-notes are handed over.

You have a wild idea of protesting, in the name of economy. How can our diminished trade stand such an oncost?

You postpone your petty transactions, and go over to the station. Your train is a busy one, and there is a queue at the booking-office.

An elderly Englishman in plus-fours is inquiring about availability and alternative routes. He goes off, half-satisfied. Then comes a lady who is not sure about her destination, and who has to peck up her money from amid miscellaneous objects at the bottom of a handbag. She has difficulty in lifting her change with her gloved hand.

The booking-clerk surveys her with stern impassivity. He has a coign of vantage. We have to bow ungracefully, and speak up to him from under the window. There is an oval aperture for vocal communication, but few passengers seem to use it. One doesn't like to address a fellow-being through a chink.

There are a few more knots in the plank, but at last we get to the window, determined to show the footlers how business should be done. We slap down our money, state our demand in a sharp voice, snatch the change—and let a sixpence fall.

There is a deep growl behind us. We retrieve the coin, and, with half a minute to spare, run for the train.

§ ii

In the early days of the cinema, European beholders of transatlantic films were intrigued by the mobility of the American male.

Travel and Return

The strong, silent man received a telephone message that his wife had skipped to Reno, that his son was making an ass of himself at Harvard, or that his mine in Nevada had collapsed.

Without removing his cigar from his lips, he stuck a Derby hat on his head, flung a flimsy overcoat over his arm, seized a pup suitcase, known as a gripsack, and vanished.

Immediately thereafter, one saw him leap on to the footboard of a long-distance train, and take his seat in the car. Doubtless he had his gun in his hip-pocket, but one looked in vain for an umbrella. Sticks and umbrellas, in America, are reserved for comic "business".

Our American traveller, of course, could get a shave and a shampoo on the cars. He could buy cigars at the first stopping-place. In his hotel he could purchase anything from a collar to a tuxedo.

Why did he take the gripsack at all? Probably it contained only a few soiled collars, a shirt that ought to have been sent to the wash, and a week-old newspaper.

The gripsack was vestigial, like man's appendix or rudimentary tail. It was a relic of the primitive age when travellers trailed their furniture with them.

Sadie and Daisy are not content with a gripsack. The armoury of beauty calls for trunks. On these the baggage-smasher—the American citizen in revolt against the indignity of carrying things—wreaks his savage will.

Perhaps that is why Sadie and Daisy are so fond of travelling in feudal Europe, where luggage is still handled with reverence. The labelled cottages that emerge from the baggage-holds of American liners are an impressive spectacle for "impoverished" peoples.

In Europe, the tendency is to work down to the minimum of travel impedimenta. Few of us possess anything in the nature of a trunk or a portmanteau. We contrive to take nothing on a journey that we cannot, at need, carry ourselves.

Not long ago there changed hands in London the travel-bookcase of an Elizabethan nobleman. It was a large chest of fine wood, beautifully carved inside, with temple-like compartments for various kinds of classics.

Today, such loving care is reserved for smokers' cabinets and the apparatus of sport. And there are bookshops in most towns. On the Continent there is the Tauchnitz edition of English authors. And there is room for a few small volumes in a Swiss rucksack. With a rucksack you can, in safety and for nothing, cross the Alps or the Pyrenees, or even Paris. Blessings on the inventor of it!

§ iii

Travel books are preoccupied with the aesthetic and cultural aspects of towns; with their history, antiquities, churches, public buildings, monuments, gardens, and general lay-out. But the passing stranger is apt to judge a town by the facilities for getting the kind of meal he happens to want, at the price he feels inclined to pay. The tourist army moves upon its stomach.

"Do you remember the Trossachs?" one English traveller asked another. "Yes." "Do you remember that delicious cold roast beef we had there?" "Yes." "Well, I've regretted ever since that I didn't take another helping."

It is the proper thing for the Scot, a devotee of plain living and high thinking, cultivating literature on a little oatmeal, to sneer at that ingenuous Sassenach. But the worst of that kind of superior attitude is that sooner or later you get caught out.

Thus it happened to me on a Harwich and Hook of Holland boat. Light-heartedly I strolled along for supper. There was no oatmeal on the menu, so I had to content myself with cold roast beef, salad, and coffee.

When I had finished, a magnanimous emotion possessed me. I called the steward, and expatiated poetically upon the roast beef of old England: which, by the way, it was. My enthusiasm increased when a moderate sum was demanded.

There may be finer cities than Warsaw, but, when marooned there alone from eight in the morning till midnight, I had three excellent meals and two "pit-byes", in five different restaurants, at prices which even a Glasgow man found moderate. When the stars are mirrored in the broad Vistula, the main streets are alight with cafés where hefty Sarmatians put away the solid and liquid products of their native land; and it is not assumed that the need for hot meals and other creature comforts ceases at seven, nine, or ten.

One remembers the scene in *Great Expectations* where Pip takes Estella for tea to a fashionable London hotel:

the sepulchral dining-room, the long delay, the weak tea, the tiger-like toast, the exorbitant charge. Even yet, in many country hotels, the assumption is that there is nothing midway between a full meal and a glass of beer or a cup of tea.

What a piece of work is man! He builds mighty motor ships, motors at hundreds of miles an hour, flies over Everest, and achieves miracles in radio and tele-photography; but his farms are without electricity, his rooms and furniture are dust-traps, and in otherwise happy homes the housewife is heard weeping over kitchen grates of a design patented by some fat-headed ironfounder in the year of the Disruption.

Little wonder that the roadside purveyor beyond the Highland line has not yet heard of the omelette or the rarebit, and, like Dorothy Wordsworth's Scottish landladies, has a congenital reluctance to "gi'e fire".

§ iv

When Napoleon was in Syria, he had chapters from the Old Testament read aloud every evening in his tent. His staff were impressed by the fidelity of the descriptive passages to the life and scenery of the country around them.

This fidelity extends to the Egyptian pages in Genesis and Exodus. The mention of a chief butler and a chief baker—not to speak of a wanton woman, wife of a captain of the guard—marks a luxurious society, contrasting with the pastoral Semitic tribes.

The chief butler and the chief baker had offended Pharaoh and been put in prison. Probably the butler had been doing a little wine-merchanting on his own account. That was a venial offence, and he was restored to favour. The baker may have been using inferior flour or rancid butter, with disastrous effects upon the Royal digestion and temper. Anyhow, he was hanged. His fate may have given a cue to the concocters of the old puppet-plays, in which the baker was seized by the devil—"Pull devil, pull baker"—and shoved into the flames of hell. In the Middle Ages, millers and bakers were regarded as "enemies of the people".

Pharaoh's baker was not a mere dough-tramper and baker of loaves. He was an all-round artist. Before his fall, he may have won prizes for wedding-cake at the Luxor Bakers' Exhibition.

Here, perhaps, we have the explanation of the prowess of Scottish bakers. Scota, the foundress of our race, was an Egyptian princess. She would have bakers in her train. The scone and the cookie may have been evolved on the banks of the Nile. There is something exotic about "parlie". Sections of Scotch bun may have been built into the Pyramids.

At all events, it is remarkable that, whereas in contiguous countries the baker is merely a breadmaker —turning out tubular crust by the mile and cutting it off by the yard, or producing loaves like curling-stones (in Brittany I have seen a loaf trundled home like a "girr", or hurled in a wheelbarrow)—in Scotland the baker is equal to anything from a "pan" loaf to a super-pie, a "snap" to a castellated cake.

From time immemorial, every Scottish village, especially along the East Coast, had an attractive

85

baker's shop, locally famous for some kind of biscuit, "bap", cake, or fancy-bread. In towns, the finest shops were the bakers'. They formed an oasis of wholesomeness in the slummiest quarters.

The absence of anything like this in England struck me as a child. A country where "teabread" was almost unknown, and "cakes" were an infrequent kind of dessert, eaten with fork and spoon, couldn't, I thought, be civilized.

Perhaps the difference indicated the greater daintiness of the Scot. We are less carnivorous than the English, less the slaves of knife and fork. But we have overdone this characteristic. A stranger entering a Glasgow tearoom in the afternoon must have the impression that the hardy Caledonian lives mainly on pastry. We are still "the land of cakes", in a sense that would have astonished Fergusson or Burns.

§ v

There are certain human customs that seem to have been designed with the purpose of abating the pride of life.

Tipping is the skeleton at the feast, the fly in the ointment, the bugbear that waits for us in moments when we are soaring towards a dangerous felicity.

"It'll be a fine holiday, won't it?"

"But what about gratuities?"

The flower of hope withers. From the contemplation of Nature's marvels and man's achievements, you crash down to anticipation of those awful moments when you will be wondering how much is expected, how much you ought to give, how it is to be divided, and whether you have the right change.

Twice or thrice I have had narrow escapes from sudden death. My recollection of them has grown faint. But I shudder when I recall a moment, many years ago, at the gate of one of the Cambridge colleges.

It was in the vacation, and I had been shown over the place by a lodge-keeper. When we got back to the gate, I found that, apart from pound notes, I had only three pennies and a halfpenny in my pocket.

I remembered the story of the two guests who were leaving a Scottish mansion. The generous tips of one of them to the ranged-up servants had been glumly received. The other had evoked smiles. "You must have given an awful lot."—"I gave nothing. I just kittled their luifs."

That expedient would not serve. I stood well off, on a line of retreat, muttered fervent thanks, shoved the coppers into the man's hand without looking at him—and fled.

We picture the "people" in the Middle Ages as trembling in presence of the gentry. The reality may have been very different.

Even from Ariosto, we gather that the onset of a hostile champion must have worried a knight-errant much less than the approach of a proud servitor, who would not be put off with a spear-point in the gizzard, but expected to be thrown the customary purse of gold.

Some of those medieval servitors must have done almost as well as the head gamekeeper in the North whose employer went bankrupt and who left nearly £40,000.

This ironic tax levied upon the taxers reached its height in Western Europe in the eighteenth century. Noblemen were powerless to check the exorbitance of the "vails" exacted by their servants. To accept an invitation to a castle meant ruin for a poor author.

Most of us would be willing to subscribe for a monument to the man who invented the plan of adding to the hotel bill 10 per cent. for "service". The dubiety still surrounding casual services is removed in France, where porters shout "*Pas assez! Pas assez!*" until the astonished foreigner has dealt forth a satisfactory sum.

Had that incident that so upset me happened in France, my guide would have seen that I changed one of my sovereigns and gave him what was right. But neither he nor I, nor the Head of the College, nor the Professor of Mathematics, had any idea what was right—except that it was more than $3\frac{1}{2}$d. and less than a sovereign.

§ vi

To one who has been brought up on Spartan principles, it is disconcerting to find how deeply mankind are sunk in sloth and luxury.

The revelation begins on your first morning on board ship. There is a discreet rustle in your cabin, and, when you open your eyes, you perceive a cup of tea, with two small biscuits, placed within your reach.

It is the cup of Circe. Touch it not. The apple and bananas, supplied over-night, are another matter. They are blessed by the goddess Hygeia, and by Mr.

Dugald Semple. On such healthful fare did Adam breakfast. Partake of it while you dress, and hasten to the upper deck, to acquire an appetite for a manly meal.

You will have few companions in your promenade, and not many more at the breakfast-table. With a shock, you realize that most of your fellow-passengers are having breakfast in bed.

It is the same in Continental hotels. Breakfast in bed seems to be the order of the day. The assumption stings the national pride of the Scot. By taking a cold bath, and getting downstairs for breakfast before eight, he will show those foreigners that Écosse is not in Angleterre.

Jock and Hughoc never breakfasted in bed. Toil called them forth betimes, though not the allurements of their miserable fare. And the "quality" had to get out of bed in order to have a cut at the cold venison pasty, and a swig of ale or malmsey, ere sallying forth to slit each other's throats.

A change came with the advent of breakfast beverages. Tea was not among them at first. Belinda and Roxana, when they "oped those eyes that must eclipse the day", sipped a cup of steaming chocolate, freathed with whipped cream. The very idea gives one a headache.

Tea at least "kittles up the notion", and conscience is placated when the after-breakfast hour in bed is devoted to the study of the news of a world whose violent activity astonishes the recumbent reader. But to begin on a novel is fatal.

Our friends the ancient Romans took all their meals

in bed, so to speak. They used Nature's implements, however, and their food was of a kind according. Complications began with the introduction of knives, forks, and spoons. Their manipulation is fatiguing when the body forms a right angle. "The halesome parritch, chief o' Scotia's food", presupposes a Caledonian rampant, in a posture adapted to competitive supping.

A census on the matter would show that a large percentage of hardy Scots breakfast in bed on Sundays and holidays. They are entitled to a restorative luxury prompted by overwrought Nature. Breakfast in bed, however, means that someone, instead of resting, is doing a little more work than usual. If the luxury goes round, we can enjoy our turn of it with a clear conscience.

§ vii

On a fine July morning in 1923 I was having breakfast on the deck of a Rhine steamer near Coblenz. It was the stringent period of the French occupation, and notices were posted up in the companion-ways, forbidding the singing of patriotic songs.

At one of the tables a young German, with horn spectacles, rose to his feet and began to sing. His voice was of the fireside order, but he looked respectable, and his motives were not mercenary. His compatriots listened sympathetically.

The song he sang was one I had not heard since I was a boy. A soldier stood on the village street to bid his love adieu—in waltz time, with chromatics—

Travel and Return

O love, dear love, be true;
    For this heart is ever thine;
When the war is o'er, we'll part no more
    At Ehren on the Rhine.

We were passing a village called Stolzenfels, and I learned that the song was German, dating from the Franco-Prussian War, and that its title was "*Zu Stolzenfels am Rhein*".

One doesn't associate musical Germany with that kind of thing. Yet I am certain there is a German Angus MacDonald haunting the concert halls of the Fatherland, to the annoyance of connoisseurs. One touch of treacle makes the whole world kin.

There is no such place as Ehren on the Rhine. Yet down the streets of that ghost-village Fritz and Gretchen waltz solemnly for ever, to the strains of an old German band.

Once, when leaving Dublin for Cork, I nearly changed my destination. For one of the carriages on the train was labelled "*Lisdoonvarna*". I believe Lisdoonvarna exists, but I have refrained from visiting it. No Irish town could live up to such a name.

I had no hesitation about visiting Killaloe, which was associated with a comic song. The loveliness of the place washed out that smudge. But I am sure I should have had a vision even more entrancing if I had gone to Ballyjamesduff.

"Camlachie, Ecclefechan, Auchtermuchty, and Milngavie." The list is not euphonious, but the harshest Scots name has a dignity that does not pertain to Pudsey, Hog's Norton, Muggleswick, or Hockley-in-the-Hole.

The lure of place-names is mainly a matter of association. Perth and Stirling might not appeal to us as names of villages. The partiality of poets for "Dunedin", "Edina", "Embro", "Auld Reekie", is significant. But poetry gives salute to Dunfermline, Dundee, Aberdeen, Melrose, Flodden, Bothwell Brig, Culloden. Morven, Lorne, Lochaber, Nevis, Lomond, Iona, the Hebrides, Greenloaning, Aviemore, Lillies-leaf, Colmonell, Durisdeer, are each as lovely as Lisdoonvarna. Bruce's crowning day was further crowned when the English were driven across a little stream named Bannockburn.

§ viii

It was said of a famous ruler of Israel that he went out to seek his father's asses, and found a kingdom.

The experience of most people is just the opposite. They go out looking for something grand and august, and stumble into a series of trivial adventures.

On a beautiful afternoon I was walking along a little road on a ridge of the Wicklow Mountains. The slopes were golden with broom. On one side, across a broad green valley, was the main range. On the other, a deep glen, densely wooded, wound down to the Irish Sea.

The shadows were dark blue. The sunlit hill-sides were moist green and gold, flecked with autumnal russets. I was trying to raise my mind to the height of this glory, when I heard a strange wailing cry.

What bird could it be? I gazed about. No bird

was visible. Still the cry went on. At last I located it. It came from the ground, near my feet.

Right in the track of a cart that had just passed was a grey kitten, uninjured, with its eyes not yet open. I took it up, and soon got it a good home at a little farm close by.

Pleased with my good deed, I turned and walked downhill. I was getting into the poetic vein again when I was startled by a series of unearthly howls. My heart missed a beat or two—and then I saw a donkey on the hill-side, with his mouth open. A relative across the glen brayed in response. The antiphonal effect was tremendous.

> O listen, for the vale profound
> Is overflowing with the sound!

Round the next corner came a man in a donkey-cart, with his name scratched on the side, and some iron bars and three stone of potatoes at his feet. He stopped for a chat, and offered to sell me the whole outfit cheap. He was very persuasive—and the donkey gave me a fraternal glance when I stroked his ears.

Next day I was studying Dublin's architectural vistas, and looking for an old church whose crypt has the bad habit of preserving bodies for centuries. A crowd in a side street drew my attention.

On the steps of a house two ladies were leaping and yelling in convulsions of rage. A man who looked good for a heavy-weight championship was being urged to battle with another heavy-weight. He was speechless with terror.

A policeman pushed his way through the crowd,

asked a few questions—keeping carefully out of reach of the ladies—and led off to the "office" two coatless youths whose rôles in the drama were unrevealed. The heavy-weights were yanked indoors by the battling Bridgets—and late-comers were left guessing.

If all domestic quarrels were conducted *coram populo*, in the old fashion of Celtic tribes and Norse republics, there would be few serious assaults, and no murders. And if travellers had the courage to ignore the guide-book now and then, and follow up the possibilities of chance encounters, there would be fewer dull travel-books, and more good poems, plays, and novels.

§ ix

I read in a newspaper of two young Cockneys, of a very prosaic type, who, while travelling on a Glasgow tram-car, were roused to uncouth exclamation by the sudden glory of a sunset.

I remember a September evening, many years ago, when I was travelling south on a West Highland train. A blond young German-American from Michigan, with whom I had forgathered, was expatiating on the scenery of the Mississippi, the Lake of the Woods, the Rockies, and Norway.

As we passed Bridge of Orchy, the rain-clouds lifted in the west, and a brilliant sunset lit up the heather and brackens and streaming rocks, and filled with golden vapour the hollows of the mountains round Glen Orchy.

The young fellow rose, and gazed silently at the spectacle till we came to Tyndrum. As he sat down he remarked, "I have never seen anything like that, and I don't expect I ever shall, again."

I remembered, too, how a chattering, cosmopolitan crowd on a MacBrayne steamer were awed into silence by a vast golden sunset in which Mull swam like a huge jewel and the isles of the sea were like galleys of dreams. Tir nan Og had come east upon us.

And I remembered how, from a high cliff above Bergen, I saw that strange little city transformed, by a vaporous sunset over the fjord, into a marvellous translucence of ivory, purple, green, and rose-pink, like a drowned city compact of sea-ware, shining up through clear water.

That was the only sunset I ever saw abroad that approached any of the sunsets I have seen from my own window in Scotland.

Within a few hours, in this West Country, the sky will pass from a rainy dullness that blankets the soul, to a maenad wildness presaging doom, a crystalline peace that seems eternal, and a slowly mounting magnificence of gold and crimson, with a spreading wing of rosy cirrus, broadening in superb perspective to the zenith.

No wonder we have so many poets in Scotland.

> Poverty like a princess goes
> In my land.

But the glory of the skies is as far beyond poetry as beyond painting. Shelley came near it in *The Cloud*, and in the opening of the second Act of *Prometheus Unbound*. And there is that wonderful line in Keats's *Hyperion*: "Upon the gold clouds metropolitan".

My Scotland

When, one winter morning, I looked out at a sky which was crimson to the zenith, over blue-white snow, rose-spangled, I could only murmur, "God made Himself an awful rose of dawn." And I felt how strained and inadequate Tennyson's line was. Such a sky must have suggested Marlowe's terrific words: "Christ's blood streams in the firmament."

Music can do better. There are passages in Beethoven and Wagner that give the very effect of sky pageantry.

Those visions of the vesture of God reprove our earthy baseness. In the glowing folds lie our lost dreams, our wistful and vanished hopes. From our sordid little world, we glimpse, with "A.E.", ineffable and unattainable Beauty:—

> Its edges foamed with amethyst and rose,
> Withers once more the old blue flower of day. . . .

> I saw how all the trembling ages past,
> Moulded to her by deep and deeper breath,
> Neared to the hour when Beauty breathes her last
> And knows herself in death.

§ x

> I remember, I remember
> The house where I was born;
> The little window where the sun
> Came peeping in at morn. . . .

Parents and educationists have realized the importance of the view from the window out of which a child first looks with seeing eyes.

Travel and Return

My own outlook on life has been coloured by the view from a top-story window in a Glasgow tenement. Over back-greens and attics and chimneys, one looked eastward to the church-spires of Bath Street, the houses of Garnethill, and the stores and malt-houses of Port Dundas.

The sun came peeping in at morn, when cloud and smoke allowed him; and a tall tree brought spring and summer within a few yards of the window-sill. June was not a "legend empty of concern", though "idle was the rumour of the rose".

The abiding impression, however, is of wet roofs, yellow fog or livid cloud, and a dull roar like that of a river in spate. Muffled whistles of distant trains hinted at escape, but the "granny" cowls on the chimneys turned mournfully from side to side, and groaned "No use!"

From other windows, in holiday-time, I had glimpses that made me less forlorn. But they seemed too good to be true. I had the disdain of a sour realist for stage scenes in which the golden-haired maiden opened her rose-embowered casement and sang forth her heart to the birds and flowers. It was astonishing to find that such windows existed, and not only in Devonshire.

"The bonnie wee window", or the window that was bonnie when it framed the right person, figures prominently in Scots romance, urban as well as rustic. "Oh, Mary, at thy window be", strikes a note unknown in Latin lands, where the lady had to remain secluded, or compromise herself by coming out on the balcony. In Leopardi's beautiful elegy, Silvia is heard singing in her room, but never appears at a window.

Old country houses in Scotland nearly always turn their backs on an open view, even masking it with trees, and face inward to a wood or a hill-side.

The fashion seems absurd. Yet there are moods in which, with a choice between a window commanding a view of half a county, and a window looking across a small garden to a road and a fir plantation, one prefers the narrower prospect.

It is more human—more like the windows from which Hawthorne, Mrs. Gaskell, and Barrie made their immortal surveys.

The front windows of the house where I was born looked into a dull side street. Over the way, several ladies every afternoon sat at their respective windows, from which, at a painful angle, they could glimpse a small section of a main thoroughfare.

But for genteel inhibitions, they would doubtless have done what a Glasgow child, in a school essay, expressed her intention of doing when she grew up and was married. When her dinner-time work was done, she would go to the window and "have a good hing-oot".

I do not recommend the practice, but on the few occasions when I have ventured on it, I have found it exciting. Mr. Sean O'Casey, I am certain, must have had many a "good hing-oot".

§ xi

It is seldom that one comes across an old-fashioned wooden signpost, relic of the pre-motor age, pointing down a side-road with wooden persistence, as if to say: "I'm doing my bit in telling you it's three miles by this road to Clattering Shaws: won't you please justify my existence by going there?"

In a lonely place, of an evening, the gibbet-like signpost suggested hanged highwaymen and Crack-skull Common; and the solitary traveller shivered, and hastened his steps. His creepiness was intensified if he found the signpost decrepit and defaced. A broken signpost figures in old drawings of *The End of the World*.

Cycling to St. Abb's one summer day, I came at dusk upon an old signpost bearing the name, Old-hamstocks. Had I overshot the Border, or been carried by enchantment deep into Saxondom?

The road led into a rolling, grey-green dimness, darkening on the horizon into moorland hills. The Lammermoors, unmistakably. There was really a Scottish village called Oldhamstocks!

Scotland, being Celtic, is richer than England in names of natural features. But England beats us in respect of towns and villages. Her old signposts were minions of feudal romance, inviting us to walk out of the world of steel rails and trade unions into Compton Wynyates, Yatton Keynel, Childs Ercall, Stanton Harcourt, or Audley End; into the world of *Baker's Chronicle*, Miss Braddon, and the *Family Herald Supplement*.

A few miles west of Chipping Norton, signposts gave the tramper the choice of Moreton in the Marsh, Stow on the Wold, and Bourton on the Water. Bourton sounds the nicest, but a wise man would take all three and include Burford.

The modern iron signposts are more reliable than the old wooden ones. One can even manage to read them from a motor car. But they do not allure to brighter worlds; they merely state a geographical fact. They have a hard and alien air. They are not part of the scenery.

As for the large yellow discs that announce to the motorist that he is passing through Melrose, Yarrow, Falkland, Bridge-of-Orchy, or Appin, their convenience only emphasizes their affinity with the petrol pump. Their perpetual announcement of the distance from London—Glasgow and Edinburgh are ignored—is a subtle annoyance. The distance from Jerusalem would be as useful—and it would be less invidious and more interesting.

Mr. Pecksniff was likened by Dickens to a signpost, which shows the way to a place but never goes there. The comparison is apter than Dickens intended, for Pecksniff does little to deserve the ridicule and punishment visited upon him.

I wish the yellow discs that show the distance to London would go there.

§ xii

Our village has a wayside station on the main line from Glasgow and the North to London. The gradient is heavy, and even the Royal Scot, southward bound, has to abate her speed so much that an alert person might manage to swing on to an end platform of one of the coaches, though the action would be as ill-advised as the one contemplated by a passenger on an express train between Aberdeen and Inverness. "I'm feeling very ill," he told the guard; "indeed, I think I'm going to die." "I'd stroangly advise ye no to dae onything o' the sort," said the guard, "for a corpse on this train's a shilling a mile."

Had Stevenson spent his childhood in this district, his *Child's Garden of Verses* would have included a poem about the trains thundering past—the three brither Scots, the socially even more august North trains, the all-England expresses, the postal train, and the fish and meat train, which has priority of "locals".

> At night I hear the London train;
> I see it through the window pane;
> It's like a fire that's run away
> With shops and houses bright as day.
>
> The engine-driver and his mate
> Are used to being up so late;
> They do not fear the wind and rain,
> For nothing stops the London train.
>
> And at the station I can see
> The people sitting down to tea,
> With buttered toast, and cakes and honey—
> Those people must have lots of money!
>
> I wave to them, but they are proud,
> They do not see the village crowd:
> I'm going to tea with Jimmy Brown—
> But they are going to London town!
>
> Some day, when I have saved a lot,
> I'll travel by the Royal Scot,
> And see the sights of London town,—
> But I'd like to go with Jimmy Brown!

Those trains give me the go-fever sometimes—but not the London fever. How friendly the word "Glasgow" looks on a railway carriage at Euston!

When the London suburbs are cleared, one breathes freely—but there are still the dull, scarred, depopulated Midlands to pass through. The vigorous industrialism of Lancashire is better; the Pennines bring a foretaste of Scotland; Carlisle is a neutral interlude —and then the blink of the Solway, and the closing in of the hills of sheep in Annandale, and the stertorous climb from Beattock.

The London fever persists among Scots who have not wakened up to realities. As they watch the trains go past, they sigh because it is so far to London and the fare is so dear. But let them take heart. If they manage to live long enough (and here is an inducement), they will not need to go to London. London will come to them. It will at least meet them more than half-way.

For Sir Halford Mackinder contemplates, evidently without a shudder, a London of about twenty-five million inhabitants, covering a great part of England. Already the area which to all intents is London extends to nearly 2000 square miles!

With more spacious town-planning, that area will easily treble. London is already over the Chilterns. The touch of it is perceived forty miles from Temple Bar. In time it will comprise the whole Thames basin as far up as Oxford, the whole of the country between the Thames and the English Channel, and the country north as far almost as Birmingham, Leicester, and Cambridge.

To this nightmare of pullulation must be added another. Liverpool, Manchester, and Leeds, with all the towns between, will coalesce into one vast city, spreading out tentacles towards Hull and Newcastle.

There will be no more England. There will only be two terrible urban tumours eating up every acre of farmland and forest, and racing for Sheffield. The Peak district of Derbyshire will perhaps be made a National Reserve, and called England, in memory of the "green and pleasant land" of that name.

Scotland will have become merely a meat-and-milk, sporting, and tourist area, with a few coal-pits and minor industries.

§ xiii

"Kennst du das Land?"

Those words, the beginning of the most beautiful song Italy has inspired, are familiar throughout the world; and the song itself, in the original, or in translations that seem to have been made from one another—so ineffably bad are they—has been sung in every theatre, concert-hall, and drawing-room, "from China to Peru".

In that brief song, and in the beautiful, passionate, pathetic, fairy-like little creature who sings it in *Wilhelm Meister*, Goethe expressed the wild longing for Italy that had tormented him since childhood.

When, at thirty-seven, he was able to satisfy this longing, he virtually fled from Germany, and posted south through the Alps, and on to Rome, by day and night, terrified lest by some chance he might be re-called.

My Scotland

Italy was all his fancy painted it, and he lingered in it for nearly two years. But his *Italy* is a disappointing book.

Goethe was blind to the greatest things in Italian art, and obsessed by Palladian architecture, and the late, over-blown school of Italian painting: probably because both were in extreme contrast to Gothic, and recalled the Italian prints in his father's house.

When he returned, brimming over with Italy, he was chagrined at finding no one to share his Italian enthusiasms. Boswell, in a like condition of travel-ebullience, was nicknamed "Corsican Boswell". No one in Germany would have dared to dub the Olympian poet "Italian Goethe"; but his friends yawned behind their hands while he raved about Naples and Sicily—and turned with relief to gossip about Weimar and Jena.

Have we not all had the same experience, when home our footsteps we have turned from wandering on a foreign strand? We described and narrated, raved and rhapsodied—unconscious, or repressing our half-consciousness, that our hearers were either bored or envious, or both—in any case, wishing to goodness we would shut up.

Later in life, our experience as listeners may have taught us that the things in travel tales that interest hearers most are those the traveller enjoyed least. Things pleasant and beautiful interest not at all.

That is why the most enthralling travel books are those—like Mrs. Trollope's, or Arthur Young's, or Norman Douglas's, or George Gissing's—in which there is a dash of the repellent, *outré*, whimsical, tragic, fearsome, or macabre.

We want, incidentally, to have some slight consolation for not having been there!

And the "land" we seek, when we fare forth ourselves, is, like Goethe's, a homeland of our own soul, compact of childish dreams and impressions: of which, on a first visit, we seem to find realization, though a second may bring to us, as it did to Goethe, sordid disillusion.

The "land" is not Italy or Greece, Tahiti or Tidore. It lies still farther on—

> Over the Mountains of the Moon,
> Down the Valley of the Shadow.

It is El Dorado, Avalon, Tir nan Og, the Lost Atlantis. When we have given up cruising in search of it, it may reveal itself as our own native land, "the place where, in the end, we find our happiness, or not at all".

§ xiv

It is hypocritical for elderly people to pretend not to wish they were young again. The pretence vanishes, for me, when I look over a Ramblers' Annual.

I do not envy modern youth its fashions, games, motor cars, film stars, jazz songs, or stupid dances. Were such things the most of life, there would be "something to be said for being dead". But when I read that in the near future the Highlands of Scotland are likely to be opened up to "the feet of the young men", I echo the cry of Faust: "Oh, give me back my youth again." Bliss is it in this dawn to be alive, but to be young is very heaven.

In my penurious youth, I made several tours on foot through the enchanted land of bens and glens and gamekeepers. The scenery entranced me, but I discovered that, beyond certain well-defined areas on the fringe of the Highlands, I was an undesirable alien in my own country.

The grandest scenes were associated with extortionate bills in hotels where the "Highland welcome" was conspicuous by its absence; the most alluring vistas recalled the impossibility of proceeding farther, either through lack of paths or shelter, or because of the decree of the landowner. In some places I was lodged secretly—like the hunted Stuart!

I turned my back upon the whole domain of sporting snobbery. Books about the Highlands added insult to injury. I tossed them aside.

During the years when Goethe cherished his dream of beholding Italy, but saw no chance of its fulfilment, he could hardly bear to hear Italy mentioned. Many Scots have felt that way about their own Highlands.

Now the ban is to be lifted. Provision is to be made throughout the Highlands for ordinary folk who go there, not to kill things at a heavy fee, but to enjoy Nature and mix with the people.

Fortunate young people, who for a few pounds will taste the rarest and purest delights earth can afford —tramping and climbing from ben to ben, and sleeping amid the haunts of eagles and the mountain winds —give a thought ('twill heighten your bliss) to those who were pushed back from your Eden, and scarcely dared to dream what you enjoy!

§ xv

The saddest tale I read in my boyhood was in our school reading-book, colloquially termed "the shillin'y". It was about a boy named Solomon Slow, the son of a gentleman who lived on the borders of the New Forest.

Solomon was a boy of lazy and unpunctual habits. He was invited to a picnic. It was to be an all-day affair, and the party were to leave in a horse bus at an early hour, with all kinds of hampers on board.

The morning was fine, with promise of a glorious day. At this point my pen falters. Somebody ought to have flung cold water over Solomon, or dragged him out of bed by the heels. But nobody did. They only hammered and shouted, and appealed to his better nature. Solomon overslept himself, as they put it in the South.

An illustration showed the wretched boy, dishevelled and desperate, panting along the road, and waving frantically to a huge bus disappearing over a crest. They might have stopped for him, I thought. But they were good Victorians, with a moral to point. They jeered at him from the bus, and shouted "Serve you right!" or words to that effect.

Picture the long misery of that lonely day for the hapless Solomon. Pleasures and palaces might be his in after years, but nothing could ever make up to him for that lost picnic.

I was the more ready to weep for Solomon because

I had always managed to miss the Sunday School picnic, or "trip". It was to Busby. I have seen Busby many times since, but it was not the Busby of the Sunday School trip. That remains a nook of Never-Never-Land.

The real kind of Sunday School picnic is the one that goes in country carts, with ribbons on the big horses, and mothers and grannies taking charge of the younger bairns. The minister in the front cart may look a little self-conscious. Church picnics are a test of pastoral qualities.

In Victorian days only well-off folk picnicked. They went in carriages, in their best clothes, the ladies with poke-bonnets, voluminous skirts, dainty shoes, and little parasols, the gentlemen with tight-waisted tail-coats, wide white trousers, and broad-brimmed hats. On a shady lawn beside a stream they spread a table-cloth, and from the hampers were unloaded cold fowls, potted meats, and all the apparatus of a heavy meal. The whiskered gallants made play with the uncorking of bottles and the serving of wine. The ladies screamed in a refined manner when caterpillars and spiders appeared.

Nowadays all the world picnics. The hikers' fires and spirit-stoves are everywhere. Motorists spread their tables in the wilderness, and enjoy elaborate meals. The sight may bring salutary reflections to hotel-keepers and landowners. Our tradition of rural solitariness and inhospitality is depriving our country-sides of a big amount of trade.

The picnic fire is discouraged, and rightly. It is a menace to woodlands. But the lighting of a fire was the charm of the old-fashioned picnic. The kettle might take an hour to boil, the tea might be smoked —but there was "our" fire. Delight in it may be a survival of fire-worship.

That cult is still strong among tinkers: and those children of the wild retain the real secret of picnicking.

§ xvi

Twice I have had the experience of saying farewell to a country-side after living for some years in it. In neither case did I have any profound regrets.

The truth of the matter may be that I never dared to harbour regrets. When one has "flitted" several times, one develops a providential stoicism.

In both cases, also, my location had been determined by accidental circumstances. The country-sides were healthful, pleasant, and beautiful; and I took delight in exploring them. But in both I was a preoccupied "in-comer", with no local affinities.

Our country-side is where we have spent our youth. Mine had its centre in Kelvingrove; and it widened out to include Cathkin, Waterfoot, Mearns, Glanderston, Caldwell, Gleniffer, Erskine, Bowling, Stockiemuir, Strathblane, Campsie, and Cadder.

Farther and farther it widened, till it took in Galloway and the Lowthers, Ettrick and Tweedside, the Pentlands and Edinburgh, the Ochils and Lomonds, Menteith and Strathearn, the Sidlaws and the Braes of Angus. There it linked up with the country-side of my ancestors, and with Aberdeen and beyond.

Improved communications, the "rambling" habit,

Mòds and Community Drama, the study of Scots literature and social history, and the movements for national reconstruction, have given us something which our rustic ancestors, with all their love of home, did not possess. They have given us the "sense of Scotland".

The old barriers between East and West, North and South, Highlands and Lowlands, have broken down. Our country-side extends from Maidenkirk to Unst, and from Fife Ness to the Butt of Lewis.

One does not forget that Shakespeare, who wrote:

> All places that the eye of heaven visits
> Are to the wise man ports and happy havens,

found his haven in his native Stratford; and one remembers Scott's cry in Italy, when he heard of Goethe's death: "He at least died at home. Let's to Abbotsford!"

That intensive love of home is necessary to our spiritual health as a nation. *Sunset Song* shows why we had repressed it. The death of a country-side is painful to contemplate.

A reawakened and reunited Scotland brings hope to those moribund regions. When the national "circulation" has been fully restored, we shall be able to give play to our local affections without fear of being left lonely among graves, or of being provincially marooned.

> O look! the sun begins to shine, the heavens are in a
>   glow;
> He shines upon a hundred fields, and all of them I
>   know.

Travel and Return

The rising sun of Scotland shines on Galloway and Glenelg, the Lothians and the Hebrides, Buchan and the Lennox. Edinburgh and Glasgow, Dundee and Aberdeen, Perth and Dunfermline, Inverness and Oban, are virtually one great city. Country-side is linked vitally with country-side, "and all of them I know".

The new sense of Scotland may even absorb the incurable nostalgia of a Glasgow man for the Firth of Clyde.

CHAPTER V

PEOPLES AND PEOPLE

§ i

I UNDERSTAND that the British-Israelites do not include the inhabitants of the Irish Free State. The Scots, however, are numbered among the Chosen People. Scottish Nationalists might contend that Scotland had a prior claim in this matter. The Scottish Kingdom was founded by an Egyptian Princess—doubtless a convert to Judaism—and in the seventeenth century the Scots identified themselves with Israel to an extent that makes it difficult to follow their itineraries on the map.

France believes itself to be the citadel of civilization. Houston Stewart Chamberlain wrote a big book to prove that the future of humanity lay with the Germans. The world-destiny of Italy has been modestly set forth by Mussolini. As for England and the United States . . .

I wonder what the real Israelites think about it. Perhaps they recall Disraeli's retort to O'Connell, who had hinted at a lineal descent from the impenitent thief on the cross: "When the honourable gentleman's ancestors were running about naked in the Bog of Allen, mine were princes in Israel."

Or perhaps a sad smile expresses the tolerant wisdom

of a race that has learned for what variety of destiny a people may be "chosen".

Mr. Dick, in *David Copperfield*, who could not get on with his wonderful Memorial because King Charles's head was always coming into it, is typical of most people who are "past a certain age".

Now and then we revolt against this tendency of the mind to move in "a circle that ever returneth in to the self-same spot". Beloved Ithaca imprisons us. At evening, when the lights begin to twinkle from the rocks, we will launch our patched-up boat and sail towards the bath of the western stars.

But a strange thing has happened. The fixed idea from which we try to escape has become the fixed idea of the brightest young minds about us. Ithaca has become more to them than Atlantis.

The Scottish national movement expresses the awareness of active-minded young Scots that they cannot realize themselves fully unless within a nationally developed Scotland. Their activities give me assurance that the working round of all my thoughts to this point is not monomania. It is a life-impulse; the search of the mind for a missing nucleus of effort; the working out of sum after sum to a point where a missing integer declares itself.

In Sir Willoughby Patterne, Meredith has portrayed the immortal type of the systematically selfish man. His ideals, his duties, his irreproachable conduct, reduce themselves to the level of a carefully played game, in which everybody and everything about him minister to his pride, convenience, and pleasure. His game has a fixed ambit, and it involves the restriction of his own personality. He has no cranks or hobbies, no designs upon the general scheme of things. As the perfect egoist, he is the antithesis of an egotist.

Sir Willoughby is a distinctively English type. Stevenson's *mot* about the Shorter Catechism and drink expresses the inability of the Scot to cultivate a perfect egoism.

The Scot has no desire to be the petted tyrant of a domestic and social circle. His ambitions, for good or evil, are in the wide sense spiritual. He wants to reform the world, to subdue a portion of it, or to destroy it; to impress upon it his own will and personality. He is an egotist.

In Scotland, Celtic tribalism and Norman feudalism infected each other with their worst features. The result was a chaos of blind egotisms. Lowland lords and Highland chiefs vied with each other in raids, murders, and plottings.

The people, loyal so long amid disloyalty, caught the infection of schism when their turn of power came. The insane sectarianism of the Scots Presbyterian Church made Scotland the laughing-stock of Europe.

This malady of blind schism, of insatiate egotism, persists amongst us. It expresses itself in narrow regionalism, suspicion of anything nationally Scots, the impulse to split up national movements and carry off sections of them into the wilderness, or to assail them destructively from the outside, instead of helping them by constructive criticism from the inside.

That Scotland ceased to be a nation is no mystery

to anyone who has traced in her history the workings of this destructive vice of egotism. Our present effort to subdue it to a national purpose is tantamount to a second Reformation.

§ ii

" *There* is a man!" Napoleon exclaimed when his eyes lighted on Goethe. Beneath the words lay annoyance that this majestic creature was roaming outside the Napoleonic menagerie.

There were two other figures, living within Napoleon's lifetime, to whom he might have paid the same tribute. One was a Scottish farmer and exciseman, who had died at thirty-seven. The other was an English nobleman, half a Scot by blood, and wholly by temperament and training, who was to perish also at thirty-seven.

These, Napoleon included, were great elementalists, experimenters in life, creating for themselves "impossible" situations, as if to see how their minds would react to them, escape from them, absorb them, or transcend them. Their function was the dangerous one of extending human consciousness.

Later, the daemonic influence passed into politics, though Tennyson showed an external trace of it. It reached its height in Gladstone and Disraeli, and with them it faded out. One of its last exponents was the Scottish actor, William Mackintosh.

Today the daemonic influence seems to have vanished. There are vital personalities amongst us, but their range is limited.

Slavery to the machine is making us a supine race.

We have lost the sense of human dignity possessed by those fine old Victorian whiskerandoes who walked like exiled monarchs, and put impressive style into a demand for a pint of beer.

The beautiful series of photographs by David Octavius Hill, which a German writer has brought into prominence, are of sociological as well as artistic interest.

Their beauty is mainly due to Hill's Rembrandtesque sense of character, grouping, and chiaroscuro, and to the fortunate imperfections of photography. But Hill found his original inspiration in his sitters. They possessed the picturesque and grandiose elements which his genius assembled and grouped.

The Victorians were prejudiced, narrow-minded, and unenlightened. But they had coherent and stable individualities. Every one of them was an independent "system" of will, belief, opinion, taste, temperament, and idiosyncrasy.

Whether they were saints or criminals, they were consistently themselves—and sure of themselves. They were always "in character", and stuck to their parts throughout the play. We, in the disintegratory torrent of modern life, can attain only a transient pose. The Victorians had poise.

Those old photographic pictures make us realize what is amiss in modern literature, art, music, and social life. Art, the dignity of life, is bound up with the conservation of personality.

If the "lord of creation" becomes a mere nebula of uncoordinated reflexes, of no interest to a Shakespeare or a Dickens, a Rembrandt or a David Octavius Hill, what is the value of "progress" ?

I should like to make a collection of old prints and photographs showing the various schools of what the late Frank Richardson called "face-fungus".

When I come across a photograph of about 1870, showing a group of lusty and leisured Scots—large men, large whiskers—out to maintain national prestige in curling, shooting, golf, cricket, bowling, football—not to speak of whiskers—I am spell-bound, and forget all time.

Those were the days when Scots who were not slaves of the machine ran to the cultivation of height, fighting-weight, thews, masculine good looks—and whiskers. "There were seven brothers, all over six-feet-three"—and each with his own fancy in whiskers.

The fascination lies in the fact that whiskers are a disguise. The big braw man with the ecclesiastical side-whiskers may be a freethinker and a Bohemian. The man with the military moustache and mutton-chops combination may be a born pacifist. The man who peers sideward over a dark, tangled forest is probably not a blood-stained bushranger but a Sabbath-school teacher.

Each of them seems to be asking us to guess what he really is.

A well-known advertisement has been showing us famous men of the whisker period with and without their disguise. The result is disillusioning.

W. G. Grace denuded of his beard is living Grace no more. He is only an insignificant type of English-

man with an ugly cap. Not thus could he have ruled
the field. Henry VIII. is like a stockbroker and
gentleman-farmer. Dickens clean-shaven is as un-
thinkable as Wellington with a Prussian moustache or
Napoleon with Dundrearies.

Why did the spade beard of Tudor times give way
to the pointed beard of the Cavalier, the upper-lip
smudge of the Restoration, and the smooth-facedness
that lasted till the nineteenth century?

"Side-galleries" came from Spain during the Penin-
sular War. The "cavalry moustache" came from
Poland via the *Grande Armée*. I saw some choice
specimens of it in the Carpathians.

The Crimean War was responsible for the epidemic
of large side-whiskers in the 'sixties. Scotland contributed chin-whiskers—"the Celtic fringe". The
Knoxian super-beard had revived on land, and the
short-pointed beard at sea. The wild medley of those
motifs from 1870 to our own time provoked a desperate
return to eighteenth century hairlessness.

But is it not also the case that, whereas the young
men of 1860 or 1870 wanted to look mature and responsible, the older men nowadays want to look as
young as possible? Until middle-agedness and elderli-
ness become fashionable again, we are not likely to see
a return of whiskers. But you never can tell. The
young might turn the tables on the old by adopting
flowing whiskers as a badge of youth.

The rapt interest with which Edinburgh audiences
witnessed a play on Robert Burns would have been a
revelation to a foreigner.

Peoples and People

According to received notions, the figure that would most appeal to a Scots audience would be one in which the rigidly moral element was always uppermost, and whose energies were directed towards repressive righteousness and the gathering of gear.

But the man upon whose stage effigy those hard-headed Scots gazed with moist-eyed sympathy was an unsuccessful farmer and rebellious exciseman, who was guilty of moral lapses, loved conviviality, flouted the "unco guid", expressed subversive sentiments, championed the outcast, and devoted his powers to the unprofitable art of verse-making. He even refused money for his songs!

"Character", in so far as it consists in repression of impulses for a moral or "practical" end, had been overdone in Scotland. Personality, which consists in the harmonious release of impulses, had suffered.

Burns broke the conventional mould of Scots character, and aimed at a bigger synthesis of human qualities.

Burns achieved personality. That is why Scotland worships him.

The modern world has its heroes, but their function seems the reverse of that of Burns or Goethe. They do not stand for release of faculties, but for their fixation.

Lenin checked the divagations of the Russian mind, and forced it into channels of doctrinaire materialism. Mussolini persuaded the Italians to adopt a discipline foreign to their modern tradition. Hitler invoked the disciplinary tradition which the Hohenzollerns imposed upon the dreamy Germans. He released the impulses of anti-release!

But restriction and expansion are alike effected by dominant personalities. The hero is the expression of the "quantum theory" in the moral and social sphere.

If anyone is a good judge of manhood, it is the courageous, massive-minded, deep-thinking author of *An American Tragedy*. Dreiser learned life in a rough school, where a man's very existence often depended upon his ability to think quickly, decide promptly, and act boldly.

Not all of Dreiser's "Twelve Men" are heroes, in the conventional sense. Only one is a saint. But each has a certain definiteness and forthrightness of character, a general consistency of taste and aim, that makes him individually distinctive.

The most striking of the group is "Culhane, the Solid Man", a stalwart Irish exponent of Spartan ideals, who in his toning-up establishment addressed his swell clients in the manner of a Carlyle turned sergeant-major. Culhane sought inspiration—and vocabulary—in books like Lecky's *History of European Morals*. It is remarkable, however, that only one of Dreiser's "men" was, strictly speaking, of his own profession.

The price the gods exact for song—"to become what we sing"—is paid by most people whose trade is writing. They have to expend so much of their will and imagination in writing that they have little to spare for their own lives. Many of them go through life without developing any definite character at all.

"A talent is formed in quietude, a character in the stream of the world."

Most of the authors who are remembered as personalities belonged to periods when personality in general was richer than it is to-day. They are remembered as men because they wrote about themselves or were written about by other authors. Their lives and characters were probably less interesting than those of thousands of their unliterary contemporaries.

Literary men are not below the moral level of their period. They are usually well above it. But, if they are prolifically creative, they cannot cultivate the art of living. When they venture into active life they are apt to lose sense of proportion and show up badly. Witness certain episodes in the lives of Pope, Swift, Rousseau, Voltaire, Shelley, Musset, Dumas, and Balzac.

Things have changed nowadays. Most writers are, to a greater or less extent, men of action and affairs. They travel and have adventures, and write, as men to men, of that which they have known and experienced.

That is all to the good—up to a certain point. But it may explain why our age is deficient in great creative work. The gods still exact the "price of song" —the suppression and even mutilation of the author's personal life.

The greatest of all writers occulted himself so completely in his works that the little that is definitely known of his life seems a tale told by the village idiot, signifying less than nothing.

§ iii

The late Lord Rosebery, one of the greatest bibliophiles, once described large public libraries as "cemeteries".

The description is found painfully apt by the book-lover who, rummaging in odd corners of a great library on a summer day, comes upon rows of volumes which once ranked among best-sellers, but now yellow in semi-darkness, touched only by the feather-brush of a cleaner.

Outside in the sunshine, trees sway, motor-horns sound, and young folk chaff and laugh. The dance of life goes merrily on. But those once-popular authors are dead and forgotten.

> They have no share in all that's done
> Beneath the circuit of the sun.

The irony of it is that their share, when they lived, was considerable. They were not recluses, living laborious days in the hope of posthumous fame. They did not chisel and polish phrases that would resist the "ever-rolling stream". They turned out in hot haste the stuff that would bring them money and current reputation. They sampled existence, floated on topical currents, and "cashed their cheques".

Here, for example, is an attractive-looking volume, *Doctor Syntax's Three Tours, in search of the Picturesque, Consolation, and a Wife*. Who, nowadays, knows or cares anything about the man who, week after week, furnished R. Ackerman with a chapter in facile octo-syllabics, to accompany Rowlandson's drawings?

Born at Bristol in 1741, William Combe, by 1771, had travelled on the Continent with Sterne, figured as "Duke Combe", gambled away a fortune, served in the British and French armies, and been a cook in Douay College. He wrote or compiled Travels, Voyages, and Histories innumerable, besides at least two thousand columns in the newspapers, and a large collection of sermons for clergymen. At seventy, when he wrote his once-famous "Tour", he had amorous experiences of an invidious nature. At eighty, bankrupt and ill, he was still writing, and he died at eighty-two.

"If, therefore, a long experience of the world, an enlarged view of its affairs, the habits of diligence and intellectual toil, a mind not wholly unstored, a versatile faculty in constant practice, with a decorum of manners that suits conduct to situation, be qualifications" (the words are from an office-seeking letter to Lord Mulgrave, soon after Combe's "moistened eye" had "followed the remains of Mr. Pitt to his ever-honoured sepulchre"), Combe has a permanent claim to notice.

But those things weigh not with posterity, unless they have resulted in something permanently vital. Defoe was as topical as Combe, and even less scrupulous; but Defoe wrote with his "eye on the object", and also on Everyman, who is the same to-day as in 1729.

There is a sadly bitter poem of Musset's on an evening at the Comédie Française, when Molière's *Misanthrope* was being performed. The audience was small, and the half-empty house seemed to echo

Alceste's denunciations of the frivolous obtuseness of fashionable society. The melancholy poet felt himself in solitary communion with the most sadly wise of humorists.

A lover of great drama has much the same feeling at a modern performance of a Shakespeare play. Even "cultured" Edinburgh fails to show appreciation of disinterested efforts to keep the prince of poets and dramatists on the stage. There must be something in what has been said as to the deficiency of our Scots universities on the cultural side. What is the net value of education if it does not bring young people out to hear the supreme voice of immortal youth?

The Germans pay Shakespeare the tribute of constant performance, while in the English-speaking countries he has become a literary antique. Germany, however, is exceptional in her appreciation both of foreign and of native genius. Shakespeare has never been naturalized in France, and Britain's record of Shakespearean performances is better than France's record in regard to her own great dramatists.

And yet is it not a wonderful thing that plays written for audiences three centuries ago should have any appeal for modern audiences? When I saw a crowd at the "Old Vic" spell-bound by *Lear*, I was aware that I was witnessing a miracle of genius.

Most of Shakespeare's comedies have a lot of dead wood in the shape of topical cross-talk, fashionable "wit", conventional clowning, and mechanical "mistake" plots.

A few of the comedies have become hopeless for the stage; in others, some of the dead wood might be cut out. The tragedies and the historical plays have worn best; indeed, they have probably gained in effectiveness by the lapse of time.

What we want is a public prepared to rise to the height of strong presentations of all the plays in which Shakespeare is at his greatest as dramatist, poet, and humorist. There is a touch of modishness, almost of school-bookishness, about the conventional Shakespeare repertory. We want a fresh and bigger one, which should include *Julius Cæsar, Antony and Cleopatra, Measure for Measure,* and *Cymbeline.*

From the stage point of view, the best of Shakespeare is yet to be—if the young public will come along and make its wishes known.

The worst sin of which anyone can be guilty is that of flattering the "people". The finest thinkers in all ages have held the demagogue in horror.

One can go too far in the other direction, however— as Voltaire did when, in a private and very frank letter, written when he was at the height of his fame, he declared that manual workers—the people who "had only their arms to live by"—were unworthy and incapable of intellectual instruction. It was desirable, indeed, that it should be withheld from them, because the only effect of it would be to make them less useful to the *bon bourgeois.*

An extraordinary comment on this is another letter, written twelve years later, in 1778, by a girl named Marie Phlipon, afterwards known to tragic fame as Madame Roland. Her father was an engraver, and the family were "of the people". Yet Marie and her friends were able to put Voltaire "in his place".

"We admire him", she wrote, "as a poet" (that seems queer; but taste has altered), "as a man of taste and esprit, but we give him only a very limited authority in regard to politics and philosophy."

If Voltaire had seen himself ticked off in this cool fashion by a working-class girl—who anticipated the considered judgment of great critics in our own day—he would have died of rage and mortification.

Many an acclaimed writer is being subjected to a like process. In mines, factories, shipyards, bothies, engine-rooms, judgments are being passed which will be confirmed, years hence, by critics who are not yet out of the nursery.

Why not, then, accept popular verdicts in literature, art, music? Because they can seldom be authoritatively delivered, with any assurance that the work in question has been judged on its merits.

Even Mademoiselle Phlipon did not perceive that Voltaire was no poet. It was sufficient that she "placed" him as a political philosopher. One thing at a time!

In matters that can be tested by common sense and experience of real life, the "people" are the ultimate jury—when they choose to serve. It is their verdict, in such matters, that filters into literature and is pronounced at length by the high court of criticism.

Even in Voltaire's day the "populace" was ceasing to be delimited by occupation. Where taste and thought do not rise above the jazz and sentimental-fiction level—there is "populace". Where they rise

to Wagner, Hardy, Guthrie, MacDougall, von Hügel
—there is "the head of the table".

When, in a public square of Oslò or Bergen, we come
across a statue of Ibsen or Bjӧrnson, Grieg or Ole Bull,
we feel it is exactly right. Nansen and Amundsen will,
naturally, be added. It is chiefly through such people
that Norway is known to the world.

The matter is more complicated in a large and composite country like Britain. It is particularly difficult
in Scotland, which has a national tradition of its own,
and also a share in Imperial history.

The best plan is to put ourselves in the place of the
"intelligent foreigner" who has a sympathetic knowledge of Scotland. He would not expect to find massive
monuments to Hanoverian personages who had little
to do with Scotland, to forgotten aristocratic and legal
magnates, or to statesmen, sailors, and soldiers who
were not of Scottish birth or affinity.

In the centre of the Scottish Capital he would look
for monuments to Wallace, Bruce, Dunbar, Knox,
Mary Stuart, Montrose, William Paterson, Adam
Smith, Watt, Burns, Scott, Galt, Camperdown,
Cochrane, Chalmers, Livingstone, Simpson, Carlyle,
Stevenson, and Haig.

If the intelligent foreigner knew anything of Glasgow's history, he would decide that among those who
should be conspicuously commemorated were Wallace,
Bishops Jocelyn, Wishart, Cameron, and Turnbull,
George Buchanan, John Cameron, Alexander Hen-
derson, Francis Hutcheson, Cullen, Reid, Adam Smith,
James Watt, Professor Anderson, the Foulises, Smollett,

Patrick Colquhoun, Campbell, Henry Bell, Lord Clyde, the Napiers, Livingstone, Lister, the Cairds, Kelvin, Macewen, and Neil Munro.

That list is sufficient to show that in the matter of public monuments Glasgow does not need to draw upon rolls of fame that do not touch her borders. Outside the capital, the visitor does not look for repetitions of national commemorations. He looks for the local contribution.

The Glasgow list suggests that a multiplicity of statues is undesirable. The inscription on a building, with, where possible, a bust within a sculptured niche, is a good method. And every city ought to have something like the Dean Cemetery of Edinburgh, and Dublin's Glasnevin.

Monuments form the most emphatic item in the "publicity" of a nation. For that reason alone there is need for some agreement on the principles governing their erection.

§ iv

A waterfall plunging from canyon into canyon induces a feeling of exultation. The soul is strengthened by the sight of a cliff with the Atlantic rollers breaking at its base. And what can be more tranquillizing than a beautiful old English village, like Bablock Hythe, with an old-fashioned ferry on a slow-moving river?

But a higher degree of exultation, of strength, and of tranquillity is experienced as one ascends from a river-valley to a boldly undulating upland.

We have forgotten what it was that depressed us an

hour before. The tasks ahead that frightened us seem child's play. Nervousness and languor have been subdued by an Olympian calm, modified by a profound awe.

We understand the spirit of the Waldensians, the "Israel of the Alps"; of the Huguenots of the Cevennes, who chanted their wild Psalm-tunes as they met the charge of the dragoons; of the Covenanters at Drumclog and the Highlanders at Killiecrankie.

The hills have been the sanatoria of vanquished races. Driven up into them, they have gathered new strength that in time their former conquerors had to respect. Even the tepid Muse of Mrs. Hemans was moved to epic greatness by the vision of the Swiss mountaineers driving the Austrians down the defile of Morgarten.

It was the strength of the hills that was manifested at Bannockburn. Sadly reduced by depopulation and the sporting system, it displayed itself in the immortal exploits of the 51st Division. There was a terrible social irony—foreshadowed by the writer of "The Canadian Boat Song"—in that last hecatomb of Scotland's mountaineers. What penal laws, punitive oppression, and armed might could not subdue has succumbed to the power of the purse and the lure of cities.

Where is the strength of the Highland hills today? The whirring grouse, metallically mocking, answers "Where?" The requiem of the vanished races is sounded by the melancholy whaup.

Not long ago I paid a visit to a farm on the Lanarkshire uplands, near the Ayrshire border.

"Winds, austere and pure," blew about us. The eye, following the swift cloud-shadows, ran up over grey-green slopes to rounded cones nearly two thousand feet above sea-level.

Though the land was less fertile than that of many deserted straths in the Highlands, the hill-sides were dotted with white farmhouses, each with its little garden and grove. Near-by, a river flowed through a wooded glen.

Our host, a working farmer, stood upon the ground his ancestors had owned and farmed since before the Reformation. A monument on the hill-side marked the spot where one of them had been martyred for the Covenant.

As we went up over the moor we discussed biology, geology, astronomy, and archæology. On all these subjects our host was an authority.

The object of our quest was a group of ancient burial chambers on a hill-side, with a couple of stone circles on the crest. This was one of the holy places of the Britons of Strathclyde. I understood why the same region was a stronghold of the Covenanters.

The fruitful valleys and the fairy-haunted groves were shut out from view. Only the clean uplands and hill-tops were visible. The sky was close above, and all around.

In the stars, the clouds, the thunder and the winds, and in the awesome silences of noon or night, Heaven spoke here to the sons of Scotland, as to patriarchs and prophets in Palestine. On this mountain altar the Covenant seemed a real thing.

On the fringes of this Scottish Carmel are other hills,

inspiring no mystic rhapsody. They are coal-bings. Between those dreary mining settlements and the sky-roofed temples of the Druids and Covenanters there is no perceptible link. The life of the black-country seems as bleakly inorganic, as foreign to the soil, as the bings that adorn it.

Yet the miners are Covenanters, of a modern type, with ideals of solidarity and brotherhood. Their lives have the elements of romance. They are subterranean foresters, living in several geological periods, and hewing trees that sheltered the dragons of the prime.

Perhaps the miner is too easily pleased with home surroundings that, at the worst, are more cheerful than the places where he works. Will his town or village always seem a raw and grimy intruder in the land of the Covenanters?

§ v

I took note of him when I entered the restaurant, and, in order to study him more closely, I sat down opposite him, at the same table.

Having disposed of a large basin of soup, he was hacking his way, in the good old English fashion, through an extensive acreage of Châteaubriant steak, with numerous vegetables, staying himself with a tall flagon of beer. Now and then he sighed—but he never gave in.

He was a big man, with wavy, yellow hair, an aquiline nose, and blue eyes. He wore a sailor-looking suit of dark blue, with a pink shirt and a flowing bow-tie. He looked like an artist with a taste for yachting, or a yachtsman who painted pictures. His age might

be about forty, but he was the kind of man who looks
thirty-five till he is sixty, and sags into senility in a
night.

We exchanged condiments, and animadversions
upon the weather and the state of trade.

"It's those Dagos," he said, sighing deeply, as he
stolidly began a frontal attack upon a kopje of apple-
dumpling.

"Dagos and Jews. The dark-skinned races. Turning, in mean ways, upon their conquerors. Like
jackals upon an old lion."

I wasn't sure about the zoological accuracy of that
illustration; but I merely remarked that an ethno-
logical friend had assured me that the proportion of
dark people in Britain was steadily increasing.

The big fair man looked sadly at me for a few
moments, but said nothing. He had biscuits and
cheese to deal with, and a second bottle of beer. I had
been toying with two courses.

We went into the smoke-room together. We had
coffee; the big fair man had also a liqueur brandy. He
unrolled a monster tobacco pouch and slowly filled
a corn-cob pipe. I thought, inconsequently, of William
Morris; and, in the next moment, of a Captain Miller,
who used to paint sea-pictures that won the approval
of his fellow-mariners.

"What you were saying about the increase of dark
people?" he said, when he had enveloped himself in
smoke. "It's ominous. It's sinister. You're fair yourself."

"I once was. My hair was like faded straw. These
boiled-gooseberry eyes were once blue. But if I dyed

my hair I suppose it would have to be dark brown. That's the fashion."

"Just so. Now, when I was a boy, all the books I read—boys' books, you know—*Freddy and the Slavers*, and all that—they all made you believe that the blond people were top-dogs everywhere—doing all the really big and noble things, and bossing the 'lesser breeds', you know.

"That seems to be changing. I haven't been able to do much bossing. It takes me all my time to earn a living. I've actually been employed by an Italian Jew. What do you make of it?"

"Make of it? How?"

"I mean—have we been deceived—taken in? Is this blond supremacy a mere superstition? Look at me! I'm six feet two—a boxer, runner, wrestler, all-round athlete—pure Celto-Saxon or Celto-Norse strain, I'm informed—just the type we were told was born to command.

"But nobody's made way for me. The lesser breeds don't weep with delight when I give them a smile, or tremble with fear at my frown—not so far as I've noticed, anyhow. I was cheeked by an Italian waiter in London just last week. . . . And there's that fellow Maurice Walsh——"

"Maurice which?"

"The writer, you know. Making game of a man of my type; humiliating him; representing him as being knocked out, chaffed, deprived of his girl, by a 'small dark man' from Ireland—not even a Gael, I believe, but an Iberian, a Fomorian, or something like that. The Irish invasion—there you have it.

'One of our conquerors'—eh? What do you make of it?"

"It's easier to state the facts than to find reasons," I said. "Achilles, Agamemnon, Helen—all those conquering Hellenes were blond, and the *Iliad* describes their victory over the dark Trojans. Alexander the Great was fair. The old Romans were probably fair folk from the hills; they beat the dark Latians, Etruscans, and Carthaginians. But the fair elements in Greece and Rome were swamped by the swarthy slave-races.

"Then Rome was conquered by the blond barbarians from the North. Alaric, Odoacer, Charlemagne, Kenneth MacAlpine, Alfred the Great, William the Conqueror, Godfrey of Bouillon, Tancred of Jerusalem, Henry the Fowler, even Charles V and Ferdinand and Isabella—all were blonds. The Englishmen who beat the Spaniards and the French were fair. And the Germans——"

"The Germans, yes—who played a wicked mugs' game and wrecked the fortunes of the blond races— so it seems to me. Hitler's trying to redeem the blunder by shoving out the Jews; but it's too late."

"I don't think that has much to do with it. It's economic and social."

"What *do* you mean?"

I was forced to a theory, and put it forth desperately.

"Just this. Blondness is partly climatic, but it depends also on wide, free ways of living—lots of leisure, space, open air, sport, flesh food, and so forth —the things that become scarcer as people increase in numbers, and crowd together, and compete hard for subsistence. Blondness is like a rare flower, that flourishes only in favourable conditions. When conditions get bad, it is overborne by lower but hardier forms of life. The blonds pass out, like the dinosaurs, or elephants, or tigers—because the world isn't big enough for them."

"Now you're talking. That's me. I want lots of elbow-room. If I was a millionaire I'd show you what depopulation meant—I'd buy Mull, clear out all the people, and live in a big castle in Glen More. I want to go yachting and fishing and climbing, half my time. I love to loaf, between. I need lots of beef and lots of beer. I like to live in the best hotels. I refuse to get married, if it means living like a troglodyte. So I pass out, the last of my race, leaving this rabbit-warren of a world to the swarthy little degenerates who are content to huddle and stew and starve in it."

"War," I remarked, "used to be the trump card of the blonds. But it's no good now. The blonds would be killed off, and the troglodytes would win through, and go on multiplying. Still, they may evolve a better civilization than the blond one. Amyas Leigh, Tom Brown, and blond barbarians of that kind, were rather dull and insufferable, don't you think?"

"Maybe—but the blonds had the fine brains, too. And it isn't a question merely of brain in the narrow sense, but of big, free, generous, all-round living. Those scientific chaps are right: the superior type, mostly blonds, aren't reproducing themselves; and the lower types, mostly dark Iberians and swarthy wops and Yids, go on increasing. Look here, sir, it's simply degeneration—a working back to Neolithic Man and cave-dwellers."

My Scotland

We went out into the street. As we stood chatting for a moment at a corner, I was struck by the fine build and handsome appearance of the big fair man. He would have looked even finer with a beard. Vaguely I recalled a vision of my childhood: Frederick of Prussia, tall and fair and golden-bearded, the beau ideal of old Northern manhood, passing on horseback along a street in Stettin. I recalled, too, the old-time skippers I had seen as a boy—British, Scandinavian, German —tall men with fair, pointed beards, and eyes as blue as the sea, calm, but with the deep reflections of many tempests; kings of the bridge and quarter-deck. Vanishing types, in a world of small dark men.

"Big-game shooting would have suited you," I remarked.

"Yes—I suppose so. But it's beyond me. And I don't quite care, somehow." His eyes were lymphatic, and there was a droop of the mouth. "I've lost interest." As he looked round despondently I thought of a long-captive lion escaped into a noisy world that dismayed him. "I might go back to Australia, but this—this kind of thing follows you. It's everywhere."

We exchanged cards, and parted. When he was out of sight I looked at his card. At the left-hand bottom corner were the words: "Manufacturers' Agent. Buttons and Dress Trimmings."

A group of shop-girls came along the pavement. They were smartly dressed, alert, laughing, radiating vigour and the joy of life. All were, in their way, bonny, but none was tall. And, as they passed, I noticed that not one of them was blonde.

§ vi

The Adventures of an Obscure Victorian reminded us
how inarticulate—outside of the engine-room and
the captain's cabin—the "seagoing engineer" has
hitherto been.

Kipling's famous poem is a clever composite of
received ideas and actual observation, but it is
mechanical in conception. It lacks the subtle touches
that could be supplied only by a writer who had
absorbed the atmosphere of the Paisley Road.

The apprenticeship of the marine engineer, old
style, did not conduce to *joie de vivre* or lyrical self-
expression. On foggy mornings, when the rest of the
household were still in dreamland, he rose at the
summons of an alarm-clock, donned his working
clothes, and boiled coffee for himself in a pan, set over
an old-fashioned gas-jet, on two irons on the bedroom
mantelpiece.

With other ghosts, he crossed the Stygian Clyde
in a ferry-boat, to live a laborious and oily day in a
"shop" in Finnieston Street. In the evening, after
"cleaning" himself, he made his way to the "Tec",
armed with scale-drawings and a T-square, to grapple
with the theoretical aspects of cylinders, gauges, valves,
and feed-pumps.

When, at last, he found his way to sea, it was only to
bury himself in a floating "shop", cramped and dark.
Not for him those glorious first displays of brass buttons
and authority on the bridge. Not for him the sextant or
binoculars, or the cord of the bellowing siren. Nothing
but lubrication, revolutions, and the relation between

coal consumption and steam pressure; not to speak of
recalcitrant firemen in the lower depths.

Yet the Clyde-trained engineer, seagoing or land-
faring, is one of our great national figures. A French
engineer who had worked on the Clyde was impressed
by the fine way the railways were run in the Malay
States, especially as the train personnel was entirely
native—with one exception. The engine-driver was a
Glasgow man, restoring instant order when any hitch
or dispute arose—with a spanner as sceptre.

Kipling's divination was in the main accurate.
Calvinism—the sense of the inter-linking of duty and
divine destiny—found congenial expression in association with machinery, and a better medium than the
theological voids in which Scots mental machinery had
hurtfully "raced".

§ vii

It is a solemn thing to attend the jubilee reunion
of a school where one had been among the first
pupils. Yet when I had this experience I did not find
it depressing. The oldest of my former comrades were
remarkably perky. They would have been ashamed
to be otherwise, for some of their old teachers were
present. There was another circumstance that gave
special interest to the rally of veterans. Their school
had been only an ordinary "Board" school. But it has
established a tradition. It has its badge, magazine,
societies, sport teams, and so forth. It has developed
esprit de corps.

One noticed the interest of the present teachers in
the tributes paid by the veteran former-pupils to the

influence wielded by their teachers in the years long gone. Here was the revelation of a defect in our system of education. Teachers are discouraged when they never see the results of their labours, or receive any recognition from those they taught.

One of the evils of the massing of population in big monotonous towns was the destruction of all that was connoted by the village, its school, and the dominie. Society became inorganic. The surest way to restore organic life to Society is to extend the "great school" idea, with its loyalties, pride, associations, and enduring camaraderie, to every school in Scotland.

The Public School is the most distinctive of English institutions. Yet the English Public School as we know it is not an immemorial institution.

The five or six "great" Public Schools were originally semi-monastic. They had no particular cachet of swellness until the middle of the eighteenth century, when the English gentry, jostled by the trading and professional classes, tried to reinforce the barrier of caste by making certain of the old schools aristocratic preserves.

Naturally, that increased the attraction of those schools for well-off non-patricians, some of whom forced the barriers early in last century; and the "model" of the great Public School was adopted by old schools of humbler tradition, and by new schools.

The process was favoured by the growth of the British Empire. A large number of the Public School pupils were sons of military and naval officers and of Indian and Colonial Civil Servants, planters, and merchants.

Class-feeling and inhuman narrowness are not necessary features of the Public School. They were temporary blemishes, due to circumstances of development. The real evil is class-segregation, but the solution of the problem in England does not lie in the abolition of the Public School, but in the extension of the best of its traditions to every kind of school.

Many Scots forget that the strength of Scotland was the education of the sons of lairds, lawyers, doctors, ministers, alongside the sons of farmers, crofters, blacksmiths, or shepherds. How to retain that feature, and to apply it in the development of genuinely Scottish schools that will counter the pull of English or Anglified "Public Schools", is an urgent problem for Scotland. Part of the solution is provided by a school like Dollar Academy. The other part lies in the general process that has converted my old school from an education mill into a genuine academy, with an *esprit de corps* as strong as that of a Scottish regiment.

§ viii

Being by nature a Pyrrhonist, I have always been envious of those compatriots of mine who are able to make up their minds at once on any subject.

There was Francis Jeffrey, leader of Scottish criticism in the early days of the *Edinburgh Review*. He lived in the full height of the Romantic Revival, when strange new stars were climbing the literary heavens.

But he remained as calm as Horace's just man amid the crash of worlds.

It never occurred to him that genius adds to the body of law which it obeys, and creates the taste by which it is to be enjoyed. He never felt called upon to re-adjust his canons. His mind was made up. He raxed down a Sinaitic table of stone, and heaved it at the innovation.

Lockhart and Wilson seized crude boulders from the Caledonian mountains, and, with mocking laughter, hurled them at the Cockney Sansculottes who impudently aspired to literary heights reserved for gentlemen and scholars sealed of the tribe of "Sir Walter".

De Quincey, though a "Manchester man", had lived much in the shadow of Arthur's Seat, and acquired "aye-richtness". He drew out the German leviathan with a hook, and told the listening earth that Goethe, though he might pose as an Olympian on the Continent, was classed by Grasmere and Dalkeith as a lewd fellow of the baser sort.

Macaulay had so little difficulty in making up his mind that political bias, or the mere turn of a phrase, would send him clattering alliteratively through sixteen pages of cheap rhetorical sophistry.

Poe was unconscious of ever having borrowed a line or an image, but he was so sure that Longfellow had plagiarized from him that he quoted long "parallel" passages, between which the ordinary reader can detect no resemblance.

Poe, in his turn, came under the lash of the youthful R.L.S., who found an unpleasant taint in the man and his works, and dealt with him and his French translator, Baudelaire, much as Johnson dealt with Voltaire and Rousseau.

R.L.S. thought Scots literature had been overpraised. To compare Dunbar with Spenser or Rabelais was donkeyish; and Burns's "difficult and crude patois" was to the Englishman "a raucous gibberish".

This suggests an easy way with the so-called Scots Literary Renaissance. To examine its products in detail is tedious, and lands us up all kinds of streets. It is simpler to dismiss new experiments in the vernacular as "raucous gibberish", and to declare a Scottish Literary Renaissance to be in the same category as a Scottish vintage. Simplest rule and safest guiding—"This will never do."

There is an old Scots law-book called *Dirleton's Doubts*. I have never read it, and I know nothing about Dirleton except that he can't have been a happy man. He was not of the sturdy breed of those Scots ministers whom Cromwell (the thing is pathetic) entreated to consider it possible that they might be mistaken!

There was nothing of Dirleton about grand old Andrew Carnegie. When discussion arose, he would exclaim: "Yes, but listen to me." The Gordian knot was cut. The law was given forth. Even Kaiser Wilhelm II fell mute, and gave ear.

Ah, my friends, the secret of success, happiness, and long life is very simple. Have your mind made up. Incidentally, if you do that, the question of whether you have a mind will never arise.

§ ix

I am not a whole-hearted admirer of Sir Harry Lauder. And I am not any kind of admirer of his admirers. Most of them seem to know remarkably little about Scotland or Scots song. They also appear to be unaware that comedy which is not balanced by tragedy, humour which is not set off by true lyrical pathos and beauty, are like light without shade, or a colour without its complementary, or *hors d'œuvres* and condiments without solid viands.

Shakespeare is the greatest English poet and tragic dramatist: he is also the greatest English humorist. The decline in dramatic poetry after the Restoration was accompanied by a decline in real humour. For these are Siamese twins; and when one is sickly or dull, the other cannot be healthy or bright. True humour is a frictional discharge of all-round imaginative activity. It has got to be "earned", so to speak.

Sir Harry Lauder himself has "earned" his humour. In a touching speech at Arbroath, he told how, after his period there as half-timer, he worked in the mill for twelve hours a day and then teased ropes with his mother till midnight. Two years of that were followed by a spell of work in a coal mine, often from dark to dark. "That", he told a friend, "is how you learn to be a comic." He added, "You cannot learn to be a comic."

Both propositions are true. You require to be born a comic; and you require to have had early experiences that awoke the need for comic relief. You must have lived in the dark to appreciate the light.

143

What Sir Harry Lauder has told us of his early years makes us think of Dickens, who spent part of his boyhood in dismal slavery in a blacking factory, with the doubtful "comic relief" of possessing a father who had some of the traits of Wilkins Micawber. The real though elementary humour of Sir Harry's songs contrasts with the conventional banality of his "serious" ditties. Similarly—to compare small things with great—the inimitable humour of Swiveller and the Brasses, of Mr. Guppy and his circle, contrasts with the bathos of Little Nell and the stiltedness of Lady Dedlock.

Sir Harry Lauder and the early Dickens are both lopsided in their development. They put piquant sauces and inferior tinned tripe on the same menu. Even Cervantes was a little bit like that. His Exemplary Novels, and the serious tales intercalated in *Don Quixote*, are not on the same artistic plane as the adventures of the Knight of the Sorrowful Countenance. Smollett is another example: when he essays the tragic or romantic, he descends to commonplace dithyramb. Miss Ferrier, who invented some of the best comic and farcical characters in Scots fiction, has only waxworks for heroes and heroines, villains and villainesses, and their entrance is the occasion for pietistic declamations of frightful verbosity.

Scott is not exempt from the same failing. Galt is more free from it, and so is Fielding. Thackeray got almost entirely rid of it. In Meredith, Hardy, Bennett, Wells, and Galsworthy, the serious and comic elements run well balanced side by side, and mingle on equal terms. But these last—except, at times, Wells, who

had sat in darkness and "learned to be a comic"—
are not among the great mirthmakers.

What is the psychology of it? I think it is found in
the idea of "escape". The Dickens of the early novels
did not grapple with the serious side of life, which for
him had been intolerably grim. He hid it from himself with a screen of amusing types, droll scenes, and
melodramatic episodes. In his great autobiographical
novel he began to come to terms with actuality.
Thereafter he was more and more a "serious" and
artistic novelist. But his seriousness had a morbid
taint. The theme of his finest novel, *Great Expectations*,
is depressing rather than tragic, and in *Our Mutual
Friend* he broods over dust-heaps and skeletons and
drowned corpses and living *simulacra*. His early experiences had saddened him, and left a bad taste in
his mouth.

That is the tragedy of many of the world's great
jesters. When their period of "escape" is over, they
are apt to find the real world melancholy or forbidding. They become conscious of the iron in their
souls. Then they either become morbid, and sadly
cynical, as Dickens did in his three last books; or else
they preach sermons on the virtue of self-help, as Sir
Harry Lauder has been a good deal in the habit of
doing. Perhaps the beginning of a less didactic phase
was marked by his confession that the memory of
early struggles makes one "very, very humble". It
need not do that. It should make one proud and
strong. But it should also make one sympathetic with
those who, not having the instincts of a Carnegie or
the comic talents of a Lauder, have got to remain in

the ranks of the proletariat, and who try to raise the status of their whole class. Self-help alone would never have improved the working conditions which Sir Harry endured as a boy and a young man. Mutual help and an awakened social conscience were needed for that.

The most delightful of French humorists had a youthful experience as hard as that of Dickens or Sir Harry Lauder. But Daudet was too much of an artist to evade realities. The sadness of his school-days is reflected not only in his stories of childhood but also in the pessimism of *Sapho* and the asperity of *Numa Roumestan*. These, however, are genuine studies of life. He had his "escape", of course: without it, a man of his sensitiveness and with his experiences could scarcely have remained sane. But the "escape" of Alphonse Daudet is not represented only by his "Tartarin" books. The delicious humour of these is balanced by the lyrical beauty of his short stories and sketches, notably those included in *Lettres de Mon Moulin.*

Humour is thus not the only "escape". From the mine one may glimpse the stars. There are men working in Scottish pits today who have a vision of beauty and of art that has not been vouchsafed to Sir Harry Lauder and his admirers.

The public are more to blame than Sir Harry himself for his travesties of our song-literature. He has earned the right to be a comic. But they have not earned, by knowledge of really fine serious songs —and very few of them have earned by youthful experiences like his—the right to enjoy his "comic relief". They lack the "complementary". They remind one of the stories of the Clydeside miners, in the boom many years ago, sitting down to champagne and beef sausages, or the munition-workers whom a friend of mine saw in a swell Highland hotel, in 1917, washing down dubious mince with choice French wines.

No doubt Sir Harry, who is said to have had ambitions in the way of oratorio, would give his public the true, serious "complementary" to his humour, if they wanted it. But they don't want it; and, consequently, since red cannot for ever exist without green, or male without female, or irreverence without reverence, or laughter without tears, or parody without serious poetry, humour of the Lauder type is doomed to decay and extinction.

§ x

The fact that many Scots object to be called Celts, and fancy themselves something else, is not without interest. Celticism is exclusively associated by them with the Gaelic fringe in the Highlands, compulsory Gaelic, land-leagues, economic futility, squalor and laziness, Mr. De Valera and the Irish Republican Army.

Celticism is supposed to be too much mixed up with art, music, poetry, picturesque costume and other falderals, and to be inimical to industrial rationalization, economic imperialism, the sporting system, Knox, Carlyle, and Kipling. It is not regarded as friendly to "those things which".

It would be a poor look-out if Celticism were the

only corrective of the commercial pseudo-Calvinism which descended upon Scotland in the early days of the industrial era. But the corrective influence of genuine Celticism, being spiritual and positive, is perhaps the best kind.

If the nations of Western Europe and their off-shoots oversea get through their troubles without plunging into Communism or Fascism, it will be largely due to the tradition that resisted feudalism for centuries. That tradition is spiritual humanism: the belief that society exists for the individual and not the individual for society; that the test of society is the spiritual and imaginative quality of its average member. To call that Celticism is to use a convenient term warranted by what we know of history.

The use of the term Anglo-Saxon with regard to Scotland is historically ridiculous. No Saxon ever came into the old Scotland save as an enemy soldier, or as an office-seeker under an Anglifying king. The Angles of Northumbria held the Lothians for a while, and may have pushed as far west as Yarrowdale, sowing a few place-names among the older Celtic names; but they were driven out at Carham, and thenceforth were represented only, and doubtfully, by a few Border families.

The Norse influence was permanent only in Orkney and Shetland and to a lesser extent in Caithness, Lewis, and Skye. All the rest of Scotland was Pictish, Brythonic, and Gaelic; and that the Picts were Celts as well as the Brythons and the Gaels is proved by the ease with which they all coalesced into a nation.

That from the thirteenth century the Celtic tongues

148

in Scotland began to give way in the Lowlands to a variant of northern English was due to Court influence, the Church, and trade, and to the convenience of a simple speech like English as a lingua franca. But Gaelic was the dominant speech at Bannockburn, and the earliest "English" poems associated with Scotland deal with Arthurian themes.

Even in England, Anglo-Saxonism is largely a myth. As Arthur Weigall has shown, in his *Wanderings in Roman Britain*, the racial basis of England was firmly laid before a pirate from Lower Germany settled in the country. For probably fifteen hundred years before a Roman appeared, the population was purely Celtic or Celtiberian, and Britain long ere Caesar's time had attained a civilization that yielded little to Rome in practical matters, and in art was ahead of her.

After the vicious battle—in the Euston Road—with Boudicca and her Iceni, the Romans settled down to peaceful occupation. During nearly four centuries, thousands on thousands of legionaries, officials, and traders from all parts of Europe and from North Africa and Western Asia married British women and retired to live on the land. By the time the Roman armies were withdrawn, the population of Britain, as far as the Welsh border and Hadrian's Wall, was Celtic plus a bewildering cosmopolitan mixture.

The Anglo-Saxons cannot have been nearly as numerous as the Roman legionaries of ten generations. They killed very few of the Britons, but drove them west, or made them serfs, or intermarried with them. They forced a language on them, but were in time absorbed racially, and the weakness of their hold was shown by Canute's conquest and the Norman conquest.

Scotland invited Normans in, much to her sorrow. Scotland was the only part of north-west Europe that had not been conquered by Canute. Scotland had flung out the Angles. Scotland had stopped the Roman advance, and only a small section of the central south and the south-west was ever Romanized, and only for a few years.

In A.D. 116 the Ninth Legion, one of the biggest and finest in the Roman army, marched north from Yorkshire to put down a rising in Scotland. Not a man of the legion returned or was seen again; not a trace of the legion has ever been found. Rome shuddered at the news. Purely Celtic Scotland was the only country that ever put the wind up on the Roman.

The Normans were little interested in the Anglo-Saxons, but they became fascinated by the British legends of Arthur, and, being *arrivistes* of doubtful ancestry, they tried to identify themselves with the old British swells. France caught the infection, scrapped her Charlemagne stuff, and fastened on to the *Matière de Bretagne.* Welsh and Breton bards became the rage, until Wales and Brittany tried for independence and had to be chastised.

The Arthurian cycle, with its centre in Kymria, widened out over half Europe. It is the biggest cycle in literature.

When the Elizabethans wanted old native themes, they elided the Anglo-Saxons—if they knew anything about them—and went back to the real Britons.

Beaumont and Fletcher wrote a rousing play on
Boudicca or "Boadicea". Two of Shakespeare's
tragedies deal with Celtic kings. His Cymbeline was
a British king contemporary with Caesar, and the
play was read by the dying eyes of the author of the
Idylls of the King. Milton had intended to make Arthur
the subject of his great epic. The first we hear of the
Anglo-Saxons is in Thomson's *Masque of Alfred,* to
whom "Rule, Britannia!" was barely appropriate.

Then came the great Celtic rage of the Welsh and
"Ossian" period, followed by the revival of Irish and
Breton study. From Germany, mainly through literature and philosophy, came a strong anti-Celtic wave
in which Coleridge and Carlyle were caught up.
Irish rebellion and Roman Catholicism may have
had something to do with it.

Freeman, Stubbs, and Green were the exponents
of the idea that everything worth while in English
life went back to the Anglo-Saxons and to Germania.
Scotland, demonstrably eighty per cent. Celtic, had
to be in the fashion and call herself Anglo-Saxon.
Perhaps the war abated that absurd assumption of
Teutonism. But one finds traces of it even today.

Anglo-Saxon literature was at last studied. That
was all to the good, though it is preposterous for a
Scot to study Anglo-Saxon and neglect Gaelic. The
remarkable thing about Anglo-Saxon literature is
that it is not anti-poetical and Gradgrindish. It has
many of the characteristics of the old Norse literature,
though on the moral and epical sides it is finer.

Thus the Anglo-Saxon idea was doubly mythical.
The real Anglo-Saxons, after their piratical phase,

were not the kind of people their modern admirers wanted them to be. They were a peace-loving, land-loving, religious, unambitious folk, fond of learning, art, minstrelsy, and fine costumes. Left to themselves, they would have built up a happy England, and let France and Scotland alone. World conquest was not in their line.

It was the Norman and Angevin elements, themselves mixed with Celtic, that acted as the catalytic to the amazing racial compost that had formed itself in England upon a Celtic basis. They impelled the nation to a world career and the production of a literature whose richness is the more astonishing when one considers the defects of the language.

To have made a real literary tongue out of a mixture of broken-down Anglo-Saxon and bad Norman-French, as Chaucer did, was an unexampled feat. In performing it, he produced, and made possible, effects beyond the compass of a structurally coherent language. Still, English was only an exceedingly "practicable" conglomerate at the best, and one cannot but regret that the greatest poet of all time had not as fine an instrument at his command as was possessed by his contemporary, Cervantes.

Shakespeare would have had such an instrument if Gaelic, the finest of the Celtic tongues, had dominated in Britain, and, without losing its structure, been developed in accordance with the increasing complexity of social and intellectual life. The biggest crime of the Gaels has been the surrender and neglect of a language that ought to have vied with Spanish.

Peoples and People

§ xi

Lewis Grassic Gibbon's novel, *Sunset Song*, has drawn attention to a region of Scotland already celebrated in the poems of Violet Jacob. The outlook of the realistic novelist is very different from that of the lyric poet. Yet there is an underlying note common to both. It is the note of wistfulness, of elegy.

The tender grace of a day that is dead envelops Craigo Woods. The theme of "Tam in the Kirk" is eternal, yet we feel that Tam and Jean are of yesterday. The almost hectic coarseness of certain pages in *Sunset Song* expresses the blind struggle of rustic life to perpetuate itself in the face of approaching decay and death. It is the final battle of the vanishing races fighting with their backs to a setting sun that for them will never rise.

My own ancestors, for centuries back, lived in that same country-side, in which they were descendants of the ancient Picts who have left traces of their mysterious language in place-names and surnames; but all my kinsfolk, now, are furth of Scotland. In Pictavia there are only graves.

The Howe of the Mearns is one of the regions of Scotland that have passed into twilight, the deeper because of the human brightness of former days. From the middle of the eighteenth century down to the 'fifties or 'sixties of last century, it was a busily prosperous country-side. The effect of the Repeal of the Corn Laws was counteracted for a while by the advent of railways, the growth of fishing and of local manufactures, and the expenditure of wealthy incomers or retired folk. But decay had begun when farm was joined to farm and the area of "permanent grass" extended. And now there is decay over all.

The twilight effect of the region is deepened by the Highland glens and mountains on its western side, from which solitude descends like a mist, creeping over the once-peopled plain; and also by its mysterious history. Near Auchinblae is Fenella's Castle, where a Pictish princess murdered a Scottish king in an early-Greek fashion. Brechin has its "Pictish" Tower. Fordun, the chronicler, whose name connects itself with that of a Mearns village, said that in his time a half or more of the people still spoke Gaelic. There is a vanished county "town", Kincardine, of which no stone remains. Dying Fettercairn, with memories of Gladstone, is pathetically overshadowed by a big arch commemorating a visit of Queen Victoria and the Prince Consort.

Up over the heather slopes are the Ladder, Mount Keen, Cairn-o'-Mount, and Bridge of Dye, in a Highland *terra incognita* from which, as quaintly related in *The Fortunate Shepherdess* of Alexander Ross, schoolmaster in Glenesk, Highland caterans used to descend and carry off cattle and even children. That came to an end with the '45, in which Mearns folk were strongly Jacobite. Many were "'Piskies", and some of the raciest traditions of the region are associated with the old Scottish Episcopal Church, which in those days was as Scottish as Atholl brose.

The Howe of the Mearns is neighboured on the south-west by another region that has always affected me in a slightly eerie fashion. Even the invasion of buses from Dundee cannot destroy the crepuscular glamour of Meigle, Newtyle, Eassie, Glamis, Kin-purnie, Glen Ogilvie. Walking alone in that region, on a bright summer day, I have been overcome by a sudden feeling of utter strangeness. The fields and woods and hills seemed to be whispering ominous secrets of an age long past.

Is this a lingering emanation of the old Picto-Scottish life, and of the mysterious "Arthurian" con-flicts between Celt and Teuton, commemorated by the Meigle stones? Or is Strathmore a part of the realm of Faerie? It is not by a mere accident that Barrie belongs to Kirriemuir, which is near the High-land edge of this twilight region.

Menteith is decidedly a twilight and haunted region. That was brought home to me before I had read Cunninghame Graham's book on the district. When, in my early rambles, I discovered Fintry and Balfron, and wandered out over Flanders Moss, I felt as if I had crossed the Mountains of the Moon. It did not seem as if there was really any way back, and I was quite surprised when I picked up a familiar trail and stepped out of Never-Never-Land.

The eeriest experience I have ever had was boating alone on the Lake of Menteith in thundery July weather, when the Fintry Hills were heavy with gloom and the bright sunlight from over the inky clouds was livid on the stones and tree-trunks of the islands. Beauty had become sinister. The whole valley seemed peopled with the ghosts of tribes and races long gone. On such a day, it was easy to believe that the Rev. Robert Kirk, M.A., had really been kidnapped by the elves for revealing their polity, and carried off into the Fairy Hill.

Appin is another ghostly region, but the ghosts there are more friendly, more definitely poetic and romantic; and it is the same throughout the Highlands. One may feel depressed or exalted, but somehow not disquieted. Nature's part is positive, inspiring, and engrossing. It is in the equivocal borderlands, devoid of eponymous mythology, that one feels vaguely afraid.

Other countries have their twilight lands. I have had a glimpse of one or two in France and Ireland. In Scotland we have more of them than we require for purposes of poetry. Their elegiac charm is darkening into a taint of spreading death. We might reserve a region like Menteith, perhaps, for a certain touch of ghostly and sombre beauty. But we cannot sacrifice our whole country for the sake of exquisite morbidity. We have got to bring back most of Scotland into the major scale of healthy vigorous rusticity in which the real classics of rustic poetry—Theocritus, Virgil, Horace, Goethe, Burns—have been written.

§ xii

You have sailed through the far-famed Kyles of Bute to Loch Fyne, or you know it from the pages of Neil Munro. But you are probably unaware that, ages ago, there dwelt on the shores of Loch Fyne—the Lac Beau—a creature named Trilby.

He was a lutin, an elf or brownie, of the salamander type (*vide* Pope's *Rape of the Lock* and Anatole France's

Rôtisserie de la Reine Pédauque). In Minard or Dundarave he would have been an honoured guest, but he chose to consort with the crickets about the peat-fire of a humble fisherman named Dougal. For Trilby was in love with Dougal's bonny young wife, Jeannie, and his delicate courtship surrounded her in the colour and perfume of flowers and in the incidents of her daily toil. Trilby also took delight in annoying decent, stupid Dougal.

Dougal and Jeannie talked the matter over, and they sent for the venerable Ronald, the hermit of Balvaig.

Ronald exorcized Trilby, and for a time there was peace. But Jeannie began to be haunted by visions of a handsome young chief of the clan Macfarlane, who years before had come under the ban of the Church and mysteriously disappeared; and Dougal missed the help of the brownie in his fishing. So the pair joined a pilgrimage by way of Tarbet and Loch Katrine to the shrine of Balvaig, near Callander. At that time, evidently, Loch Fyne, Loch Long, Argyll's Bowling-green and the Cobbler formed a geographical unit, and Portincaple had high chimneys.

At Balvaig Ronald and his monks pronounced a malediction on the pagan persecutors of St. Columba's successors. In the gallery of the shrine was a row of portraits of Scottish heroes; the last in the row was veiled. Lifting the veil, Jeannie beheld the features of the young chief who had haunted her dreams. Beneath in Gothic letters was his name: JOHN TRILBY MACFARLANE.

The brownie and the chief were one. Jeannie fell

on her knees before the shrine of St. Columba and murmured: "Charity!"

One day in late autumn, as Jeannie was rowing home after ferrying a party (tourists, probably) over Loch Fyne, she saw a funny wee old man on the shore. He leaped into the boat, reproached Jeannie with her treatment of the brownie, and then suddenly grew and freshened into the young Macfarlane. His sentence, he said, was but for a thousand years—and her love could atone for an eternity of torment—might he return to the peat-fire? Ere Jeannie could answer, Dougal came in sight and Trilby Macfarlane disappeared.

Dougal thereupon brought up in his net a richly carved ivory casket, which he presented to Jeannie. From within the casket she heard a voice—Trilby's— she could unlock it if she declared her love. She refused. . . .

Going out into the darkness, she heard her husband and Ronald. The latter was cursing. As the northern dawn began to whiten over the Cobbler, she stole into a haunted graveyard where there was a birch known as the Saint's Tree. There "she heard a two-fold sound", easily recognized, "as of an ivory casket breaking and a tree-trunk bursting open". Following a glimmer of light, she found Ronald and Dougal. A faint voice within the tree-trunk murmured Jeannie's name and died away. "A thousand years are nothing on the earth," said Jeannie to her husband, and expired. Ronald went on with his prayer.

Twittering of birds. The sky reddens over the Cobbler. Hebridean music by the orchestra. Curtain.

Peoples and People

That is a tabloid version of a story called *Trilby*, written about a century ago by Charles Nodier, one of the earliest of the French Romantics. Du Maurier appropriated the name *Trilby* for his famous novel. Nodier says he found it in Scott, but he didn't. Probably he dreamt it. It has proved a stayer—but it's certainly not Highland.

The early Romantics were great masqueraders. Nodier wrote stories of Spanish, Bosnian, and Italian life; of their fidelity we can judge by his Highland tale—and his French stories are said to be not much better. Scott, Hewlett, and Maurois are among the few writers who have trod with sureness on foreign soil. The ordinary writer can never hope to deal faithfully with territory more than fifty miles distant from his home. Ouida's novels must be almost as funny to an Italian as Nodier's *Trilby* is to a Highlander.

CHAPTER VI

FROM *WORK NOT YET BEGUN*

§ i

A LL the best people are publishing excerpts from *Work in Progress*. I can go one better with a fragment from *Work Not Yet Begun*. It is the outline of a preface to a book I want to write on "England".

England, Mr. Bernard Shaw remarked, produced Shakespeare: the British Empire produced Marie Corelli. The British Empire produced also Mr. Bernard Shaw, but he is the voice of one crying in the wilderness, whereas Shakespeare was the voice of a proud, self-contained country, where every rood of ground maintained its man, and every village had its poet or composer: "a little body with a mighty mind".

It was a misfortune for England that in Napoleonic days she became the workshop and *entrepôt* of the world, and that in later times her capital became the world's financial centre, and her fairest counties the cosmopolitan playground of a huge Empire. England was too beautiful, too precious, for such a crude destiny.

France, Italy, even Germany, present a picture of steady social development, for good or evil, since medieval times—a picture in which foundation and superstructure are harmonized. In England the agrarian foundation crumbled and almost disappeared.

From *Work not yet Begun*

England is like a beautiful Gainsborough canvas, or Crome drawing, which some bilious modernist has smudged over, to the extent of one-half, with nightmare atrocities in black, ochre, and dirty grey, while obscuring half of the remainder with splashes of dull green.

It is pathetic to notice how in Victorian literature and art, down to Tennyson and Meredith, the old England of cathedral and market towns, village bells, and the miller's daughter tries to assert itself. Even the London music-hall clung to the convention. But in Ruskin the note of despair is sounded. Hardy fell back upon the Wessex of the past.

Grand old minsters and their russet towns, ankle-deep in golden wheat, poppy-splashed, with sedgy rivers and their barges, and elms, poplars, and wind-mills far out in the mellow haze; distant chimes like a swarm of golden bees; Morris's *Summer Dawn* and the Midland landscapes of Clausen; the odour of brewing, grain stores, soft coal, and tree-blossom; Oxford and Cambridge; the Garden of Kent in June sunshine; the wonderland of Severn and the Mendips, culminating in the Eden of the West, Devon—such is my dream-picture of England.

An Englishman would object to it as strongly as I would object to his guide-book picture of Scotland, missing out Glasgow and most of the Central Belt.

But if one misses out Manchester, Liverpool, Bolton, Leeds, Huddersfield, Newcastle, the Five Towns, Sheffield, Birmingham, and so forth, it is simply because they are in monotonous excess. Reduced in volume by two-thirds, they would come naturally into the picture. As for greater industrial London, where our industries drift to, it is a sheer horror.

And yet beneath the wen-like proliferation of London there remain traces of "the biggest village in the world". In the old London there were assembled, as in a huge living museum, all the characteristic features of all the old English towns and villages, and the homely touch extended even to the palaces and Government buildings.

That was the charm of London. But the blight that has destroyed half of the real England has concentrated upon the Thames Valley. The city of Chaucer and Shakespeare, Lamb and Dickens, lies buried beneath a dreadful eruption of brick and concrete. The charm has gone for ever.

§ ii

All of us have memories of moments that we should have wished to last for ever.

Such memories are oftenest associated with evening; with music and the glow of lamps, the flash of oars on a moonlit lake, sunset on the isles beyond Jura, or

> Some hamlet-hollow which can hold
> The gloaming like a tierce of wine,
> Red rose of some white river's fold,
> Smouldering where elfin waters twine.

There was a cloudless July dawn on the wild-wood slopes of Portincaple, when the smoke from fishing-boats rose straight in air, continuous with its reflection in the still water, and Loch Long was an inverted

firmament, in which the mirrored mountains hung
dizzily. Diamonds sparkled on the hill-side, there was
the scent of briar and bog-myrtle—and I was twenty-
one.

The Garden of Eden is one of the world's memories
of a Golden Age, when the powers of the human race
were in primitive harmony, and for a brief space
mankind enjoyed innocent happiness.

When intellect moved ahead of the other powers,
discord set in, and mankind began their painful
crawl up the cliffs of progress, leaving blood on every
stone.

On those cliffs there are green ledges, where flowers
hang over the abyss. Halting there, men may have
fancied that harmony had been reattained. History
has its golden moments.

There was the age of the Antonines, when peace
enveloped the Roman world. In the thirteenth century, when the Church held the balance among the
dynasties of Western Europe, there was such another
period.

The well-known verses on the death of Alexander
III commemorate Scotland's share in the peace that
preluded the struggle between England and France.
James I and James III tried for another golden age
in Scotland, but they were frustrated by the barbarous
nobles. Under Elizabeth, Merrie England was a
reality in some country-sides.

On the most perilous ledge of all, with a roaring
torrent below, and an avalanche poised above, the
intellectuals of eighteenth-century France gathered in
salons for night-long feasts of wit and philosophy.

Feeling the shadow of a doom they could not avert, were they not wise to seize the golden moments ere the blow fell?

"O stay, thou art so fair!" Faust's enjoyment of a perfect moment was the signal for his death. But it was also the earnest of his redemption, for the perfect joy was one of selfless love. He was delivered from "the wheel".

§ iii

The April sun shone with summer fervour. The grass of the Meadows was taking on a silky sheen. In the brown trees hung a haze of yellow-green.

On a topmost branch a thrush sang loudly. Following the sweetly defiant note, passers-by looked up, and traced his brave little silhouette. Faith, hope, and love were in his song. Those who heard it forgot for a moment their troubles and fears.

In many a heart, the song passed on into the city. But it seemed as if the thrush had a special audience.

The tree on which he sang was close to a great hospital. On the balconies, patients were sunning themselves. They listened to the song, spoke of it and smiled, and listened again. Through the open windows, the notes passed into the wards.

On the other side of the building were the queues of visitors. Most of them had flowers in their hands. Flowers and the song of a bird: what had they to do with disease, injury, and suffering?

The patients and their visitors may have known, but they could not tell. These things are as mysterious as the influences that brought our hospitals into being.

From *Work not yet Begun*

Here, and not in the records of feudal murder, robbery, oppression, conspiracy, and treachery, is the glory of Scotland. Her real civilization began with the foundation of her old hospitals, and with the dedication of medical and nursing skill to the service of those who were both sick and poor.

The greatest story I have ever listened to was told me by a famous surgeon at his own fireside. It was the story of his crowning operation.

The operation, splendidly successful, had been a terrific strain upon his whole being. Yet it was performed in the ordinary course of hospital duty, without any fee.

The story was typical of the miracle represented by the temple of healing beside which the thrush was singing. One may look for explanations in growth of knowledge and wealth, scientific curiosity, love of experiment, and desire for professional prestige. The creators and organizers may have been unconscious that they were doing anything particularly noble.

Yet the miracle remains; and a St. Vincent de Paul, a Lister, or a Simpson would have had no doubt as to its nature. They would have pointed to the Gospels.

The little thrush, singing on the branch—how small and fragile he seemed, with the great city beside him, and the terrific Universe around! Yet his poise was serene, and he sang of faith, hope, and love, as if confident that his message expressed the purpose of the Universe. And his listeners understood.

§ iv

" I heard a cow low, and a bonny cow low," begins an old Scots ballad. The words keep singing in my mind as I watch some bonny cows grazing in a field next my garden.

In days when the high-piled fabric of industry, commerce, and finance quivers to its foundations, there is comfort in the dusty hum of the threshing-mill, the sturdy slow-march of the ploughman up the glistening hill-side, behind his broad-beamed horses, and the benevolent placidity of the grazing kine.

One of the finest poems in the world is Carducci's sonnet to the plough-ox, that strong, patient, beautiful creature in whose serenely austere eyes are mirrored not only "the heavenly silence of the verdant plain", but also the whole history of Italy since Virgil's day.

A poem not less noble might be written about the Ayrshire cow. Her massive build, her warm colour, her sleek skin, her fine head, are points of beauty. As she walks slowly up the field, cropping the rich grass, and curling her tongue around buttercups and clover, she is translating the beauty of the meadow into the beauty of milk and cream.

With what unutterable serenity she looks round at us with her big soft eyes, sending in our direction a warm breath as sweet as meadow gales, and gently reproving our worries and distractions. With quiet surprise she watches her animal antithesis, our fussy dog, who stops short in a bark and a run, awed by her large calmness.

Ridiculous when she runs (though her quest of

band music is an interesting feature), she is in her normal acts a creature of poetry. Think of Hogg's famous song, or Kingsley's *Sands of Dee*, or the beautiful cow-names that form part of the haunting refrain in Jean Ingelow's great ballad, *High Tide on the Coast of Lincolnshire*.

Or think of the Highland milking-songs, like *Crodh Chaillean*. These go back to the days of outdoor milking. On the high summer-meadows of Norway and Switzerland, the song of the milker may still be heard. Singing is not in the line of the stolid Dutchmen who milk the cows in the meadows of Holland, but Dutch artists like Mauve have given the cow a place in art.

There is poetry in our Scots Lowland way too: in the soft lowing of the milk-laden herd as they gather towards the gate, the slow procession in level sunlight along the leafy lane, and the soothing activity of the byre.

The poetry is not evident to the farmer and his assistants. But the consideration paid to the cow, and her quiet response to it, are significant.

One is not surprised at the veneration she commands in India. In a world of social flux and cataclysm, she remains the living assurance of elemental stability and beneficence.

§ v

It is a solemn thought that we may be contemporaries of the last European artists. The possibility is suggested by certain tendencies and theories of modernism.

There is a progressive departure from objective reality of any kind. Art ceases to be representational, to be mimetic, to be aesthetic, to be suggestive, to be constructive, to be symbolic, to be comprehensible. Its function narrows down—or widens out, it's all the same—to the arbitrary and abstract expression of states of mind not only purely subjective but also purely unconscious.

The art student in Murger's *Scènes de la Vie de Bohème* painted a large picture of the Crossing of the Red Sea. His friends came to see it. There was nothing on the canvas but a huge splash of red paint, with a splash of blue above.

"Where are the Jews?"

"They've crossed over."

"Well, what about Pharaoh and his host?"

"They're all drowned. Haven't you read your Bible?"

The modernist assumes greater privileges. He relieves himself of the need for expressing anything to which one can attach an idea.

The final stage, so far, is reached by Paul Klee, with enlargements of the kind of thing—cup-and-ring markings connected by straight or wavy lines—that bored company directors draw on their blotters while the chairman is explaining why the dividend is again being passed.

The process began long ago when a French artist became tired of perspective and painted a table that widened as it receded, and when another artist, bored by the verticality of things, represented buildings with a heavy list. A third artist went one better, and hung a section of the village upside down in the sky.

The human body was then put into the rolling-mill. It emerged broadened out or elongated, with twisted limbs, and a head like a turnip or a vegetable marrow. The next stage was to halve it vertically, and mix up one of the halves with an assortment of drawing instruments, time locks, and burglars' tools, amid which the mangled fragments of another half-body might be discerned.

From this unpleasant stage, in which the taint of objectivity still remained, art has now passed into the ethereal realm dominated by Mr. Klee. The sixpenny store provides all the objects necessary— a few cloth balls, toy birds and trees, and a piece of string.

To describe those funny things as art is playing with words. If the central tendency of art is the one analysed by writers like Herbert Read, the death of pictorial art is at hand.

That is by no means impossible. The portable picture is a relatively modern feature. Landscape painting, as a separate branch of art, dates only from the generation before Claude Lorraine. Painting may not be able to survive except by return to the old "Alexandrian Empire" of architecture. There may be no art save public art.

Public art, declare some modernists, is merely a stereotyping of conventional forms. That it is the only real art is equally arguable. One would willingly sacrifice modernist pictorial art for the city beautiful.

§ vi

In the National Gallery of Scotland there is a very fine Monet. It has suggested to me that the pleasure I derived from it was nothing in comparison with the pleasure Monet must have experienced while he was painting it.

I am aware of the grinding toil that must have gone to the making of such a painter; the anxieties, the agonies, that he must have suffered in the initial stages of a picture.

But there must have come a moment when painful calculation gave place to creative ecstasy. From that moment the painter's imagination was perfectly in tune with Nature, and he lived in a wonderland of beauty.

The poet also has his wonderland, but it is shadowed by sadness, and sicklied o'er with the pale cast of thought. The soaring and singing skylark draws a sigh from Shelley. The poet is a slave to his own moods and fancies, which may lead him into a joyless psychological labyrinth, or a region of unreal splendour or morbid gloom—Xanadu, the City of Dreadful Night, or Waste Land.

The landscapist has his moods and fancies; but they are kept in touch with healthy realities. His creative ecstasy is a sublimation of sanity.

The picture begun in face of Nature is finished indoors. The winter skies are forgotten by the man who is composing the visions gathered in his sketching season. He is creating a brave new world, whose elements are sanatively real.

From *Work not yet Begun*

These are the reasons why, if I had my life over again, I should wish to be a landscape painter. Even if I were not a good one, it would not matter, so long as I was absorbed in my work.

Some of the happiest men on earth have been mediocre landscapists. What they lacked in technique they made up for in delight in their subjects. Their tanned faces beamed under their big hats. They sang as they painted in the glen. They told good stories in the inn parlour, slept without dreams, and went forth singing in the dewy morning. They were good companions.

If I could not be a landscapist, I should be in doubt whether to be a farmer, a country joiner, or a rural policeman.

The notion that the farmer is a disgruntled person is erroneous. But the farmer, large or small, is ill at ease in a non-farming community. It is a case of the more the merrier. A lesson for Scotland!

When I was a "clerk in ta offish", I envied the young men with cloth caps and leggings, who went about in country places, doing mysterious things with rods, chains, and theodolites. A civil engineer's life would be ideal, if one could get the right things to engineer.

In a country where native styles and talent were recognized, it would be fine to be an architect. But the Scottish youth whose dreams lie in that direction should consider the fate of Mackintosh's Glasgow creations, and make for Sweden or America. This is not a land for him.

I fall back upon my boyish dream of commanding

a puffer, trading from Glasgow to Ardentinny and Colintraive.

§ vii

Our grandchildren will behold something which has been denied to us and to many generations before. They will behold the Caledonian Forest.

The operations of the Forestry Commissioners are slow but steady. Year by year, in about seventy areas of State forest throughout Scotland, from eight to ten thousand acres are planted or replanted, mainly with conifers; and, in addition, grants are given for similar operations on about 2500 acres of land owned by private individuals and local authorities.

The Caledonian Forest is beginning to creep back over our hill-sides. In a few years there will be a distinct change in the aspect of many parts of Scotland.

In the inner and northern Highlands the new forest will be largely a re-creation of the old one, which was "all of black pine and the dark oak tree", and of which some portions remain.

In the Lowlands, and the coastal and south-west Highlands, the original, natural forest was probably a medley of oak, ash, birch, and thorn, with willows along the quieter streams, and groves of Scots fir on the ridges.

Place-names in Clydesdale indicate that a forest of the latter kind must have swathed the whole country from above the Falls down to Bothwell. Its existence accounts for the periodic lapses of Strathclyde into obscurity, and also for the exploits of Wallace and the Douglases.

From *Work not yet Begun*

The lonely forest of Clydesdale, shadowing fearsome canyons, and thinning out on upland moors, was the rallying base of a resurgent Scotland.

It is against the background of this kind of mixed wild-wood, covering most of the land below the 1,500-feet level, that we must place the forays, battles, progresses, huntings, and pilgrimages of medieval days.

Many of the summer "pictures" must have been very beautiful, and it was merry in the greenwood when the hunting-horn sounded and the dogs gave forth a note like a peal of bells. But the old ballads recall the secret tragedies of the forest, and at nightfall a freezing horror must have exhaled from those dark, inscrutable depths.

The vandalism of the Scots after the Reformation is not surprising. They had destroyed something finer than cathedrals. They had destroyed most of the Caledonian Forest.

The forest-fringe is the home of fairy-tales like *Hänsel und Gretel*, *The Babes in the Wood*, and *Little Red Riding-Hood*, and for these Lowland Scotland had to be dependent on other lands, borrowing from England, for example, the Robin Hood "cycle".

The carefully preserved forests of France and Germany were the inspiration of most of the nursery-tales of Western Europe. To the mystic influences of her forests, Germany, in all likelihood, owes her supremacy in music.

In re-afforesting Scotland we are not merely creating a reserve of timber. We are building a realm of secret beauty and of haunting dreams. We are planting the seeds of sonnets and symphonies, of wonderful new pictures, songs, dramas, tales, and rhapsodies. We are raising a new shrine for the Scottish soul.

§ viii

In the main street the motor-cars were whizzing past in a steady stream that had the dizzying effect of an accelerated cinema film. The pedestrians hurrying across the street, or clustered on the "islands", seemed the nerve-racked survivors in a losing battle of humanity with its own machines. One had an impression of the retreat of organic and sentient life before the gathering forces of the inorganic, invoked by mages who had made thoughtless use of a potent spell they could not revoke. So Hyperion felt when he turned to his desecrated palace:—

> Also, when he would taste the spicy wreaths
> Of incense, breathed aloft from sacred hills,
> Instead of sweets, his ample palate took
> Savour of poisonous brass and metal sick.

A few yards down the side street was a wide, high opening, leading into a big, cave-like place, from whose shadowed depths came forth a pleasantly acrid odour. There was a heavy, breathing sound, and one of the corners leaped into reddish light, revealing a big man with black hair, and shirt-sleeves rolled up. With long pincers he withdrew from the fire a glowing bar, and began hammering it on the anvil, like an harmonious blacksmith of Handelian days.

On the left, in a patient row, were four big strapping Clydesdales, handsomely caparisoned. The nearest one, who looked like a relative of the tallest horse in Scotland, glanced round at me in a friendly way as I entered. He was being shod. The stone floor was carpeted with hoof-clippings.

My errand was to obtain first-aid for an injured dog. In a few minutes two of the smiths were free to attend to him. The skill and speed and gentleness with which they dressed and bound up his wound were characteristic of their calling. A smiddy is a school of humanity.

That the smiddy, which has all but vanished from the country-side, should survive in the centre of a big city, is one of the curiosities of modern life. For certain kinds of door-to-door traffic the horse is more suitable than the motor.

Those fine-looking animals in the smiddy were brewery horses. They were a good advertisement for the oldest of British beverages, inspiring envy for other reasons than the one given in the old rhyme:—

> I wish I were a brewer's horse;
> I'd cost the brewer dear:
> I'd turn my head where my tail should be,
> And drink up all the beer.

Even strict teetotallers, wandering weary in roaring and restless London on a hot or foggy day, must have been cheered by the sight of those solid-looking brewery drays, with their burly drivers and big, sleek horses—giving earnest of a social stability underlying the gyrations of politics and finance. At the height of the Irish "troubles" did not Guinness's remain a sanctuary of peaceful activity?

It is fitting that the brewery should help to keep alive the smiddy, whose musical ding-dong and ruddy altar-fires marked the centre of old village life, where men and animals convened, gossip and stories were exchanged, and world problems discussed.

"The smith, a mighty man is he", with an air of the gods and demi-gods—Hephaestus, Vulcan, Thor, Tubal Cain, Wayland the Smith (Wieland der Schmidt), and the rest—from whom he sprang. He forged magic swords and armour of proof, but disdained the use of them, relying upon the native manhood of brawny thews, useful skill, and simple faith, with a dignity that daunted Norman tyrants. Figures like Hal o' the Wynd and Joe Gargery are in the true line of succession.

Is it any wonder that romantic young folk should want to be married over an anvil? Leaning on his hammer-helve at the anvil, and looking the whole world in the face, with a fine Clydesdale beside him, a dog near his feet, and the smiddy fire in the background, the blacksmith seems a priest of a very real kind, with a message that mankind need today.

§ ix

The farm is rather under than over average size, half arable and half moorland, in a district so purely agricultural that the gentry come only for fishing and shooting, and local enterprises are carried through by the farmers themselves.

The century-old farmhouse is whitewashed, with dormer-windows in the upper story, a bee-loud garden on one side, and the byre and farmyard on the other. The bedrooms are cosily slumbrous, the comfortable little parlour is used mainly for meals, and the frigidly Victorian drawing-room is reserved for genteel visitors and state occasions.

Life centres in the big kitchen, facing over the farmyard to thorn hedges and a slope white with clover.

At the back of the kitchen are a grandfather clock and a high dresser, bright with dishes. Along the side is a huge girnel, used as a settle.

At the big peat fire, with its swivels and chains, something is always boiling, baking, or stewing, and the teapot is always on the hob. The prevailing odour is of newly baked scones.

The presiding genius is the farmer's wife. She sees after the milking, churning, the pigs and poultry, and supervises the cooking. Her work is never done.

Yet she has a kindly word for everybody. She is the providence of the district, the resort of all who are troubled in mind, body, or estate. She can shout across the "heathery hill", or whisper comfort to the dying. Big, jolly, shrewd, infinitely sympathetic—a mother in Israel.

As she moves about, with her eye on everything, she issues orders, and talks with postie or the carrier, who are refreshing themselves at the window table, where tea and scones and butter are always laid out.

The guidman, fresh-coloured, with bright blue eyes that belie his sixty-five years, comes in from the field, with a neighbouring farmer, and the company bring themselves up to date in local history.

The sturdy pet lamb "mehs" at the door and gets its

bottle of milk. Clucking hens intrude, and are chased out by the cats. The kitchen empties, and the hay or harvest field becomes the centre of activity and talk.

And so the cheerful and changeful day slips by, until the lamp is lit and the guidman gants and greins, giving the signal for bed.

But the kitchen never sleeps. The visitor, returning late across the eerie moor, sees a glow in the peat fire, reflected in the eyes of dogs speldered on the floor, and hears the purring of cats in cosy corners. They take him for a brownie, perhaps.

The cry of night-birds and the waving of the branch in the moonlight at his window bring no mournful thoughts. He feels the friendly presence of the household gods.

"From scenes like these . . ." When I feel despondent about Scotland's future, I am cheered by the thought of the farm kitchen. From its kindly hearth goes out the virtue that will save us from decay.

§ x

Scott's famous rhapsody on Scotland is the expression of a well-founded article of faith. Foreign travel, even in the loveliest regions of Hellas and Italy, confirms the Scot in his belief that his own country is the most beautiful in the world.

Too beautiful, perhaps. Scotland's attractiveness for wealthy idlers and sportsmen from other lands has been a demoralizing influence, paralysing native effort, destroying agrarian life, and fostering a parasitical order of things.

From *Work not yet Begun*

Even over ourselves the beauty of Scotland has cast a lethal spell. Far too much of the imaginative energy of our writers is devoted to expatiation on the empty and de-humanized beauty of Scotland, and the romance of a past that is not permitted to connect itself with the life of Scotland today.

Lost in admiration for these things, we huddle meanly in the ugly towns and villages of the Central Belt, oblivious to the dreadful discord between our own works and those of Nature, and to the national shame of the desolated two-thirds of Scotland.

Our extraordinary way of treating our own country is incomprehensible to the purposeful Scandinavians, who have achieved a harmony between Man and Nature; still more to the Dutch, who have created out of the ocean ooze a land that artists love to paint.

The Scottish way results in some astonishing contrasts. From the frowsy slums of congested Greenock one looks over the water to miles and miles of lonely green hills. A mere ferry trip on a river steamer takes one across to Kilmun, and a gentle walk of a mile or so up the side of the salmoniferous Echaig brings one to the point where the slaty rocks of the hills along the Firth give place to the rugged schists of the inner Highlands.

The buses go on to Loch Eck, but our way lies past the foot of Glen Lean, with its forgotten village of Clachaig, and up the west side of the Echaig valley. The road winds leftward amid woods and bluffs into a side valley between rough hills of rocks and grass and heather, clad nearly half-way up with wild-wood.

The road ascends sharply, the hidden river down on the left gives voice, and we come out upon a tumbled grassy space. In the middle the river is disporting itself amid an incredible confusion of limestone rocks, like the columns of a great Cyclopean temple, overthrown and shattered by an earthquake. The river makes falls, races, pot-holes, and whirlpools, and at one point loses itself beneath the mass of riven shafts and pillars. Between and above the rock-masses are beautiful smooth pools.

Here, legend has it, Deirdre of Ireland and her lover Naisi and his pair of faithful brothers dwelt for a time during their idyllic sojourn in Scotland. And not even in haunted Benderloch, or in Glenetive or Glendaruel, had they found a lovelier camping-ground than amid the wild-wood of Glen Massan

Looking down towards the Holy Loch, Deirdre and Naisi may have glimpsed the coracles of hostile Picts or Britons, and divined the eastern frontier of their paradise. In the bay of Crinan lay the galleys of the jealous Conchubar, eager for a mean and cruel revenge. It is the same theme, essentially, as that of *Manon Lescaut* and Conrad's *Victory*. The world is unfriendly to love and happiness.

Glen Massan may remain sacred to Deirdre, but the transition from its idyllic solitude back to slummy Greenock is far too sharp. It will be better graded now that the new forests are spreading from Benmore up to Glenbranter. That is the way out of our overcrowded industrial Goshen into the Promised Land, which is our own land.

From *Work not yet Begun*

§ xi

We live in a noisy age. So we are told by people who are too young to remember the pre-motor age, or have forgotten what it was like.

The gathering morning roar of London in those days, as heard from a bedroom in a city hotel by a guest from the North Countrie, was awesome. Its component sounds were the stamping of horses' hooves, the rumble and clatter of hard-rimmed wheels, the shouts of drivers, the puffing and whistling of trains, and the shuffle of innumerable feet. Heard at close hand in one of the main approaches to the river, those sounds attained a *fortissimo* that stunned the senses.

The pedal-note of traffic was peculiar to London; but, after all, her main streets were mostly of wood, and their din was less painful than the clatter and crepitation of lorries, vans, cabs, and trams on the granite setts of Glasgow.

In depth and sheer volume, city noise has declined in the last twenty years, but it has got on to a higher register, worse for the nerves. Motor-horns, motor-bike exhausts, and the rattle of vehicles of the Tin Lizzie order are the chief offenders. In certain Continental cities the "musical" motor-horn, leaping erratically up and down the scale like a crazy bugle, is a murderer of sleep.

What interests me is the amount of din people can create with quite simple materials. With a few empty milk-cans, boldly handled in a large railway station having good acoustics, two porters can wake up all the sleepers in a trans-Continental express, and fill the concavity of night with the reverberations of a violent revolution. An effect of this kind which I heard in the station of the city of Cracow, between two and three in the morning, went far beyond Tchaikovski's "*1812*" Overture.

The night loading of a passenger vessel with steel or iron ware is also something to be remembered. The inhibitions and spasmodic movements of the throttled and gasping winch compel one to follow mentally the whole process, particularly in a French port, where it is vocally dramatized.

It is the delightful boyishness of the French that makes them so fond of trumpet-sounding, volley-firing, horn-blowing, shouting, whistling, and so forth. They do everything as grown-up schoolboys would do it, with the maximum of audible effect. Yet the French peasant is the most taciturn and phlegmatic of beings, and Rannoch Moor is less silent than a French country town after nine at night.

Scots people who have visited America are almost oppressed by the silence of their own country. The Americans are the noisiest and most restless of peoples, whereas in silence and restfulness the Scots are rivalled only by the Baltic races.

That is why in Scotland one hears more of Nature's voices than in almost any other country. Nocturnal moorland birds haunt Glasgow's fringes. In Edinburgh's Meadows, after the last tram is gone, the hoot of the owl is heard.

Is there a more exquisite picture of restfulness than Dorothy Wordsworth's account of a night in a farmhouse on the shore of Loch Katrine? In the fleeting moonlight the dark rafters of the house and the swaying trees outside were just visible; the slow, quiet voices of the farm-folk in another room died away; there was the intermittent rushing of rain upon the solid roof, and the lapping of the lake against an outer wall.

There are those who prefer the crooning of a nearby burn as lullaby, with the faint roar of a distant waterfall, rising and dying on the breeze. It is only in Scotland that one can exercise so fastidious a choice. Fortunate people that we are, we have become epicures in natural beauty, and connoisseurs in restful noise.

CHAPTER VII

SUCCESS

A Variation on a Theme
by R. B. Cunninghame Graham

§ i

"SUCCESS which touches nothing that it does not vulgarize, should be its own reward. In fact, rewards of any kind are but vulgarities."

"How few successful men are interesting! Hannibal, Alcibiades, Raleigh, Mithridates, Napoleon—who would compare them for a moment with their mere conquerors?"

The unlucky Stuarts, with all their faults, leave the solid Hanoverians far behind, sunk in pudding and prosperity. What is the fame of the wise and prosperous Elizabeth compared with that of the ill-starred Queen of Scots whom she sent to the block at forty-nine?

The European War has extinguished the memory of America's easy victory over Spain, but the seal of immortality rests on Cunninghame Graham's picture of the skeleton of the Spanish general, in mouldering rags of uniform, found seated in a rough chair on the beach near El Caney: "Nothing can vulgarize him; no fool will crown him with a tin-foiled laurel wreath,

184

no poetaster sing his praise in maudlin ode or halting threnody, for he has passed into the realm of those who by misfortune claim the sympathy of writers who are dumb."

In his essay on "Success" and in the preface to the volume in which it was published Cunninghame Graham has said all that needs to be said. But a footnote suggests itself: Why should mankind, made up of individuals the majority of whom are more or less interesting failures, be so hugely interested in what is vulgarly called success?

The reason is that most people live vicariously. Realizing their own social insignificance, and their failure to fulfil the vague ambitions with which they started out, they seek consolation in mentally identifying themselves with people whom the world has agreed to regard as distinguished and fortunate. Hence the keen public interest in the personalities and doings of royalties, aristocrats, millionaires, politicians, society beauties, prize-fighters, film stars, football players, tennis champions, and the writers of best-sellers.

Hence also the popularity of novels and plays dealing with high life, and the public distaste for books and plays which have tragic endings, or which deal unsentimentally with the lives of poor and struggling folk. It is not in the world of art that the public mind rests and expatiates (for art is a higher power of reality), but in a land of Cockaigne. There lollipops and bank-notes grow on trees, and birds fly into pies and fine clothes on to people's backs, and the poor but deserving lady-teacher marries the agreeable

young man in plus-fours who rescued her (or whom
she rescued) from the clutches of predatory hooligans,
and who turns out to be the lord of the manor. There
every Jack gets his Jill, and Jack Horner his plum
for being a good boy.

This vicarious solace is always in demand, since
the secret self-audit of most of us reveals only failure.
Yet it is difficult to know what would have constituted
success in our own eyes. It would have had to be
something quite personal, at any rate. None of us
would really change identities with any of the people
who are regarded as successful. Some of them we
secretly despise; and we know that the triumph of
most of them will be paid for by disillusion and
defeat. The fallen star has no worshippers till he is
posthumously "translated" and becomes a fixed star.

> He sang Darius great and good,
> By too severe a fate
> Fallen, fallen, fallen, fallen,
> Fallen from his high estate,
> And weltering in his blood.
> Deserted in his utmost need
> By those his former bounty fed,
> On the cold earth alone he lies,
> With not a friend to close his eyes.

Darius dead and deserted, however, achieved a
higher success than his conqueror. Wallace, betrayed
and executed, has a warmer place in the popular
heart than the successful Bruce. "Scots wha hae" is
not a song of victory: it discounts failure; and Flodden
strikes a deeper note than Bannockburn. Montrose
and Dundee, by their deaths in lost causes, redeemed

their errors and won apotheosis. The fame of one of
Scotland's greatest men, John Knox, has been dimmed
by success, and his name does not ring in popular
imagination like those of the Covenanting martyrs.
Mary Stuart is the heroine of hundreds of dramas in
every tongue: her fortunate son has become a laughing-stock. Prince Charlie and his supporters live for
ever in song and story: the only one of his opponents
whose name is popularly remembered is the Mac-
Crimmon of the *Lament*.

Fergusson, Michael Bruce, and David Gray were
poor men and died in their twenties. Hogg was a
bankrupt farmer. The last years of Burns and Scott
were clouded with ruin, suffering, and despair. "The
City of Dreadful Night" was the habitation of its
author's soul during nearly the whole of his brief
existence, which belonged to London. In Scotland
there were no fallen stars of magnitude between the
death of Scott and the advent of Stevenson; because
in the northern firmament there were no bright stars
—only the glow of the great star of Carlyle, shining
in the south, and, for the rest, the fuliginous glare of
industrial prosperity. Genius and tragedy begin
again with Stevenson and John Davidson.

And so the tale goes on, in every land beneath the
sun. The history of genius is thick-starred with stories
of neglect, poverty, and early death. Meryon and
Monticelli lived in obscure poverty and sold their
priceless masterpieces for a few francs. America, the
land of material success, has the deepest tragedy of
all: that of Poe. Goldsmith won European fame in
his short lifetime; but the exquisite essays of his that

are read today gained him no success as an editor: his *Bee* had a brief flight and gathered no honey. Lord Asquith rose to greatness, not by political success, but by his noble acceptance of apparent failure. Mr. Lloyd George at Versailles missed the chance of a splendid failure that would have set his name higher than that of Wilson.

Meredith was neglected or sneered at for the greater part of his life, and I doubt if he had ever more than £300 a year. Conrad at one period was granted a Civil List pension. Only in his later years did Hardy derive much from his books. It would shock readers if they knew how little money some of the best writers of our day get from royalties. The money-prizes go to a few ultra-popular writers, scarcely one of whom has any rank in literature. Wells, Bennett, and Bernard Shaw are notable exceptions; but they had to fight long and hard for recognition.

It is instructive to turn, by way of contrast, to an example of unqualified success. The chief factor in it is to be born with an enthusiastic attachment to the *status quo*, established privilege, and the big battalions. Such was the fortunate position of Lord Braxfield, for whom the law of the land, or his own interpretation of it, was the law of God. His zest in the hanging of sheep-stealers and political reformers has been graphically recorded by Cockburn, the first advocate to challenge him. "The reporter of Gerald's case could not venture to make the prisoner say more than that 'Christianity was an innovation'. But the full truth is, that in stating this view he added that all

great men had been reformers, 'Even our Saviour Himself'. 'Muckle He made o' that,' chuckled Braxfield
in an undertone. 'He was hangit.'"

Therein this pagan Caledonian gave out a most
tremendous text. The shadow of the Cross extends
the whole way down from Calvary, not only in religious and personal life, but in every noble sphere of
human activity. One can easily make too much of
this idea, especially where the person who suffers is
following the line of inward inclination and life is not
involved. But the central fact remains that there can
be no human progress unless in every generation there
are men and women who for the sake of a principle
or an ideal are prepared to forgo success and face
poverty, misunderstanding, and obloquy.

There are deeper issues involved: for example, the
apparent frustration and defeat of life's object, and of
love; as in the life-stories, gathered by a pious priest,
of the five people who were killed by the breaking of
a rope-bridge in Peru. All, it turned out, had arrived
at a point where life was really hopeless, but they
were hoping for something—beyond the bridge.
"Soon we shall all die," says the Abbess, the only
person who had known them all, "and all memory of
those five will have left the earth, and we ourselves
shall be loved for a while and forgotten. But the love
will have been enough; all those impulses of love
return to the love that made them. Even memory is
not necessary for love. There is a land of the living
and a land of the dead, and the bridge is love, the
only survival, the only meaning."

That is not very clear, though it is very beautiful;

and "it's only a story", anyhow. *The Bridge of San Luis Rey* is not an artistically satisfying book. It could hardly be; for, in attempting to deal with the last and deepest of mysteries, a story-writer has to adopt an artificial method and contrive a *tour de force*. But the epilogue of the Abbess, one may note, sums up much of the "new theology" of Karl Barth.

§ ii

Hamish's father was a bien Glasgow shopkeeper, of a line that had been "sma' corks" in St. Mungo's city since the days when the bakers went out to ding papacy at Langside. Hamish's mother was a dark, handsome Highland woman, daughter of a Cowal fisherman whose ancestors had fought the Campbells. On the paternal side there was no record of colourful adventure, but in the mother's family there were men who had sailed the Seven Seas, and come to violent ends on Malayan rivers and Pacific beaches.

Those hard-fisted sailormen had lived thrilling romances; but of romance they were unconscious, and it was the call of the city rather than of the wild that was felt in Cowal. In Hamish, the city and the wild became aware of each other. He lived romance, and also felt it. In him the observing powers of shrewd Glasgow citizens, and the temperamentalism of Highland fisher-folk, became mutually enhancive to an uncanny degree. He did not merely observe, he divined. His conversation was not mere narrative or comment, it was a series of living pictures, of vivid re-creations.

The literary faculty in Hamish was so intense that it could never express itself in writing. He was so busy living, picturing, and mentally acting, that he never learned a lesson. His grammar was more than shaky. His letters were a medley of *naïveté* and conventionality.

Only in his curiously elegant, almost feminine calligraphy, and in his fitful enthusiasm for Wagner and Tchaikovski, did his artistic temperament shine forth.

His dreamy nature and his red hair made him the butt of his school-fellows, but they respected him because of his loyalty and adventurousness, and his remarkable physical strength, which he never exercised save on behalf of weaker boys who were being bullied. "Brave as man is, soft as woman", was Hamish. He "plunked", of course, and was the Little John of a band of revoltees against the educational system, who haunted the docks and the purlieus of New City Road, pursued by parents and attendance officers.

At thirteen Hamish was apprenticed in a big engineering work. He learned little of mechanics, but he had the whole personnel of his "shop" off by heart, and became the hero and confidant of all the odd characters about the place. Seeing he was "wasting his time" his parents sent him off to learn farming in Kansas. He was a prodigious worker when work had to be done. The tornadoes and terrific thunderstorms of Kansas interested him, but he grew tired of the dull Middle West mentality, and made his way to Canada. He quarrelled with his Fundamentalist employer over the Biblical warrant for smoking, and shipped as a stoker on a cattle boat for Glasgow.

Then came his Odyssey, a round-the-world voyage as ordinary seaman on an old barque. He delved deep into the experiences and minds of old shellbacks, men whose lives were a succession of hard voyages punctuated by wrecks and wild sprees. Fights with knives and bootings from the mate they took as a matter of course. Such things disturbed not the infinite serenity of their discussions in the dog-watch, under the blazing stars, when the pipe went round, and every man told peacefully his biggest and longest lie, or delivered himself of his childlike fancies concerning religion, love, politics, and the origin of the daedal earth.

Hamish's fragmentary accounts of all this, and of the incredible personalities of the cosmopolitan crew, were so lifelike that I had the illusion of having lived it all myself. Pieced together coherently by a literary artist, it would have been finer than Dana, Clark Russell, or Conrad. That amazing life of the old sailing-ship passed away without ever finding its true chronicler.

"I am willing to try any drink once." Jurgen's motto was Hamish's. On his way to join another ship he disappeared into the wild. He roamed for weeks in Perthshire and Argyllshire, working with farmers here and there, and turned up at last in a Highland town, not far from a gloriously situated farm where he had spent holidays as a boy. His people were well-off, and he was fond of them. A good table and a cosy bedroom were at his disposal. But bourgeois comfort he disdained. He preferred a bunk to a bed, and trees and the stars to Victorian furniture and electric light.

In the city he dwelt with strange out-of-the-way people, stepchildren of fortune, whose minds and lives were a phantasmagoria of broken lights. A circus clown become undertaker was one of his hosts, and many a quaint symposium we had by gaslight among the coffins. Dickens was added to Conrad and Dana in Hamish's mental make-up. His humour, lambent and quaint, was too atmospheric for crude "literary" purposes. It was the ineffable emanation of unrecurring circumstances.

Hamish cared little for his own interest or comfort. I doubt if he ever noticed what he ate. It was curious how slightly he himself or his own notions figured in his entrancing monologues. That was the Shakespeare touch. He died of pneumonia in his twenties. If all the people who loved him had come to his funeral it would have been the biggest and queerest turn-out ever seen in a Glasgow cemetery. By Gradgrind or even Carlylean standards, his life had been a failure. But his friends knew well that they would never look upon his like again.

§ iii

There she weaves by night and day
A magic web with colours gay.
She has heard a whisper say,
A curse is on her if she stay
    To look down to Camelot.

My Scotland

And moving thro' a mirror clear
That hangs before her all the year,
Shadows of the world appear.
There she sees the highway near
    Winding down to Camelot.

．   ．   ．   ．   ．

She left the web, she left the loom,
She made three paces thro' the room,
She saw the water-lily bloom,
She saw the helmet and the plume,
    She look'd down to Camelot.
Out flew the web and floated wide;
The mirror crack'd from side to side;
"The curse is come upon me," cried
    The Lady of Shalott.

I never sit down to write without a feeling of diffidence and almost of shame. For, since I am not a specialist, my only subject is life; and there are few people who know less about real life than I do. I am not a father. I have never had a severe illness, nor crossed the ocean, nor worked in a coal pit or a stokehole, nor missed a meal, nor tramped the country in search of work, nor slept in a barn or beneath a hedge. I have never hived a swarm of bees. I haven't even kept hens.

The nearest I ever got to hard facts was when I "did for myself" once, for a whole fortnight. I didn't "make the bed", considering that a superfluous refinement; I "dined out", and tea'd, generally, at someone's hospitable board; and I let the dishes wash themselves under the tap. I concentrated on breakfast, and became an expert at omelettes, made of two eggs, milk, flour, cheese, and Yorkshire relish. Once

I added meal and barley. The result was something that seemed to need boiling. Boiling turned it into a dumpling as hard as a cricket ball. I dropped it out of the window. It fell, uninjured, with a dull thud on the pavement four stories below, narrowly missing a cat, which tried to eat it but failed.

From my infancy I was a dodger of life and a burker of issues. I contrived to put off going to school till I was nine, and to leave it at thirteen. Mental energy was conserved by means of a morning clearing-house where the products of all the talents were profitably exchanged. The lion in my path was the grim Tod-hunter, but I managed to outflank him, and remained innocent of algebra. Two things I could not evade: the tawse, and fighting; and I was licked in every fight. From the inferiority complex thus created I was delivered not so many years ago. It was at a big English railway junction, on the Friday night before Bank holiday. A stodgy Saxon "pushed" me, as Mr. Dooley would have put it, at the door of a compartment. Pride of race suddenly awoke in me, and I let him have what the Rev. Mr. Spalding called "a great blow" in the chest. His look of astonishment made me realize what I had missed by being a moolie.

While I mooned about and read romances and pottered with evening classes, theatres, and concerts, my friends tasted the salt savour of raw life. They went to sea, they learned engineering, they worked on farms, they even went on tramp. I lived vicariously, through them, and the mirror in which I saw their adventures was so enthralling that it never occurred to me to ride down to Camelot myself. In the mirror, also, were other things so entrancing—the deeds of Achilles, Wallace, Rob Roy, Rienzi, Tom Cringle, Peter Simple — that everyday life seemed poor in comparison. I retreated into a mock-ivory tower.

And yet how few of those who have fared on the open seas of life are able to make literary capital out of their experiences. The number of Jack Londons and Bart Kennedys and W. H. Davieses is singularly small, and they are not half as interesting as Hazlitt, who spent most of his days among books. The newspaper memoirs of many people who have had thrilling encounters with life are written for them by young journalists who have never been out of their own city. How the mirror can be exploited even by uncreative minds was discovered by me when, many years ago, I wrote some booklets of ocean travel for a publishing agency. With the aid of maps and encyclopaedias, I composed glowing pictures of scenes in the West Indies, West Africa, India, Australasia, and the Far East. The odours of exotic regions exhaled from my rhapsodical pages. I nearly became sea-sick over my account of a storm in the Southern Ocean. The booklets lay about in the saloons of liners, and I pictured them being solemnly consulted, amid the scenes described, by elderly ladies and gentlemen with carefully adjusted eyeglasses. They may have copied bits out of them into their travel diaries.

The most interesting travel books are by bookish folk who have a taste for adventure or who have overcome their initial fear of real life. Examples are

Gissing's *By the Ionian Sea*, Norman Douglas's *Old Calabria*, and the writings of Cunninghame Graham and H. M. Tomlinson. Henry W. Nevinson is perhaps the most scholarly and most cultured of working journalists; and as knight-errant of freedom he has followed the bright eyes of danger in Greece, South Africa, Russia, Portuguese West Africa, India and Gallipoli. He was in deadly peril during his investigations into the slavery of the cocoa plantations, and I remember his telling me that the only weapon he carried was a javelin, not because it was of any use, but because it had a romantic look. He made me aware of what I might have done, in a far humbler way, had I broken the spell of timidity and sloth. For when, at last, I turned round and faced towards Camelot—though I quaked inwardly, and walked "delicately", like poor Agag — the web did not fly out nor the mirror crack.

And at least I have the grace of humility. I salute, as my masters in life, those who have passed out of the sheltered and cosy circle on to the wind-swept open roads of life. And I feel that in some future existence my being must complete its university course of living, and take those hard classes it has missed here. The faith we live by is that for every discord there is a resolving harmony. There are notes in the diapason of life that are unknown to pundits and professors and ministers, and revealed to the stoker, the cattleman, the tramp, the man or woman at the "hot plate", the convict in his cell, the condemned murderer on the scaffold. For when we kill him, his pang, for us, "a fibre from the brain doth tear", and his agony is brought into the spiritual scheme of things. Every-man is the saint and the sinner, the mage and the shepherd, the malefactor on the gallows and the judge who sentenced him. Therein is the unescapable mystery of life.

CHAPTER VIII

LITERARY SOCIETIES

§ i

" ' THE minutes of the previous meeting were read and approved. . . . Mr. —— then read a paper on *The Ring and the Book*, by Robert Browning. Beginning with the actual case on which the poem is founded, he went on to . . . rapt attention . . . brought to a close an interesting discussion.' "

"Are those minutes approved?" asks the chairman. Subdued applause signifies assent. The chairman puts on his spectacles and consults his notes.

"This evening we are to be favoured with a paper on—er—on 'The Cathedrals of Belgium', by one who is *facile princeps* . . . acknowledged authority . . . fascinating subject . . . can safely promise ourselves a literary treat."

The acknowledged authority rises—by tentative degrees—amid slightly less subdued applause. . . . Is the light all right? Oh, yes, thanks. . . . He looks at his manuscript as if he were making its acquaintance for the first time, and clears his throat. "I am sorry, gentlemen . . . lack of time . . . pressure of business . . . could not do justice." He clears his throat again, takes a sip of water, and begins. His hearers settle down into comfortable postures and try to fix their eyes on vacancy. Time goes on. Sheet after sheet is laid reverently aside. Suddenly the voice of the speaker receives an organ-like accompaniment. An elderly member has become so absorbed in Flemish cathedrals that he has begun to dream about them. A "horrid silence" invades his ears, and he wakes up. The essay is finished; or rather, the essayist is. He has broken off half-way down the nave of Antwerp. "That's all I had written." Acute disappointment is depicted on every countenance.

Successively, on the appeal of the chairman, several members get up, slowly and painfully, as if they had lumbago. Each of them feels about for a dependable article of furniture; one gentleman puts his chair in front of him, leans on its back, cants it, lifts it, and does everything with it but the thing his hearers wish he would do—sit down on it.

The speakers comport themselves like reluctant witnesses in a criminal trial. But they all manage to say that they knew nothing about the subject, and that what they really want now is time to assimilate the rich feast of information they have just received.

One speaker wonders if the money it took to build these cathedrals wouldn't have been better spent on the distribution of Bibles; another remarks that there was evidently no Communism or ca' canny when these great edifices were erected. (*Some applause.*)

The chairman sums up in a gracefully rhetorical fashion, the lecturer modestly replies, the next meeting is announced, and the assembly thaws into human conversation.

.   .   .   .   .

Literary Societies

The Mermaid gatherings of Shakespeare's day were not the first of their kind in Europe; but privacy, regular meetings, and restricted membership came in with Queen Anne. The immortal Club of Dr. Johnson has been the model for countless coteries throughout the world. The literary tradition was maintained in some of the Edinburgh and Glasgow clubs of the eighteenth century. But at the industrial revolution town prevailed over gown and gown withdrew into its cloisters; the more famous of the Glasgow clubs were gastronomic and convivial, though "drink and no brains" is too severe a description of them.

The cultural paths deserted by the well-to-do were invaded by the new democracy. Mutual Improvement societies sprang up in the industrial areas; the Muses, still with Freedom found, repaired to gatherings of Renfrewshire weavers, where poets like Alexander Wilson and Robert Tannahill gave wing to their fledgeling strains. It is from these societies that the modern literary club mainly derives.

There is another and a more ancient source. In the primitive democracies of the Celts, as among African tribes today, songs were sung and stories told and riddles propounded round the village fires at night. In the semi-feudal period in the Highlands these symposia were confined mainly to the halls of the chiefs. But when Culloden had blasted racial hopes, and the chiefs were in exile or had become mere landlords, primitive custom was resumed. The people of the Western Isles gathered in their cottages at night and consoled themselves with music and poetry and tales of other years. These were the ceilidhs. Their story

has been told by Kenneth Macleod, himself a product
of the ceilidh.

The cosmopolitan critic may sneer at the literary
society as a provincial institution motived by the
"uplift" fallacy. But for many of us it was an oasis of
cultural interest in a desert of sordid commercialism;
it gave us assurance that we were not alone in our desire
for the finer things in life; in the preparation of essays
we learned to systematize our reading and clarify our
thoughts, and the discussions taught us to think on our
feet and express ourselves in language a little less slip-
shod than that of ordinary conversation. At the worst,
we learned patience. When I come across the inter-
minable essays I wrote in youth on Elizabethan
dramatists, eighteenth-century French literature, the
English romantic poets, and so forth, I marvel at the
forbearance of those who listened to them.

We were more interested in pure literature than
people seem to be today, though in our anxiety to extract
a "lesson" from the life and writings of a great author
we often missed his real power and charm. That is a
traditional Scottish failing, illustrated by the "morals"
Henryson appended to his Fables. But the "uplift"
fallacy is not wholly bad if it leads us to study poets
like Wordsworth, Browning, and Arnold. When the
didactic thirst has been slaked, our palates become
aware of the artistic savour of sterling poetry, drama,
or fiction. Possibly it was really that savour that
attracted us, and the moralizing was a concession to
national tradition. It was our only concession. Our
syllabuses rarely contained the name of a Scottish author.
Dunbar, Henryson, Lyndsay, Ramsay, Fergusson might

have been Chinese authors so far as we were concerned. Nor do I remember hearing a paper on the Scottish Ballads or the Gaelic literature of Ireland and the West Highlands. Contemporary literature, also, was practically ignored. An author was of no use to us unless he was English and dead.

The church "literaries" with which I had acquaintance were bigger than the private ones, but they were less intimate, and the presence of ladies and of the minister had a daunting effect. It was at a church literary that I heard a debate in which the respective merits of Burial and Cremation were so eloquently presented that one was filled with a deep regret that it was impossible to enjoy the advantages of both. Most of the old church literaries seem to have died out. A few have grown into big lecture societies, at whose weekly sessions lions roar you as softly as sucking-doves, with no one to say them nay. Those organizations can never take the place of the small semi-private literaries, to which they bear the same relation as a big professional football club to a multitude of small amateur clubs.

§ ii

Literature, to those who love books and have read much and written seriously, remains always the most interesting subject in the world. It is as big and as various as the universe; and the longest, most productive, and most successful literary life cannot do more than touch the fringe of it. Is there any good reason why authors should not meet together and have set discussions on selected literary topics? One would think not; and yet one gathers that in some countries authors of standing have a prejudice against anything of the kind. Can it be that they object to discuss purely literary matters unless with their literary peers, and are afraid of prejudicing their own status by engaging in the debates of a literary House of Commons? Or, as creative writers, dealing directly with life itself, do they consider the discussion of literary questions a waste of time?

Ministers, one is aware, do not like listening to sermons, and they form the very worst audience for a preacher. Authors are even more strongly individualist than clergymen, and they may have a distaste for *ex cathedra* utterances by people of their own profession, unless they happen to be writers of the very first rank, to whom the whole world listens. Ministers have their "fraternals", where theological and social questions are discussed by all who care to speak. Fraternals of authors may be a little more difficult to manage, for the description of the writing clan as *genus irritabile* is not inaccurate. But that they are impossible, inexpedient, uninteresting, or useless, I emphatically deny. Indeed, there is nothing more enjoyable or more stimulating than a rousing debate in a literary society composed of authors of all kinds. A discussion of this kind on the literary movements in modern Ireland was one of the top-notes of my literary experience. It taught me more than I could ever have learned for myself. I would not have missed it for worlds.

The production and the reviewing of books do not make up the whole of literature. Literature must return now and then to its primitive origins and express itself vocally and socially. Iron must sharpen iron; authors must come down occasionally from their ivory towers and realize the solidarity of the great company of those whose central concern is literature. There are rules of the game, and literature does not suffer by their observance. No human purpose is served by blatant egotism, Sinaitic pronouncements, sweeping condemnations without reasons annexed, or denunciations of all other speakers as nit-wits and ignoramuses. There is not a literary principle or canon or judgment, however novel or recondite or severe, that cannot be set forth in a rationally persuasive fashion to an intelligent audience, and discussed intelligently by them. The humble literary society of our youth was a school of things which transcend even literature, and without which a literature of any consequence cannot exist: self-respect, respect for others, and the human decencies of debate. It set standards which must be followed by the loftiest cenacle.

It would be inconsonant with our Scottish traditions and the origins of our culture, such as it is, if our writing folk did not get together now and then, and hold discussions in the good old fashion of the literary society. There is a special need for doing so in a country whose literature is in the remaking. Questions like the literary use of the vernacular, the place of Gaelic in our cultural scheme of things, the new standards in poetry, the scope of fiction, the true function of criticism, and so forth, call for active discussion by authors of all kinds, not so much for their individual benefit—though sparks thrown out in

debate are often very illuminating—as on account of
the necessity for creating an "atmosphere" conducive
to the further development of Scottish literature.
Scots writers dealing faithfully with Scotland are as
yet swimming against the tide. They have to create
the taste by which they are to be enjoyed. They have
to make their public. They are none the worse of
feeling that they are parts of a general movement
which, however one may describe it, is at all events the
spiritual dynamic of the new Scotland. Literary technique and the creative imagination owe little or
nothing to instruction or discussion of any kind. They
are to the extent of at least seventy-five per cent. the
gifts of God, and the other twenty-five per cent. is due
to close observation, hard thinking, and painful experi-
mentation. The author will not learn much of his
own craft among fellow-authors, for his particular
business is the exploitation of his own mind, about
which nobody except himself knows anything. Also,
there have always been certain risks in bringing together at one time too many of the *genus irritabile*.
Nevertheless, set discussions among writers in a country that is still struggling out of the provincial phase of
limitations and inhibitions serve two very important
purposes that are definitely related to actual literary
production. They encourage writers to be boldly
conscientious in artistic self-expression; and they
deepen the author's sense of spiritual and national
responsibility.

CHAPTER IX

SCOTS BANKING AND BANKERS

THE first banking transaction, we used to be told, was when Messrs. Moses, Aaron & Coy. gave Pharaoh a check (Amer.) on the Bank of the Red Sea, and crossed it for their own safety. This early instance of large-scale banking was balanced by citation of the first savings bank transaction, when Peter lodged with one Simon, a tanner. The currency of those brilliant pleasantries in Victorian Scotland bespoke popular knowledge both of the Bible and of banking. The Lombardy Jews were the originators of banking; one reads of Leonardo going to draw money from his bankers in Milan, two centuries before the Bank of England was founded. But the great modern systems of banking and finance owe their birth to two Scotsmen, William Paterson and John Law; an extension of her banking system was Scotland's reaction from the Darien disaster; the cash-credit system, a Scottish invention, is referred to by Burns; and at a time when English shopkeepers were still paying accounts in gold, and the stocking was the bank of French farmers, Scottish crofters and blacksmiths were using cheques and "the meanest hind in a' Scotland" had a few pounds in a savings bank.

Banking is a curiously abstract business. Abstract in a literal sense, for our introduction to it was the withdrawal of sums we had imagined to be intended for our own delectation. The tin receptacle into which monetary gifts vanished could at least, when shaken, give audible audit of its contents. But when the sum-total disappeared into the savings bank, dissatisfaction was tinged with anxiety. What was done with the money? The sight of our bank-book yielded no comfort: this interest business, now, was it not a mere blind? And even when we were trained to conduct our own banking transactions, we regarded the whole business with gloomy suspicion, registering a vow that when we got control of that bank-book we would transmute its dull paper into crowded hours of glorious life.

A deeper mystery surrounded the ordinary banks. From our childhood we had puzzled over those dingy establishments, with the wire-gauze on the windows, through which one could make out nothing but vague forms and white paper. The public-houses had some kind of connotation. Bad men went into them, and came out wiping their mouths and talking loudly; some of the frequenters were known to us, and were regarded with a shrinking horror. But the people who went into these sepulchral banks didn't seem to have any exciting experiences inside; they emerged as sad-looking as they went in; and we never saw anyone thrown out. Occasionally a solemn countenance, with a bald head and a pen in the ear, would be visible above the wire screen; and at three o'clock a big boy, in long trousers, would take in the "bass", and lock the door upon an impecunious world.

When we penetrated the arcana, our mystification

was increased. What were those little pink or blue documents, those funny little slips, that were handled with such reverential care? What was the basis of public confidence in those huge bundles of bank-notes? What was done with all that gold, withdrawn by this weird agency from the control of people who could have made a picturesque use of it? And what was the idea of that sponge in the glass? It could not be for ablutionary purposes, for it would leave a dirty mark on the face. . . . The whole thing was beyond me. I gave it up: little dreaming I was destined to be a ministrant in this gloomy temple of Mammon.

The fine new bank premises of our days, with their neo-Hellenic architecture, their bright spaciousness, and their up-to-date equipment, signalize the change that has taken place since I was a bank apprentice. Banking has opened out to the world. In my early days the profession was cloistered, almost monastic, and every office was a museum of characters. Idiosyncrasies grew as rank as mushrooms in a tunnel, every one had a nickname, and there was a rich inheritance of cryptic jests, anecdotes, catchwords, and practical jokes. Some of these, in the days before I joined, were of a kind that would not be appreciated nowadays. A bank clerk had a touch of congestion and a mustard poultice was put on his chest at night. In the morning he remarked to his fellow-lodger, "What a pity to waste such a nice poultice!" So he parcelled it up neatly and sent it through the post to the bank-manager, a pompous martinet. Remarkable extravagances of language were indulged in. I knew of a bank accountant in a large office who, when a clerk raised any question about an order, used to lift his right hand high above his head and declare in sepulchral tones: "I have registered a vow in Heaven that this shall be done!" In the smaller offices there was an affectation of shabbiness in regard to office-jackets. One old teller I knew used to daub his jacket periodically with ink-and-water to give it an air of freshness. The bacterial world had no terrors for him: he would eat ham sandwiches in the intervals of counting dirty notes with fingers moistened on a coal-black sponge. He had a stock pleasantry for customers cashing cheques: "Will you have it in gold, silver, or precious stones?"

There was need for all the relief afforded by original characters and quaint jests. For the work, before calculating machines and typewriters and patent safes came in, was grindingly monotonous. To those who have gone through annual balances and term-times in big bank offices under the old régime, no work they are ever called upon to do can seem hard. The speed at which we used to work on busy days was equalled only in booking-offices at big railway stations; and I see nothing like it anywhere today. The country bank-accountant, who came to the office in knickerbockers, reared prize poultry, and shot and fished all over the country-side, was in a different category, though he had his own peculiar problems, the chief of them being to show face on his incredibly meagre salary. We who were in the front line had no time to worry about our poor pay. The troubles we endured encouraged a fine camaraderie among the rank-and-

file. Clypes and climbers were marked and ostracized:
the rest of us never let each other down. I only wish
I could live up to the standard of manliness, helpful-
ness, and all-round decency that prevailed among my
old colleagues.

CHAPTER X

THE SCOTS OBSERVER, 1888-1926

§ i

Oɴ October 2, 1926, appeared the first number of *The Scots Observer*: A Weekly Journal of Religious and National Interest. This fulfilment of an old plan for an unofficial organ of the Protestant Churches in Scotland was largely due to the enterprise of the late Mr. Adam B. Keay and of the late Dr. Donald Fraser, who became chairman of a board that included Neil Munro and Dr. Lauchlan MacLean Watt. I was appointed editor, and retained that post until the summer of 1929. The paper was published at first in Glasgow, but the editorial office was removed later to Hamilton, where *The Scots Observer* is still published and printed.

Such a paper ought to have been established in Scotland at least thirty years earlier. To win a circulation for it so late as 1926 was no easy task. Scotland is the world-centre of Presbyterianism, yet the idea that the religious life of Scotland could have full journalistic expression elsewhere than in London had become strange to ministers and Church members. An editorial genius with lots of money behind him might have conquered that prepossession. I was no genius of any kind; and our financial resources were limited. But I tried to make up for my editorial incapacity by working hard for fourteen hours a day, seven days in the week; and, thanks to the backing I got from the directors, and to the splendid campaigning work of that great and devoted churchman, Dr. Donald Fraser, *The Scots Observer* made a place for itself in the life of Scotland.

I was skipper of a new vessel sailing in strange waters, with no chart or compasses, and only a vague general idea of direction. Had the churches given us backing on the score of our being a Scottish paper, and made a few allowances for the difficulties of a new start, our course would have been largely determined for us from the beginning. But as we did not happen to be better in every respect than what they could get from London, they gave us only a circulation which, though good enough for an ordinary small weekly, was not half what we had a right to look for. We expected to be a liner. We had to become a "tramp", going here and there for cargoes.

Had the churches shown awareness that on their loyal support depended our ability to satisfy them, I should have endeavoured to produce a purely religious paper on as high an intellectual plane as the *Church Times*, with addition of the popular and gossipy features which Church people in Scotland seem to require. That remained my ambition; but I made the disconcerting discovery that Scots people were comparatively little interested in the scholarly or philosophical aspects of religion, or even in its application to big problems of social ethics. Newspaper correspondence about the Old Testament reveals abysmal ignorance concerning that fascinating, all-important, but highly difficult volume. The intellectual side of a purely religious paper presents a problem in a country where every man is his own Wellhausen.

In any case, it became necessary for us to organize the constituencies available to us, and, so to speak, to create the taste by which we were to be enjoyed. I proceeded, first of all, on the broad assumption that every Scot who is not a convinced atheist is actually or potentially religious, and interested in religion. A central aim for the paper was suggested by the growth of the national movement in Scotland. That movement was mainly cultural, and therefore in essence spiritual. Scotland was a spiritual entity, of which the Church, as representing the basic spiritual impulse, ought to be the centre. The idea of incongruity between an evangelistic address by a saintly genius like Dr. Fraser and a poem or novel or essay by a distinguished Scots littérateur was utterly false; and the Church could not be indifferent to questions like housing, industrial economics, land settlement, and international peace.

In my attempts to make a national, spiritual, intellectual and social synthesis of Scotland, I was backed loyally by most of the ministers and by all the Scottish writers, artists, and musicians. If I made the paper too bookish, it was by way of over-correction of church tendency and as an expression of my own tastes, for I wrote a great part of the paper myself, my own contribution to a single issue sometimes exceeding 20,000 words. Significantly enough, it was certain of the Church leaders who were most critical both of the over-intellectual character of the paper and of my "nationalist" tendencies.

With adequate financial backing and a bigger staff, my dream of a spiritual synthesis of Scotland might have been fulfilled. Dr. Fraser was a tower of strength, and I had always his confidence, though I must have given him anxious moments. But money was lacking, and we had to narrow our scope. In our attempt to win a larger popular clientèle within the Church, we were finely assisted by the racy contributions of John MacNeill, though I made him very angry by publishing an article in which it was hinted that St. Paul, while a very great man, was not the fountainhead of Christian doctrine. The experiment of placing the paper under a board officially representative of the Church did not prove very successful, and shortly after I ceased to be editor *The Scots Observer* resumed its independence.

My successors in the editorship, Mr. Livingstone, Mr. Stevenson and Mr. M'Queen, were able churchmen, and much better at the job than I was. Still, the impression of failure I had received was tempered by a fine send-off from my numerous and loyal friends among the ministers, to whom I owe more than I have ever been able to acknowledge. And, looking back, I do not think that my terrific expenditure of energy, or the splendid work put in by my brilliant young assistants, Mr. G. Macintyre Little and Mr. W. M. Ballantine, was entirely in vain. We did assist definitely in making a spiritual unity of Scotland. We were of some real use to the Church in furthering Union; and in November, 1927, I had the fortunate inspiration of writing an article outlining the plan which, thanks to the *Daily Record* and the Convention of Burghs, took shape later in the Scottish National Development Council.

In the later months of my editorship, overwork and a sense of futility induced moods of petulance, and I find a certain reflection of these in articles of a quite too personal kind, written, mostly, in the small hours of the morning. Some of them are funny enough in a way, though humour is not my strong suit; but I remember that I was admonished for them by serious-minded correspondents. Putting each other right is our national forte and mission. But these incidents were slight in comparison with the thousands of letters of warm sympathy I received from Scots men and women all over Scotland and the world.

§ ii

The title of the new *Scots Observer* was my own suggestion. I nourished a secret hope that some day the paper might take up the golden thread of Henley's famous weekly.

In 1873 William Ernest Henley, then in his twenty-fourth year, came to Edinburgh to see what Professor Joseph Lister could do for a tuberculous ankle. The treatment lasted twenty months, and proved successful. In the Edinburgh Royal Infirmary, Henley was visited by Stevenson, his junior by one year. The acquaintance ripened into a friendship which had its literary fruits in the memorable series of plays in which the young writers collaborated. Of Lister and the young Stevenson, Henley has given pen-portraits in his *Hospital Poems*. After his discharge from the

Royal Infirmary, Henley remained in Edinburgh for four months, working on the staff of the *Encyclopædia Britannica*. In 1878 he was married, in Edinburgh, to Anna Boyle, daughter of a Scottish engineer. Their one child, Margaret, who died in 1894 at the age of five, is the "Reddy" of Barrie's *Sentimental Tommy*. After Henley's death, in 1903, his widow lived with her relatives in Glasgow, and she died there in 1925.

In 1889, Henley came back to Edinburgh to become editor of a weekly paper, *The Scots Observer*, which had been started in the previous year. In November, 1890, the name of the paper was changed to *The National Observer*, and very shortly afterwards its headquarters were removed to London. Henley resigned from the editorship in 1894. Among the contributors of "middle" articles and of poems were J. M. Barrie, T. E. Brown, Thomas Hardy, Rudyard Kipling, Andrew Lang, R. L. S., H. G. Wells, and W. B. Yeats. Stevenson's *Christmas at Sea* was first published in *The Scots Observer* of December 22, 1888, and his famous letters in vindication of Father Damien were printed in the issues of May 3 and 10, 1890.

The first number of *The Scots Observer* was published on November 24, 1888. It contains thirty-two well-printed pages, mostly letterpress, two columns to the page. The advertisements are mainly of books. The paper was evidently designed to counter Gladstonian and Radical influence in Scotland. It is truculently Conservative. The Irish Nationalists are witheringly denounced, the claims of the Highland crofters are contemptuously dismissed, and the advocates of Scottish autonomy are stigmatized as disturbers of the national peace. The political and economic items are dreary and dead, while the pages dealing with books, pictures, and the varied scene of human life are as fresh as on the day they were printed.

The opening number begins with "A Political Retrospect" of two columns, a two-column article on Irish Land Purchase, and an article of well over a column on "The Governorship of Queensland". W. G. Simpson spreads himself over three-and-a-third columns on "The Spread of Golf". An article on "The Lost Works of George Meredith" bears the signature of J. M. Barrie. There are nine pages of reviews. Among the books dealt with at length are Mrs. Oliphant's Life of Principal Tulloch, a novel entitled *Tempted of the Devil*, by M. W. Macdowall (published by Gardner, of Paisley), a book on old Scottish min-strelry, by William M'Dowall, and a volume of verse by Henley, who, says the reviewer, "can already take rank with the masters".

The second number contains an article by Andrew Lang on "Literary Cadgers", and reviews of Barrie's *When a Man's Single*, Henry Drummond's *Tropical Africa*, and Zola's *Le Rêve*—the last obviously by Henley. G. A. Henty and Frankfort Moore figure in a column on Children's Books. In the third number we note that "Kaid Maclean, the Commander-in-Chief of the army of the Emperor of Morocco . . . has just arrived from the Far West of Islam, in company with Mr. Crichton Brown, who was Mr. Joseph Thomson's companion in his recent exploration of the Atlas Mountains."

Smith: A Drama, by John Davidson, is reviewed in

an early number of *The Scots Observer*; it is praised as poetry, but condemned as drama. On December 22, 1888, appears an article on Hamish MacCunn, the Scottish composer. One notes also a fine review-article on the correspondence of that brilliant "Mala-growther", Charles Kirkpatrick Sharpe, and notices of the Life of Robertson of Irvine, *The Book of Isaiah*, by the Rev. George Adam Smith, and *A Century of Artists*, the book written by Henley as a memorial of the Art Section in the Glasgow Exhibition of 1888. The question of Church Union is foreshadowed in an allusion to the U.P. Church and to the celebration at Glasgow of "the Ter-jubilee—what a word!—of the Secession". "It is still a moot point," we read in the issue of March 16, 1889, "whether Canon Liddon or Principal Caird is the first preacher in the United Kingdom."

CHAPTER XI

FROM THE PRIVATE PAPERS OF
LAWRIE TOD

§ i

"BY the way, Tod," said the Editor, "I've got something here that I think you ought to read." He handed me a letter marked "Private: Not for Publication". It ran:—

SIR,

I am astonished that you allow that elderly jackanapes, Lawrie Tod, to occupy space that ought to be devoted to serious discussion, by well-known and responsible citizens, of matters directly affecting the moral and religious welfare of Scotland,—or else to sound and healthy stories illustrating the traditional virtues and humours of our sturdy peasantry, or the solid qualities of our middle-class, who have built up the Empire. What Mr. Tod evidently intends as humour is merely the elaborate kidding and codding and clowning of a conceited highbrow, who wants to show his superiority to the average decent ratepayer. Mr. Tod's affectation of democratic feeling and of Scottish patriotism does not conceal his innate snobbery and his lack of sympathy with the genuine Scottish character as portrayed by Burns, Ian Maclaren, Barrie, and Joseph Laing Waugh. Sack Lawrie Tod.—I am, etc.,

MAN IN THE STREET.

"What do you think of that ? " asked the Editor.

"Excellent criticism, up to a point," I replied. "But where's this sturdy peasantry he talks about ? Is it in

Polmadie, or the Dalry Road, or the Blue Mountains, or the Whifflet, or Cowdenbeath ? "

"I suppose it's where he says—in the pages of those writers he mentions. Or in Alberta or Saskatchewan. Anyhow, it's up to you to say something in reply. I suggest a few notes on The Man in the Street."

.   .   .   .   .

Intellect is like a marine engine. It is apt to race when the propeller gets out of water. That was why every nation invented a figure embodying rustic common sense and mother-wit. Its literary function was to deflate the pretensions of high-flyers of every description, and bring the intellect down from rare atmospheres into the safe medium of everyday reality. It was an earth-anchor. Spain had her Sancho Panza, Germany her Hans Wurst, France her Jacques Bonhomme, and England her Piers Plowman.

In the eighteenth century England adopted the vulgar figure of John Bull, satirically invented by a witty Aberdonian, Dr. Arbuthnot. Scotland adopted the English idea of a raw-boned Lowlander in a kilt, answering to "Sandy". Ireland was represented by a stage scarecrow called "Pat". America herself invented "Uncle Sam", who has been superseded in our day by that monster known as the 100-per-cent American.

Those later types were artificial and commonplace, vulgar rather than rustic, and only nominally national. The next stage of descent was to something which had not even a national label; which was purely negative in connotation; and which, indeed, was an abstraction of mediocrity. An English statesman invented the Man in the Omnibus. A London journalist changed it to the Man in the Street.

The Man in the Street, one gathers, doesn't like poetry, he is not interested in ideas, Beethoven and Wagner to him are merely noise, so-called "art" means nothing to him, religious mysticism and the Higher Criticism are both folly in his eyes, he can't make out what people see in Dickens and Meredith and Hardy and Conrad, he has no use for Gaelic or the Scots Vernacular, and he doesn't see what is meant by a Scots Renaissance. He doesn't seem to have any intellectual attributes. Possibly he is the person who eats more fruit, pursues the elusive vitamin, wears patent sock-suspenders, and has a bad leg. Perchance in the ranks of the Frothblowers you will find him. Or he may be a member of the Mustard Club.

No one wants to be identified with him. Even the person who signs a letter "Man in the Street" would not stand to it if he were questioned. He would hold to his privileges as John Smith, with a soul to be saved, and an outlook of his own upon the world. If you flung a cake of soap at random in a public street, the person you might hit would not be the Man in the Street, but a highly individuated being. "Male and female created He them;" so, as there is no female of the Man in the Street, he cannot be a real creature. As Betsy Prig said of Mrs. Harris: "I don't believe there's no sich person."

The Man in the Street stands for the Mass Mind, and he was invented as a bogey to daunt the vendors of disturbing ideas. The Mass Mind is the negative, the fiercely orthodox mind. Its working in the Middle Ages is described in Pater's *Denys l'Auxerrois* or Balzac's *Succubus*. But it was not until the advent of popular education and universal suffrage that the Mass Mind was organized as a social force. The art with which its fears and prejudices were made to neutralize its political and economic aspirations, was something that must excite admiration: as represented by its exploiters, the Mass Mind was early-medieval in essentials, and ultra-modern in etceteras; blending Domesday Book with the Compleat Plumber. It reversed the ideal of Shelley and Mazzini: socially it was feudal, intellectually it was ultra-democratic, linking up the mob-mind of peers with that of proletarians, and making Justice Shallow, Mr. Podsnap, and Christopher Sly the arbiters of thought and taste. In Europe the Mass Mind is still held in check, to some extent, by the tradition of an aristocracy of intellect. But in America the Mass Mind has become a universal tyranny, embodied as that fearful fowl, the 100-per-cent. American.

Just as mothers used to frighten their children with Boney, or Burke and Hare, or the "Kayser"; so people who dislike new ideas, or are "afraid of that which is high", try to put the wind up on critics, poets, artists, idealists, and so forth, by evoking those fearsome dummies, the Man in the Street, and the 100-per-cent. American.

No fearless knight am I; but the things I fear are real things. The effect of turnip-lanterns and white sheets is lost on me; for your Man in the Street I care less than I do for Santa Claus or the Man in the Moon. He doesn't exist. And on that which he stands for, I declare open war. I refuse to believe that what interests or moves me deeply is of no concern to my compatriots, or that in order to engage their sympathies I must cease to be myself. On the contrary, I believe that by being boldly individual, I am assisting in that general process of individuation which is the necessary corrective to the coagulative tendency of modern life.

§ ii

From Ninian Keelevin, of Messrs. Pitwinnoch, McTavish, Keelevin, and Fash, Writers, Glasgow, to James Brathins, Merchant, Woolburgh.

You have expressed interest in my early recollections of our friend, Lawrie Tod. Trivial in themselves, perhaps, the following details derive a certain importance from the fame that has been won by the charming but inscrutable author of *Lilts from Lambhill*, *U.P. Idylls*, *Eros in Kelvinhaugh*, and *The Cruise of Clutha No. 3*.

.   .   .   .   .

Lawrie and I were born in adjacent tenements in the Middle West of Glasgow; we were classmates both in the day school and in the Sunday school. I send you a photograph of a class group in which we both figure. It was taken by an eminent artist whose name was known to us as Woalgemutt but was spelt Wohlgemuth. A period of transition is marked by the costume of the lady teacher, the moustache of the young male teacher, and the redundant whiskers of the head-

From the Private Papers of Lawrie Tod

master. Lawrie, aged ten, stands out conspicuous by
reason of a white woollen "grauvat", which he had
been wearing on account of a recent attack of mumps,
and which he had omitted to remove.

. . . . .

Lawrie was not remarkable for physical strength or
courage. I myself, who was of stocky build and phlegmatic temperament—being generally known as "Puddin'"—often acted as his protector. When things grew
dull at school, fights were arranged in this wise: A.
was informed that B. wanted to punch his head; corresponding information was conveyed to B.; and at
four o'clock A. and B. found themselves borne by their
supporters to the place of combat, where they were dis-
robed and shoved up against each other. Lawrie did
not escape his turn, and I have a lively recollection of
seeing him undergoing disfigurement for the general
entertainment; for Lawrie was like the ancient Celts,
who always went out to battle and always got licked.
Tears mingled with the blood which flowed from his
sharp little nose; but ten minutes later he would be
deep in the recital of a yarn out of Marryat or *The
Arabian Nights*.

Lawrie and I never missed seeing a fight. One,
which took place in ecclesiastical precincts, lasted for
an hour, and ended with the retreat of one of the com-
batants into an ashpit.

. . . . .

Lawrie was a lazy little beggar at school; I doubt if
he ever really learned a lesson. But by dint of what he

picked up from the teacher or from novels, he managed to put up such a good bluff that a school inspector declared he ought to be sent to the university. If Barlinnie had been proposed, Lawrie couldn't have been more frightened. His real ambition was to speculate in something—railways, or sugar, or split peas—and make a fortune, and go and live in a log hut beside a creek. Meanwhile, "what, now, about a rowing boat, with provisions—and fishing tackle—and a dog—and an anchor—and a small sail—and blankets—and a locker—and a tarpaulin to cover the boat at night—couldn't we cruise about the Firth that way?"

.　　.　　.　　.　　.

Lawrie didn't seem to have much interest in the people about him. He was a romantic dreamer, delighting to drag exploring parties into odd corners of the city. Before he was eleven he had discovered the Cathedral, the Docks, and Bowling Harbour. When he was a small chap he had been taken on a voyage by a seafaring relative, and he used to tell us he had been in Africa and seen a lion. Also, he used to kid that he was descended from an earl. We all did our share of fibbing, but Lawrie's fibs were of that irritating kind that are calculated to make folk feel cheap and common. We didn't like to hit him, because he was puny and brainy; but he may understand now why we used to call him "Sweenie".

.　　.　　.　　.　　.

Lawrie was a spoiled kid; the ethical and practical qualities didn't develop in him till Fate had tapped him once or twice on the solar plexus. Perhaps my picture of him is distorted by lingering jealousy. We were rivals in love. He was twelve and I was thirteen. The damsel was more mature. Fourteen winters had passed over her head. She was not a Jeanie Morrison, slender and winsome and gentle. She was short, plump, ruddy, bright-eyed, and cheeky. All the boys in the class were in love with her. Forty eyes gazed on the back of her round, fuzzy head. Looking back, I divine that to the teachers this gallery of mooncalves was a source of mirth. The young lady was the unconscious cause of several quite good fights. Lawrie wrote poetry about her. Both of us once bought toffee and dared each other to present her with it. Lawrie snatched the sticky tribute and, flushing to the roots of his hair, approached the proud beauty. He stammered out the first syllable of her adored name. She looked at him as if he had been a sack of potatoes. He made a half turn to the left, pretended he didn't see her, and fled; what time "the imperial votaress passed on, in maiden meditation, fancy free". And if she reads this, she will be like the lady in Arvers' sonnet:

> *Elle dira, lisant ces vers tout remplis d'elle:*
> *"Quelle est donc cette femme?" et ne comprendra pas.*

I had a note of something about a sweetmeat called money-balls, in an alleged connection with a decline in the Sunday School collections for our own black protégé in Old Calabar—he used to be introduced to us on the magic lantern screen, poor thing! An occasional penny may have dwindled to a halfpenny by the time the sweet shop was passed. Anyhow, there was nothing of Ananias about Lawrie. His pennies got through all right.

Yours,

NINIAN KEELEVIN.

§ iii

Since Keelevin elected to drag in that ridiculous stuff about the money-balls, he might at least have made himself clear. They were large coarse sweeties about the diameter of a penny, more than half an inch thick, and with a coating of bright red. They cost one halfpenny each. The purchaser had the chance of finding a threepenny bit in his mouth when he had sucked his way down to the centre of the sweet. It was a form of gambling, of course—a saccharine lottery— and as such was very properly denounced by the guardians of public morality. But the idea that it diverted money from the Old Calabar Mission is an absurd invention of Keelevin.

The money-balls were dispensed by a certain drug-gist of our acquaintance, who also sold a deadly kind of penny cigar, called Pickwicks. Our motto in those days was that of Jurgen: "I am willing to try any drink once," and "Puddin'" and I once clubbed for a Pickwick and smoked it by turns in a secluded back green. We didn't finish it. It finished us. Never have I got such a variety of sensation for so small a price. It was as good as a Channel-crossing in a gale.

Why do we indulge so inordinately in reminiscences of childhood's days? Was the Frenchman right who declared that we do all our real living before the age of

228

fourteen, and spend the rest of our lives in talking about it ? I was battling with the world at thirteen. Perhaps that is why I divagate so readily into *souvenirs d'enfance*. I never had my boyhood "out", and its premature cessation left my mind full of broken melodies which will tantalize me to the end of my life. Youth, to me, remains like that "lady sweet and kind" whom the poet saw only in passing—

And yet I love her till I die.

Frustrated boyhood went back, so to speak, "into my system". Never having been wholly young in my early 'teens, I stay half-young.

That is how I explain my inferiority in practical wisdom to the majority of my compatriots. Of this quality Scotland would seem to contain as much as would suffice Russia and China. Perhaps it would be better if the Scottish people had a little less of it; they might be able to give a freer rein to their imaginations, and press forward to the realization of their smothered dreams.

. . . . . .

We whose boyhood belongs to the period of Browning and horse cars are puzzled to know how the imagination of youth functions in this mechanized and all-technical age. The "beyondness" of the world, its atmospheric background, seems to have vanished. No wonder old folks take to Spiritualism, and young folks to chocs. and the Charleston. Do thay make love in the moonlight, and write endless love-letters, partly in bad verse? Does he give her a copy of Shakespeare's sonnets, with lines marked, and does she respond with a marked copy of Tennyson? Does he write essays for the Literary Society on Marlowe or *The Ring and the Book*? And if they don't do those things, what are their spiritual equivalents for them? How do they sustain the life-impulse?

.   .   .   .

The mind of man is like a race-horse or a hunting hound; it must be kept half hungry. Starve it of table scraps—of cheap distractions and facile pleasures—feed it sparingly on solid meat and drops of honey-dew—and it will enter for the Holy Grail, follow the horns of Elfland, and go a-hunting after Leo and the Great Bear.

> Who ne'er with tears did eat his bread,
> Who never, through the bitter hours,
> Sat nightlong weeping on his bed,
> He knows not you, ye Heavenly powers!

I fancy the people who still read poetry are not in the thick of the visible "fun" that's going. What did the "world" know about us in the days when our dreams filled the universe?

Yours,

LAWRIE TOD.

§ iv

Uncle David gone—Uncle David of the Mains! I can scarcely believe it. He seemed as much a part of the abiding scheme of things as the Craig Hill. He was nearly sixty when I first met him, yet he seemed to me then, and always since, one of the best-looking men I have ever seen: moderately tall, solidly but gracefully built, with well-trimmed beard, shapely nose, fine complexion, and bright blue eyes. I see him yet—fit match for his handsome horses—turning round from the plough to speak to me, his eyes in his sunburnt face, like corn-flowers in ripe wheat. "Boaz!" I said to myself—and ceased to wonder at Ruth's choice. How Uncle David had managed to remain a bachelor was always a puzzle.

In public matters Uncle David was not interested. I doubt if he had any political opinions, and the business side of the farm he left to his partner. Yet he was one of Scotland's most useful citizens. He had a passion for the land. He loved the farm, knew every clod and stone of it, the arable value of every square yard, and worked a big field with the intimate care of a Belgian smallholder and the swift pace of a champion Scottish ploughman. Watching his big, sure, delicate touch in "dreel-harrowing", I would say to myself, "That's how Rembrandt painted his pictures."

. . . . .

Some of you country folk do know how well off you are. Uncle David, of course, didn't know what a city was, and didn't care. Tom Jamieson of Glenwhan had visited Glasgow; he had sat out, with great amazement, a fairly bold revue, priced furs and diamond tiaras in Buchanan Street, and expressed approval of the topaz and chrysolite, bdellium and the onyx stone, that covered the walls of Gerson's restaurant; but the third day found him wearying for the stony fields and heather hills and dark mosses of

231

Glenwhan, and when he got home he walked round
the farm, stretching himself and whistling aloud for
sheer joy.

Farm life must be pleasanter than it used to be.
In Covenanting and Cameronian and even Disruption days the farmer required the solace of theological
and even philosophic literature. Today he seems to
rub along with Edgar Wallace and a popular weekly.

The old Covenanting spirit still flashes out, however. I remember one Sunday afternoon I was sitting
with Tom Jamieson in his parlour, reading an extinct
theological work. Tom was reading the *Weekly
Screamer*. Suddenly, from the other room, in which
the children were, came the gramophone voice of
Harry Lauder in "Stop yer ticklin', Jock". Tom was
in the middle of a thrilling article, by a popular execu-
tioner, describing the last moments of a famous
murderer. Nevertheless he tore himself away from
it, and went over to the other room. He rapped
loudly on the door. "Stop that this meenit," he said,
in stern accents. "D'ye no' ken what day this is?"
Silence fell; and Tom, his duty done, returned in
peace, to see the miscreant dragged to the scaffold
and launched into eternity.

.   .   .   .   .

I'm glad to learn they've got their village hall and
institute up at Moorside finished. To have raised
every penny of the cost from the farmers and villagers,
without resort to any nabob or big-wig, was a splendid
feat. How many villages in Scotland could do the

like? Most of them are withering in the shadow of the big hoose. I hope the Moorside hall will soon echo with the joyful sound of music and dancing—real dancing, not that hideous American parody of savage postures. An Italian said that the modern girl was like a bad photograph—suffering from over-exposure and insufficient development. The Moorside lassies don't give an impression of that sort when they take the floor.

.   .   .   .   .

I see the Rev. Mr. Peerie graced your board at the Burns supper, and I understand he proposed the Immortal Memory last year. At one time, I believe, the clergy frowned on Burns celebrations, the Auld Kirk ministers because of Burns's radical sentiments, the Free Kirk and U.P. ministers because of the Bacchanalian associations. Since then the Church has begun to associate herself with the Burns cult. Burns himself is being "translated". Already he is almost a teetotaller. He is becoming Tory and anti-Nationalist. There remain the amorous episodes. So far, these have defied the sand-paperer. But what has already been done gives ground for hope that Rab the Ranter may yet shine forth as the Scottish Galahad. I confess I prefer the real, imperfect, but human Burns— rebel, satirist, lover, sinner, and praiser of life.

.   .   .   .   .

Do you remember our night at the Moorside Farmers' Burns Club? The supper was at six: we arrived then. But the local contingent had assembled at four, and for two hours they had been toying with *apéritifs* in the shape of glasses of whisky and pints of beer. The "form" they had acquired was made evident when grace had been said. The first course was Scotch broth, of the consistency of porridge. It was served in basins, and vanished like dew in a tropic dawn. Then came huge helpings of boiled mutton, roast beef, and steak pie. They melted away, but, when the pie appeared, one had the feeling that the company were getting down to something solid. Then, amid a skirl of pipes and a thunder of applausive boots, came the haggis, served, not in ladylike samples, but in half-pound portions. There was a perceptible increase in the flow of beer and whisky. Last of all came massive slabs of apple dumpling. At eight o'clock the speeches and songs began. Hotter and thicker grew the atmosphere, louder the laughter: at the end of the Burns oration a tumbler was broken. They kept it up, I believe, till half-past one. That was the year before the war, wasn't it?

No, I didn't do an Immortal Memory this year. I think I made myself unpopular by my remarks about orators who couldn't tell the good from the bad in Burns, and my insistence on the need for a knowledge of Burns's predecessors, and of the new school of vernacular poets in our own day. I didn't give them the sob-stuff they wanted, about the "Cotter's Saturday Night", "Mary in Heaven", and "A Man's a Man for a' That". I babbled of Fergusson and Ramsay and the moderns—and who wants to know about them? Isn't it handier to have all your poetry, like all your religion, in one volume?

. . . . .

From the Private Papers of Lawrie Tod

Yes, I remember Mr. Sangster's venerable predecessor, Mr. M'Vicar. White tie—Celtic-fringe whiskers—ministerial to a degree—"labouring in the vineyard" and "rejoicing at this time"—a "painful" preacher, with a theology that made one blaspheme. But at a Communion service one had a glimpse of the great soul that burned behind the spiky doctrinal framework. I saw him speaking to Mrs. Thomson just an hour or two after her husband had been killed on the railway—the English caricaturist's idea of a "meenister" was transformed into an angel of the Lord—he took the poor woman's hands in his, and her hysterical wailings ceased. The farmers were a little afraid of him, but the bairns adored him, and the tinkers paid him affectionate reverence. Life, to him, was a sacrament. He knew all about the Septuagint, but the simplest banking transaction threw him into confusion, and he talked of the Stock Exchange as if it were a mystery invented by Cambridge Wranglers.

.　　　.　　　.　　　.　　　.

I see your local dramatic club has given up London "society" plays and become aware of the existence of poetic drama and plays of Scottish peasant life. That shows what a change has been wrought by Community Drama and the tours of the Scottish National Players. Some day your dramatic society will be doing *Lear* and *Macbeth* and *Dr. Faustus*, Synge's *Deirdre* and dramatized versions of Scots ballads.

A brilliant friend of mine wrote an essay to explain why modern audiences didn't like tragedy. He didn't mention Brigham Young, who was very fond of the theatre, but wouldn't have tragedy at any price. He rose indignantly during a performance of *The Lady of Lyons*. "What a fuss about one woman!" he exclaimed, and strode out, followed by his twenty-eight wives. For a man with twenty-eight wives there was "quite enough tragedy in real life". But in monogamous circles that hackneyed reason is not convincing. The real reason is simply lack of spiritual courage and a true sense of beauty.

I remember when the dramatic tastes of your burg were satisfied by a strolling company's performance of *Second to None: A Story of the Scots Greys*. The story turned, I think, on a point of regimental honour. The colonel was very grand and stiff and Anglified; he lived in an old 'all somewhere; the hero had a waxed moustache and beautifully long legs, and the villain was a trifle bandy and had a service cap two sizes too big. And they all wore mess uniform all the way through.

More vivid in my mind is a visit of some poor barn-stormers, with a cart, a bony horse, and, of course, a nursing baby, to the village of Moorside. It was the first time since before the Reformation that Thespians had entered the valley. They were received with kindness—big are the hearts of Moorside. The performance was in the little schoolhouse: the audience were farmers and ploughmen and their womenfolk, and the young people squatted on the desks. The play was that classic melodrama, *Maria Marten: or, The Murder in the Red Barn*. The acting was so superbly bad that the show had the air of a clever travesty.

From the Private Papers of Lawrie Tod

The audience didn't see it in that light; they were astounded, horrified, beyond expression moved. But the weirdest thing of all was their reception of the tragic and "bluggy" passages. They wanted to cry, to shudder, to howl with horror. Scottish country folk don't do these things. But their feelings had to get vent somehow. So they burst into shouts of hysterical laughter. The actors, poor souls, were frightfully disconcerted at first, but they tumbled to the psychology of it, and played up to the cachinnatory tribute. They had comfortable quarters in a real barn that night, and before I left the village they were showing signs of Moorside's overflowing hospitality.

Yours,

LAWRIE TOD.

§ v

I think it was Lord Northcliffe who said that the subjects in which the public was most interested were, in their order, Health, the Weather, and Sport. I must be an abnormal creature, because in the second of those subjects I am only slightly interested, in the first and third not at all. The dicta of doctors and health culturists on individual regimen I avoid as sedulously as a secret sinner avoids religious books.

The comparison suggests one possible reason. I know that I disobey every known rule of health, and I don't want to be reminded of the fact. Nor do I wish to be made aware of the number of diseases, incipient or mature, that I possess.

That lively periodical, the *British Medical Journal*,

used to pass through my hands every month. As a rule, I disposed of it at once, and with averted eyes. But once or twice it fell open, right in the middle of a realistic account, gruesomely illustrated, of some horrible disease. Fascinated into rigidity, like a bird gazing at the flickering tongue of a snake, I licked up the words at lightning speed, and with uncanny understanding. I "palped" my shuddering frame, a cold sweat broke out over me, and I gazed in wild despair at the ceiling. I reached for the telephone directory; I must see the doctor at once. . . . And then some merciful interruption broke the spell, and I flung the *B.M.J.* to the other end of the room.

The part that physical *malaise* played in Carlyle's life is well known. From his early twenties till his death at eighty-five, he was the victim of chronic dyspepsia, intensified occasionally into biliousness and what looks like hepatitis. Burns contracted in his youth the endocarditis, or whatever it was, of which he died. Boswell was a neurotic, and his inherited weaknesses were aggravated by drinking. Scott, with all his bodily vigour and manly sagacity, was a victim of some obscure nervous malady which, intensified by overwork, made his later life an agony. Physically, the case of Byron is in many ways similar to that of Scott. Stevenson was a consumptive. All these men did a prodigious amount of creative work, and all except Carlyle died prematurely.

Physical or nervous weakness, or abnormality, is one cause of phenomenal mental activity, which, in its turn, intensifies the morbid nervous condition, which, in its turn again, stimulates mental activity,

From the Private Papers of Lawrie Tod

The pearl secreted by the sick oyster is the image of the book, the picture, the symphony, the statue, the system of philosophy. Goethe, Wordsworth, and Tennyson are supposed to be exceptions to this rule; but study of their lives reveals many abnormalities. and what was strictly normal in them is expressed too often by descents into sheer dullness.

One has known of a man who, beginning with a mere knack of drawing, was converted into a fine artist by the sufferings and moral crises of early manhood; of two merely clever youths who became creative writers, the one through being torpedoed twice on end, the other through being blown up in a trench.

Or take my own humble case. I inherited a slight tendency to nervous dyspepsia, and made it acute and chronic by idiotic dieting in my 'teens. I have scarcely ever spent a day in bed, yet in my twenties I often paced the floor half the night, or went out and walked the streets till dawn. *Malaise* drove me to the study of literature, economics, art, music, and so forth, and there came in due course the desire to write, to "secrete the pearl". No pearl has been secreted, but only some small "chuckie-stanes"; but their appearance is a mystery to myself. Had I been sent to a boarding-school and kept there till sixteen, with regular meals, games, and sleep, I am fairly certain I should never have wanted to write a line, and should have been today an exemplary Kiplingite and anti-Nationalist.

Now ponder well, ye parents dear. If you want your boys to be healthy citizens and good Imperialists, free from all the morbid taints of the "lesser breeds", and immune from the dreadful desire to be artists, authors, or journalists—you know what to do. In some cases, of course, Nature may defeat you: even Eton and Harrow have—literally—turned out geniuses. But America offers an encouraging example. Education, there, has reduced morbid intellectual cravings to a minimum. The people find the secret of happiness in thinking as little as possible, and all saying the same things. We are shaping that way, but there is still an uncomfortable amount of morbid individuality about.

An important part of health culture is the "simple life". It is an extra-mural form of Puritanism, deriving from Greek stoicism, Brahmanism and Buddhism, and the "return to Nature" of the mid-eighteenth century: in our own day it has got mixed up somehow with theosophy, Yogi, and a lot of other things. Its first big apostle was Rousseau, the queerest mixture of hedonism and asceticism that the modern world has seen. Rousseau was a morbid egotist, a literary genius of the first rank, and a maker of the French Revolution. Also, his works are among the two main sources of the Romantic movement in literature. Another main source was the ballad and song literature of Scotland, revived and popularized by Allan Ramsay. And it was Allan Ramsay's son and namesake who painted that haunting portrait of Rousseau, with the sad, delicate mouth, the sorrowful, dark eyes, and the fur cap, which is one of Scotland's treasures.

In Rousseau's lifetime, certain professors of science in Scotland were discovered "rioting over a boiled turnip". "Syllabubs" were the extent of Shelley's gastronomic indulgence; and Scott, when visiting

From the Private Papers of Lawrie Tod

Wordsworth, used to walk surreptitiously to a hostelry in order to supplement the Spartan fare of Rydal Mount. "Water, bright water for me", was not the Wizard's favourite song.

Thoreau, the great American apostle of the simple life, is at times a snob of doing-without. There was a double reason for this: disdain on the one hand for the frills of European feudalism, and on the other for the American obsession by dollars, trade, gadgets, and rich food. I love that passage in which he talks of the American people marching westward to the music of the money jingling in their pockets. Thoreau's abstemiousness is a pleasant relief to the baking and boiling that goes on in the pages of Mrs. Beecher Stowe and Mrs. Wetherell. "Pies and piety" is a severe criticism of *The Wide, Wide World*, but orthodox American religion did not ban the pleasures of the table. When an ancestress of mine visited America, about sixty years ago, she was confronted at breakfast with hominy and cream, hot corn and molasses, hot biscuits and butter, beefsteaks, apple pie, and strong coffee. Hence Munyon's Remedies, Perry Davis's Pain-killer, and twelve thousand murders per annum.

The simple-lifers I have met are practical social idealists, and apart from matters of food and drink they are not bigoted; indeed, their intellectual and aesthetic sympathies are strong and wide. Two at least of the most gifted of modern writers, Bernard Shaw and R. H. Tawney, are vegetarians. But the average simple-lifer runs too much to religious eclecticism and he is inclined to eschew solid literary food and fill up on pamphlets and tracts. And he can be annoying at times.

A prominent food-reformer was invited to tea at a house in the country. The place reeked with nuttose: the hospitable board groaned with the vegetable and cereal products of three continents. Surveying the exhibition with a sad-sweet smile, the food-reformer said, "No, thank you; all I want is a little bread and milk." It was as if, to honour the visit of the King of the Cannibal Islands, one had killed and cooked his political opponent, and then been informed by His Majesty that he could take nothing but a little chicken soup.

§ vi

Ye wha are fain to hae your name
Wrote in the bonny book of fame,
Let merit nae pretension claim
        To laurel'd wreath,
But hap ye weel, baith back and wame,
        In guid Braid Claith.

Braid Claith lends fouk an unco heese,
Makes mony kail-worms butterflies,
Gies mony a doctor his degrees
        For little skaith:
In short, you may be what you please
        Wi' guid Braid Claith.

But tho' ye had as wise a snout on
As Shakespeare or Sir Isaac Newton,
Your judgment fouk wou'd hae a doot on,
        I'll tak' my aith,
Till they cou'd see ye wi' a suit on
        O' guid Braid Claith.

From the Private Papers of Lawrie Tod

When the closing hours for public-houses were changed from eleven to ten, and then from ten to nine, there was a dulling down in the appearance of city streets in the late evening. But the quenching of the light diffused by "inspiring bold John Barleycorn" has been made up for by the blazing out of other lights. Picture houses have multiplied. Sweetie-shops have achieved a marmoreal lustre. There are also the fried-fish shops. "Give me an ounce of civet, good apothecary." One can have that, too. Down the corridors of the past the echoes of the night-bell have died away; no more, beside his mortar and pestle, like knight beside his arms, the junior pharmacist sleeps; but the long-felt want is filled by the "all-night chemist".

Then there are the nocturnal illuminations of shop windows. Not book or music or print shops. "Feed them or cleed them" was the sage's advice on the choice of a business. In soft effulgence the latest fashions in coats and gowns are shown. The effigies of beautiful ladies on which they are draped are not of the old wax-work variety; their short gilt hair and impassive white features have a touch of archaic Greece. Time was when such displays concerned only what our ingenuous sires called the gentle sex. But now that electoral rights have been conferred on women, man is coming into his sartorial rights.

Oft in the stilly night, ere slumber's chain hath bound me, I gaze in wonder at those soft white shirts, those ineffable hats, those ties and handkerchiefs of tender hue, those silken dressing-gowns of Persian splendour. All this might be Grecian spoil from the wardrobe of Darius. Surely it was never intended for ordinary vulgar men like myself.

O woman, lovely woman, Nature made you
To temper man; we had been brutes without you!

For consenting to share our exile in these smoke-blighted Cimmerian regions, woman is entitled to all that the modiste can do for her. But what has man done to deserve this magnificence? Does he actually go in and buy those precious things for himself? Are they presented to him by his lady admirers? Does his wife buy them for him out of her dress allowance?

The clothes that women wear seem finer than anything one sees in the shop windows. But among my fellow-males I never see anyone whose appearance does justice to the beauty of the haberdasher's shop. The glory is concealed by rain and soot-resisting garments fashioned in the deadly style that came in with steamers and railways. Sartorially, modern man is like Stevenson's "lantern-bearers". Like the sun on a rainy day, he attains magnificence only at setting. What a scene of iridescent splendour our suburbs would present if a sudden alarm at midnight brought into the streets all the wearers of those gorgeous dressing-gowns! It would be like the chorus of the priests of Isis in *The Magic Flute*.

Women, they say, dress for the confusion of other women rather than for the admiration of men. I have seen a woman on a tram assessing the garb of a woman opposite, beginning at the foot, as with a sum in addition, and travelling up to the hat; one seemed to see the line drawn and the total announced: £15,

19s. 7½d. When they have passed the courting stage,
men dress to please themselves, or with an eye to business. Looks, grooming, and dress count for more than
slovenly intellectuals imagine: many an otherwise in-
explicable appointment was due to good tailoring
and barbering, a white "slip", and spats—in season.
My adventures in this way must have been ill-timed,
for they brought me nothing but a brief beatitude.
The main features on the first occasion were tail coat,
brilliant tie, leather waistcoat, light trousers well
pressed, spats, curled hair, and bowler. I even tried
a monocle. I must have looked like a blend of wedding
guest, bookmaker, itinerant musician, and a draper
in difficulties. At a later period I burst upon a Clyde
resort in velvet jacket and knee-breeches, purple
cummerbund, green garters, and velour hat. The
public verdict was audible and hesitant, but on the
whole favourable. Had I promptly formed a "school"
I might have initiated that movement "back to the
eighteenth century", of which I had dreamt since, as
a child, I read *King George's Middy*, with Gilbert's own
illustrations. I still nurse the unconquerable hope,
though it is less likely than ever to be realized, now
that artists have forsaken the "Dick Tinto" tradition
and learned to paint, and musicians have taken to
the Eton crop and tiny bow-ties, and youth makes
itself hideous with plus-fours.

The psychology of male costume is obscure. Not
even a Havelock Ellis could explain why at a certain
period in the nineteenth century the Aryan male
renounced form and colour in dress and fell in love
with drab clumsiness. But the phenomenon shows

the interaction of mind and garb. Costume is not a passive factor; its tonic reaction is shown in "dressing for dinner". Some day a band of young adventurers will defy the *Tailor and Cutter*, banish the trouser, and claim the freedom of the spectrum. Life will be once more a pageant and moving picture, the mental temperature of the race will rise, and dressing in the morning will cease to be a bore and become a prelude to joyous adventure.

§ viii

Modern ballroom dances of the "round" variety are not looked upon with favour by the clergy. Merely to describe such dances with crude accuracy is to condemn them. But the matter is hardly so simple as that. Nearly all the people I have known who were fond of dancing were highly respectable citizens, with a healthily normal outlook on life. That rather takes the feet away from condemnation of fox-trots and similar gyrations on moral grounds. It suggests that modern dancing is a test and earnest of normality. At all events, it lacks the insidious element of sensuous beauty, and it is not the kind of dancing favoured by corrupt races. Salome would have been more likely to dance her own head off than John the Baptist's had she performed a Charleston with a male courtier in presence of the unprincipled but aesthetic Herod.

But what of the Argentine tango and the orgiastic dances of African tribes? The Argentinos are semi-primitive and aesthetic, and their tango is danced to beautiful music and by handsome and expert performers. The African savages are unashamed worshippers of the elemental, and their dances are not "round" dances in the European sense. We are not primitive or aesthetic or savage. We are respectable barbarians.

I have put this matter to young men who were addicted to dancing, and they have laughed at the idea that insidious sex attraction had anything to do with it. What on earth *is* the attraction, then? It can't be the exercise, for the up-to-date dance is a convulsive crawl; or the music, which is a syncopated version of the tune the old cow died of; or the conversation, which, I imagine, is even worse than golf talk.

I am glad I am not called upon to pronounce judgment on this question, for I do not know anyone less capable of doing so. My career as a dancer was brief and inglorious. When I was about eleven years of age my parents observed that my gait and deportment were not all that could be desired. The parents of two of my companions came to the same conclusion about their offspring. So on Saturday forenoons we were bundled off to Mr. Burton's Select Academy at the top of Buchanan Street. For the three of us the dancing hour was one of boredom and misery, relieved only by the spectacle of Mr. Burton, a stout, elderly gentleman, giving solo demonstrations of the Highland Schottische while playing the violin. None of us was promoted to the Highland Fling or the Sailor's Hornpipe. I have a misty remembrance of falling in love with a dark-haired damsel of about thirteen, with a rather decided squint. This sentimental attraction, however, did not make me a regular attender, and latterly my two companions and I "plunked" the class and spent the hour at the docks.

My parents had given up the attempt to make me a social ornament. But in my late 'teens I became aware of the poor figure I cut in the eyes of my feminine contemporaries. So, with a heroism for which I never got any credit, I went, all alone, and enrolled at Wallace's Dancing Academy in Sauchiehall Street. My fellow-students were decent and desperately serious folk. In a long and solemn line, to the strains of an overworked fiddle, we went through the steps of La Varsovienne, the Mazurka, and so forth. Quadrille and Lancers followed in due course. Then came the Waltz. This voluptuous dance, as the learned are aware, was of German origin, and "Werther's" frank strictures on it were elaborated by Byron in a once-famous poem. My experiences of it were not of a Byronic nature: they suggested rather the chorus of a popular song, "Teaching M'Fadyen to Waltz":—

> One, two, three, balance like me;
> You are a fairy, but you have your faults;
> For your right foot is crazy, your left foot is lazy;
> But don't be unaisy; I'll taich ye to waltz.

Mr. Wallace managed to teach all the others to waltz. I was unteachable. I imitated his movements with palpitating care; I practised at home; I sought the advice of friends; I studied a manual, with diagrams like the footprints of an intoxicated Man Friday. But all I achieved was dizziness, fankled feet, and the contemptuous frown of the lady on whose corns I stepped. The climax came one evening when I was paired with a sweet young thing who weighed about seventeen stone. My arm went only half-way round her waist; and the lack of purchase, combined with the difficulty of making a complete tour round the lady in each bar, resulted in hopeless discomfiture. After about ten turns I pleaded sudden indisposition, and fled the giddy scene. My career as a waltzer was at an end.

Thereafter I confined myself to square and country dances, in which one could be shoved through by the crowd. As I write I hear the far-off echoes of the melodeon to which a company of young fishermen and town visitors danced Petronella on the road at Whistlefield, what time the evening star came out over Argyll's Bowling Green, and the briar rose gave forth its dewy sweetness. And from a lit window in dark Blairmore come the strains, played and sung, of the "Pirates of Penzance Lancers", that, on Saturday evenings long ago, roused me from green-sick melancholy to a brave ecstasy.

§ VIII

A real holiday for a journalist is not to have to write "to space". That is sheer agony at times. Half-way through an article you are haunted by the fear that you have eaten too far into your allowance and have not left yourself space for what you have still got to say. You fumble despairingly at your notes. Your style gets cramped, you slur over things you meant to emphasize, you huddle up the thing anyhow—and then find, perhaps, that you are several hundred words short. That is even worse than exceeding, for most articles gain (for the reader, at least) by being drastically cut, whereas an article that has had to be padded out has a lopsided look and shows the stitches.

In nine cases out of ten, whether the thing written be a lecture, a leader, an essay, or a story, it is the introduction that is too long. In the tenth case it is the peroration. The effective speaker is the man who plunges at once into the middle of his subject, and stops just about three minutes after he has reached his climax. If you look at a manual of gunnery, you will see that the right parabola of a sermon, or of any piece of writing that is meant to move or persuade, is pretty much that of a shell.

The long introduction is the vice of the literary man turned journalistic handyman, or of the dilettante preacher: of those who are less interested in their subject than in its background. When John Davidson, the poet, was general leader-writer on a London paper, he used to write nearly twice what was asked for. The editor would run through the leader to the sixth or seventh folio, re-head it there, and remark, "That's your leader, Mr. Davidson." The historical and literary introduction, which one may be sure was by far the finest part, he would hand back to the writer, who would be consoled by the pleasure of having written it and of re-reading it. Probably he made poems or essays out of those rejected introductions.

One has heard addresses—one has read leaders

and essays—I have written some myself—that were all background together; all scenery and no play. I remember hearing a distinguished Glasgow minister, more historian than divine, preach what purported to be a sermon on "The Ruins of Rome". It was an excellent archæological essay, as spiritual as a cold potato, and less ethical than a problem of Euclid. How the transition to the devotional mood at the close was effected I can't remember.

The long peroration is the failing of the earnest speaker or writer who doesn't happen to be something of an artist. Nowadays the clock keeps the prosy clergyman within bounds in church, and we are spared that baleful succession of "In conclusion", "Finally", and "Lastly and very briefly" that in a former age drove many a youthful hearer into the scorner's chair. But at public meetings one has heard addresses that began like a burst of great music, descended to sing-song commonplace, and tailed off in a series of barrel-organ repetitions.

The art of public speaking is mainly the art of sitting down. I think the most painful scene I ever witnessed was at a political meeting which was to be addressed by a leading Cabinet Minister. The chairman was a famous captain of industry, in his own line one of the ablest men in Britain, but not a trained speaker, nor even a reliable grammarian. When he had spoken for ten minutes there was a shuffling of feet. He mistook it for applause and carried on. The ruffing grew louder. His voice, a very strong one, grew louder too. There was a sound of booing, and the ruffing was like trucks of coal falling into an empty

hold. He shouted, gesticulated, and banged the desk.
It was like Ajax trying to bellow down the thunder.
Only when his voice gave out and his fist was sore
did he desist.

A famous scientific essayist who eschewed the type-
writer kept to space by using paper ruled like telegraph forms. As the German vendor of a poison to
be put down the throats of beetles admitted to the
Yankee farmer who said he just put his foot on them,
"Dot vos a goot vay too." But I know a better way.
Do you want to write the ineffably perfect article, the
one that will be cut out and sent abroad, and re-
printed throughout the English-speaking world? Take
copious notes, arrange them carefully, and read them
slowly, twice or thrice. Have a meal and a walk and
a talk. Then write your article, embodying as many
of your notes as you can. Then destroy your article,
and all your notes except dates, names, and apt
quotations. Next morning, with the required space
in your mind and the whole day before you, sit down
and write the real article. It will run as sweetly as
the Night Scot. I never tried this method, but I mean
to do so—some day.

As has been not infrequently remarked, this is an
age of snippets. Those who should know best declare
that an article of more than eight hundred words is of
no use for a daily or weekly paper. I must be a survival
from Gargantuan days. Smörgåsbord feeding does not
appeal to me. I want to draw in my chair and have
a hearty meal.

Brevity is the soul of poetry. In prose I require
amplitude. The two-page essay, unless it is brilliantly

funny, I can't read. An essayist is like an opera singer; he requires time to get his voice warmed. The Emerson and Carlyle scale is the right one; the best literary essay I know, that of Myers on Virgil, is a very long one. Even the short story tantalizes me; I like novels on the Balzac and Dreiser scale, that swallow me up. In a library I make instinctively for the big books, the ones I can never hope to finish. For what I am wanting all the time is atmosphere, and in prose it can't be generated save by a cumulative process. Until we have re-acquired a taste for essays of the old Edinburgh and Quarterly kind, in which there was scope for anecdote, erudition, historic setting, grave irony, reasoned argument, and all the varieties of humour, we shall have to count ourselves degenerate.

CHAPTER XII

MUSIC AND SONG

§ i

ONE of my real misfortunes happened in my boy-hood, when a coast holiday that was to have been for one month extended to two. I had received home tuition in piano-playing, and was working my way through Hemy's Instructor.

My masterpiece was "*Partant pour la Syrie*", and I was in great hopes of giving a finished rendering of "Home To Our Mountains".

But when we got home from our mountains I found I had slipped down several rungs of Hemy's ladder. The will to re-climb it was lacking; and, by the time I realized the value of piano-playing as an accomplishment, the chance to acquire it had gone for ever.

For anyone who is fond of music, the lack of ex-ecutant facility is annoying. You are dependent on the accomplishments of other people, whose tastes and moods may not accord with yours. It is almost as bad as not being able to read.

Radio and the gramophone may for a time have weakened the impulse towards personal expression. But that impulse is reasserting itself, more rationally than before. The piano is no longer an instrument of domestic torture. The convention that every girl must be taught to play it, whether she was musical or not, has gone the way of the notion that piano-playing is more suitable for women than for men. Pianos are being bought for people who really desire to play.

Music suffered through the Victorian dominance of the piano. It was Victorian snobbery that made me snigger at the American organ in a film picture of pious domesticity in California. And why should it be remembered that Mr. Smith, of the "Brides in the Bath" case, used to play the harmonium while the lady was drowning upstairs?

Association with inferior music has discredited certain instruments, but the association may be removed by their artistic use. The effect of a duet of voices and guitars can be exquisite beyond belief. By skilful arrangement and rendering, a fine orchestral effect could be given by a combination of half a dozen "plebeian" instruments, with piano and harmonium as basis.

Significant is the increasing vogue of the clarsach, or great Highland harp, declared by musical experts to be the finest of all accompaniments to the human voice.

§ ii

In the small hours of a winter night in a year long gone, I was sitting reading in a downstairs room of a house in a remote suburb of Glasgow. The night was so quiet that I could hear the ticking of my watch.

Suddenly there broke upon the stillness a thin little rivulet of music, wildly minor, and exquisitely sweet.

It was like the sound of fairy harps, serenading Titania. At first I thought it was purely subjective—one of those "unheard melodies" of which the poet writes. But the sound, as I discovered by closing my ears and opening them again, was external. My blood ran cold.

I rose, and tried to locate the fairy harping. It was in the room somewhere. At last I traced it to the lower part of the piano. A mouse was running to and fro among the wires.

Had I been a musician, I would have straightway written the score of a Mouse Symphony for muted strings, *pizzicato*. That would have been easier than to render, on our musical scales and instruments, the dulcimer notes of Hebridean tides.

Somewhere between, I suppose, would be "a certain music" which, according to the author of *The Seasons*, is

> Full easily obtained. Behoves no more,
> But sidelong, to the gently waving wind,
> To lay the well-tuned instrument inclined;
> From which, with airy flying fingers light,
> Beyond each mortal touch the most refined,
> The god of winds drew sounds of deep delight:
> Whence, with just cause, the harp of Æolus it hight.

"Awake, Æolian harp, awake," sings Gray, "and give to rapture all thy trembling strings." But this oft-cited instrument has never awaked so far as I am concerned, though I expect every Boy Scout knows how to make one. I have often thought of making one and placing it "sidelong" in an opened window of my rustic cot. The music discoursed by an

Æolian harp on these wind-vexed uplands would be very different from the voluptuous strains described by Thomson. On a stormy night it would be like a cats' conventicle and Armageddon, with the accompaniment of a hundred drunken pipers and a flock of aggrieved guillemots. In a full gale it would be like a Witches' Sabbath on the Brocken.

The Æolian harp was an appropriate musical instrument for *The Castle of Indolence*, and for the indolent author, who probably couldn't be bothered learning the flute or going to orchestral concerts. But I doubt if James Thomson had ever heard an Æolian harp in his native Border dale. Nowadays he wouldn't even have needed to place a harp in the window. He would simply have turned on the wireless. But I don't think he would have written any poetry about it.

§ iii

It sounded like high treason against the great lyrists when a distinguished critic declared that poetry became interesting only when it was divorced from music. But the critic did not say that poetry became poetry only when it was divorced from music. He merely said that it became more interesting as poetry.

The form of poetry in which most of us chiefly delight is the song. But the effect of song words depends largely upon our knowledge of the melody to which they are sung, or upon their suggestion of a familiar type of melody.

The true song is a co-operative product. Burns's artistry is most strikingly shown in his stopping down

of the "intellectual" element in his songs to give
room for the emotional co-operation of the music.

> Aft ha'e I rov'd by bonnie Doon
>   To see the rose and woodbine twine;
> And ilka bird sang o' its luve,
>   And fondly sae did I o' mine.

That seems to us one of the most beautiful verses
ever written, but it becomes almost prosaic if we shut
out the idea of the tune.

Heine's songs have a more independent poetic
interest than Burns's, but that is because they were
not, as a rule, written for existing melodies. They
presented difficulties which only great composers
could overcome, and which would have baffled even
a Rubinstein if Heine had not had musical possibilities
in mind.

The truest poets of the greatest age of English
poetry, from Blake to Wordsworth, produced scarcely
any songs that have been effectively set to music.
They did not write songs to old melodies, and there
were no contemporary English composers worthy of
English poetry; and so the poets divorced their poetry
from heard music, and made it "interesting" by
setting it to the unheard melodies of the soul.

The "songs" of those poets contained all their
music within themselves, and left no scope for the
musical composer. In later English poets, the divorce
from music was even more complete: in Browning,
because of the rough consonants and the close-packed
thought; in Swinburne, because of the rich melody
and overpoweringly euphonious diction of the verse.

The best hymns were written in periods not specially poetic, and by poets not of the first rank. A Watts
succeeded where a Milton had failed. The religious
emotion seems to transcend poetry, and to find its
true expression in music.

Inartistic must always be the effect of attempts to
give a "descriptive" musical interpretation of poetry
of any kind, however simple. Apart from the methods
of the old minstrels—a simple recitative with harp
accompaniment—there is no safety except in recognition of the principle that a vocal number is the
union of two "patterns" which, though complementary, must each possess independent beauty and
interest.

§ iv

It looks as if mankind, though they crowd into cities,
do not love them. For there are singularly few good
songs about cities.

There are many poems dealing with cities. Spenser's
stanza on "Merrie London, my most kindly nurse",
is familiar. The earliest complete poem on London
is—naturally—by a Scot, William Dunbar, in eulo-
gistic terms contrasting notably with his satire on
Edinburgh. Edinburgh has had celebrators more
sympathetic than Dunbar—Ramsay, Fergusson, Burns,
and Scott, and their successors down to Lewis Spence;
but it was Glasgow that inspired the finest poem on a
city that has been written in English.

Alexander Smith's *Glasgow* has lyrical quality,
though it is not a song; and there are stanzas in it
that a Scots Elgar might set to music. But it has a

note of reflective pessimism. Smith was the city's son, but also her captive. He was a linnet in a cage.

A like note is found even in the most popular of real songs about cities. "O Strasburg!" is the plaint of a maiden who has pled in vain with the military governor for the life of her soldier-sweetheart. The city, as in other German songs of the same class, figures as the scene of a poignant human drama. That is the case, also, with the beautiful English songs mentioning Islington, Newcastle, and other towns. In Scotland we have the same kind of reference to Glasgow in "O waly, waly"; and there is the song about the forsaken lass who was met "between Saint Johnston and bonnie Dundee".

Galashiels has fallen heir to "Braw Lads", dating from pastoral days; and the best-known song about Edinburgh—a very poor one—was written by a Huguenot Englishman and is located in a country meadow.

If "Dublin's fair city" has not yet got a city song to its mind, the chances of Scots cities do not seem bright.

§ v

When the singer, to a simple accompaniment on her harp, sang of "the auld hoose", its kind auld laird welcoming his guests, and its gracious lady who had cut a lock from the yellow hair of Prince Charlie, we were thrilled to vision.

We saw the little, grey, crow-stepped mansion on the green bank of the rippling Earn, and the smoke from its hospitable chimneys, blue against the fir grove, yellowish-grey against the pale blue sky.

Realizing what gems of heroism, faith, kindness, and patrician grace had been enshrined in such modest caskets, we felt our eyes wet with pride for that gallant old Scotland.

The Piper of Dundee swept us back to a scene of wild resolve and crazily romantic hopes, beneath the stars of a quiet Perthshire glen:—

> There's some gat swords and some gat nane,
> And some were dancin' mad their lane,
> And mony a vow o' weir was ta'en,
>   That nicht at Amulree.

And then the hall rocked and rang to the *Hundred Pipers*, and we saw the clansmen crossing the swollen Esk shouther to shouther, and dancing themselves dry to the pibroch's sound. And so on through the wild adventure to Culloden and the lonely cairns.

Songs of love or sorrow or rustic gaiety, by Lowland singers, from the mysterious Minstrel Burne of the Borders down to Burns himself and later minstrels, harped our inmost soul in three. Caustic or grim humour, and cleverly whimsical fun, received a more detailed articulation in recitations of poems like Burns's *Dr. Hornbook*, Colvin's *Melchizedek*, and Cocker's *The Deluge*.

Gaelic songs of all periods, wildly solemn, sweetly plaintive, passionately rhapsodical, or madly rollicking, delighted us by their wealth of mode, sinuous melody, and rhythm within rhythm.

Various as the streams and seas of the West is

Gaelic music. Grandest in its pibroch measures, as of slow-moving tides by moonlight amid the isles—most haunting in its brief descants of fairy music, like the evening notes of the lonely mavis of Pabal—it is most astonishing, most ravishing, when it sweeps us up in a broad ecstasy of enthusiasm for Gaeldom itself.

Billow on billow of broad, sweet, yet subtly varied melody; on the back of each billow a series of lesser waves, with a natural perfection of interval and rhythm; with alternation of sunshine, and glittering spray, and wine-dark shadow: such is the effect of a great Gaelic rhapsody sung by a Gaelic audience.

The Gaelic and the Doric Muses, sisters long estranged, met and embraced on that memorable evening. Their reunion was symbolic. Reft and divided, the Scottish soul had become provincial, timid, droopingly retrospective; seeking desperate escape in false sentiment or vulgar mockery. Reintegrated, it can become national, brave, positive, and hopeful.

"Harp of the North, that mouldering long hast hung . . ." The harp has now all its strings, and our minstrels can evoke *toute la lyre*, and go forward, as Scots, into the realm of "art" music and the European hall of song.

§ vi

There was a time when opera was the greatest of social occasions. At the opera, wealth and beauty and fashion made their most brilliant display, and notabilities forgathered.

Every city and large town in Italy, Germania, and

Music and Song

Latin America had its opera-house. In the capitals, historic appearances were made in the Royal box, and the house rang with ovations and national anthems.

In times of political excitement the opera-house was the nerve-centre. Once, in an Italian city, when a performance of *Masaniello* was expected to be the occasion of an outburst against Austrian domination, the rising curtain revealed, not a chorus of Neapolitan fisher-folk, but a company of soldiers with levelled rifles, which the officer announced would be fired if the house was not cleared in ten minutes.

Music was born in Italy, and in Italy it became decadent ere it reached maturity. General artistic decadence had been shown by the invention of the hybrid, opera; musical decadence was shown by Italian opera's breakaway, with Rossini, from "classical" forms into the musical idiom of an amiable but inartistic populace, indulging joyously in every known kind of musical "vice".

Opera, had it been left to its inventors, would have died away in the gaspings and caterwaulings of Bellini and Donizetti. But the Germans had taken it over, and given it depth and coherence.

Handel and Gluck paved the way for Mozart, whose *Marriage of Figaro* is to Rossini's *Barber of Seville* what a Greek statue is to an Italian "image".

Mozart is one of the two composers who "saved" opera. The other is Wagner, who devoted his architectonic genius to an attempt to raise opera to the plane of Greek drama.

He succeeded in all the operas in which his personages—gigantesque, weird, mystical, or primitively symbolic—are apart from the mundane life of men and women. His greatest opera musically, *The Master-singers*, is too big for its story and characters: its interest lies in its superb contrapuntal weavings of bright new patterns on a stiff old Germanic groundwork, with a total result of triumphant polyphonic geniality.

Moussorgsky's *Boris Godunov* and Strauss's *Der Rosen-kavalier* are among the few operas since Wagner that are of definitely "major" account; and it is doubtful if we should ever have heard them had not Wagner held the operatic stage open for his successors.

The theory that Wagner killed opera by his sheer greatness, as Shakespeare killed English drama, is not borne out by the history of opera down to his day. He performed the miracle of making the absurd thing called "grand opera" into a really great thing. But his "magic could not copied be".

In the strictly artistic sense, grand opera is virtually Mozart and Wagner; and another miracle of genius in the operatic region seems unlikely. Will they form sufficient basis for another fifty years of opera?

§ vii

It was on the old road between Dieppe and Rouen, on a beautiful August evening many years ago, that I had an experience which realized poetic tradition.

That part of Normandy, with its cultivated valleys, pine-clad ridges, and ancient château-farms closing vistas of lake and woodland, is one of the loveliest regions in Europe. I was cycling, alone. When the shadows lengthened, and the valley took on a golden tinge in the level sunlight that flamed in the tree-tops, I dismounted to enjoy the view.

The only other person visible was a shepherd, with a long cloak and a wide-brimmed hat, leaning on his crook, while his sheep cropped the wayside grass. From far over the valley came the sound of a bell, mellowed by distance. There was no other sound.

The shepherd uncovered and bowed his head. I did likewise. It was the Angelus.

As I went on my way I recalled the lines of Dante about the evening hour "that wakens fond desire in men at sea", and thrills the pilgrim who hears "the vesper bell from far, that seems to mourn for the expiring day".

I recalled, too, that "Ave Maria" passage in *Don Juan* in which Byron, rising above acrid cynicism, gathers his singing-robes about him, and blends some of the finest inspirations of Boccaccio, Sappho, Dante, and Gray—closing with a *cri de cœur* in the stanza on Nero.

A week or so later, as I sailed out of Dunkirk in the bright moonlight, the spire of the old church gave forth a beautiful carillon. Such a valediction must have lingered sadly in poor Mary Stuart's memory when she heard the raucous psalm-singing of her Scottish subjects, and the minatory preachments of Master John Knox.

Many of the fabrics from which Scottish chimes and peals and carillons might have sounded were laid in the dust. But in those that are restored, and in new churches and town halls, a place should be given to this beautiful art.

My Scotland

Bells may have been meant originally to scare away devils or avert thunder. But the bell-ringers gave them a higher purpose—to attract angels, and link town with village, and village with village, in a golden chain of fraternal sound.

One of the greatest views in the world is that of Edinburgh from Calton Hill in a wild sunset in late autumn, just at the moment when the street lights are lit. The one thing lacking is the effect of life and warmth that can be supplied only by an harmonious mingling of sight and sound. The suggestion is in Browning's line—"The air broke into a mist with bells".

There are the bells of St. Mary's Cathedral and of St. Cuthbert's; but these are in the West End. The chain of golden sound should extend east, and up over the Old Town.

The ordinary church bell, of the clinkum-clank variety, is tolerable in a village or a small town: heard at a distance, across fields and woods, on a bright, calm day, it is almost beautiful. In a city it is horrible. And the city ought to exercise some control over sounds that invade the ear of every inhabitant.

Public clocks striking the hours and quarters would be permitted, but all other bells would have to conform to a general scheme of harmony; and, within a certain area, there would be no church bells except chimes and peals.

Glasgow used to be famous for bells. Nowadays, in the inner city, there are only the chimes of the Tolbooth tower and the tolling bell of St. George's Church. Why should not the towers of the City Chambers and

266

St. Vincent Street Church be used as campaniles, with big strong sets of chimes and pealing bells, whose sounds, commingling about Union Street, would float over the city like a swarm of golden bees?

No Wedding Bells for Her is the title of a once-popular melodrama. The survival of an old village tradition in industrial cities may provoke a sour smile. But why should not every happy pair have a peal rung for them on the greatest day of their lives? As they drove off after the marriage, they could pass the tower where the peal was sounding, and say, "These are our wedding bells."

Chimes, carillons, and peals of bells are the unforgettable features of old minster towns in England, France, and Germany. The poems written about bells in the languages of these three countries would form a splendid anthology. I shall never forget Yvette Guilbert's rendering of *Les Cloches de Nantes*. Its effect is balanced by the Orpheus Choir's rendering of A. E. Housman's wildly wistful poem, *In Summertime on Bredon*.

Our benighted ancestors had their own broadcasting, and their own conquest of the air. They tuned in with the music of the spheres, and rang into the atmosphere the notes of their moods of worship, joy, and sorrow, weaving over land and sea a haze of golden sound.

Some day we may exchange news with Mars, and explore the craters of the moon. But the minster bells carried farther. Their echoes floated out beyond the remotest star, beyond time and space, to the heavenly thrones.

My Scotland

§ viii

Angus MacDonald" is still "coming home from the war". I can't associate him with Tunnel Trench, Devil's Wood, or any of those squalid places. He must have been in some choice section where there were no shells, bombs, gas, mud baths, vermin or corpses—nothing but brave deeds performed in the tidy manner of the operatic stage. For this is Angus the ever-young, the Highland Apollo, come from Tir nan Og via a London outfitter's shop and the studio of a music publisher.

I made his acquaintance many years ago, and I can't say I took to him. The song, I admit, was rather jolly. It suggested a "Scotch drama" with bagpipes "off", processions of white-kneed clansmen, and "The Trossachs by Moonlight", by the eminent scene-painter, Mr. William Glover.

Angus, with black whiskers, became Roderick Dhu. With red whiskers, he was Rob Roy. Clean-shaven, he was Francis Osbaldistone, singing "Though I leave thee now in sorrow". But the Protean Angus never turns into a crofter or one of Neil Gunn's intellectual and resentful gamekeepers. I picture him as the ideal Highlander of the lady novelist—brave, handsome, and slow-witted—allowing the "young lady" to think for him, and voting with the laird.

It is the young lady who is waiting for the handsome young gamekeeper. She has an English accent, and she has read poetry. She will lead Angus to the altar, and endow him with her worldly goods. Angus will rent a shooting, and shine forth at balls as a "best-

268

dressed Highlander—at his own expense". In his later years he will become fat and whiskyfied, and talk much about the Empire.

Is "Angus MacDonald" a popular item at concerts in the Highlands? If I learned that it was, I shouldn't faint with astonishment. The soldiers of the old Army were moved by songs of the "Break-the-news-to-mother" type. I have seen old shellbacks affected by "sea songs" whose sentimental unreality was evident to anyone who had done the daylight trip to Belfast and back.

People who are hard up against the "damned realities" don't want them shoved down their throats. They want to escape from them—or to have them transformed for a moment, by a little cheap magic, into attractive idealities. Only those on whom they press lightly care to see them as they are. The seven years' cycle in human personality explained the outcrop of realistic war-novels, and their popularity. Memory was released. The survivors were able, at last, to become critical spectators of their own doings and sufferings.

The tendency to evade reality, to blanket it with woolly periphrasis, or gloss it over with sentimental heroics, is present even in the old street or bothy ballads which connoisseurs value so highly. But those simple compositions are sincere to the point of *naïveté*. It is the pretentiousness of the "Song Folio" type of song that is offensive. It parts company with crude Nature, and does not attain to art, which is the way back to Nature. It is an ambiguous and equivocal product.

My Scotland

A study of old popular poetry and songs forces one to the conclusion that in old days popular taste lay closer to Nature and reality, and therefore to art, than it does nowadays. The real old Scots ballads are very beautiful, but also very simple and very grim. The farmers and hinds of old Scotland gave them the same breathless attention that some modern Scots audiences give to "Angus MacDonald".

In Allan Ramsay's day the Anglified literati of Scotland were turning out "songs" which were even worse than "Angus MacDonald":—

> When summer comes, the swains on Tweed
> Sing their successful loves.

But the ploughmen and milkmaids were singing and reciting the right stuff. Ramsay made it his business to bring back Nature and reality into poetry —and the results were the Romantic Movement and Robert Burns. By the beginning of this century the situation was reversed. The "people" were clinging to the conventional and artificial, and the "highbrows" were putting up a fight for Nature, reality, and simplicity.

To ridicule a taste which cannot rise above "Angus MacDonald"—even if the attack has been provoked by girdings at "highbrow stuff" (*e.g.* "The Dowie Dens of Yarrow"!)—smacks somewhat of the slaughter of the one ewe-lamb. It is sufficient to state one's belief that "Angus" is plated metal of a bad "period"—and to put forward the real article. The "people" will be led, but not driven.

Why people are so careful about the quality of what

270

they put into their stomachs, and so careless about the quality of what they take into their minds; why the taking of margarine instead of butter is never vaunted (though it may be a noble thing), while the gratuitous preference of bad to good music is proudly advertised; and why the man who seeks expert advice about bacon or cheese should throw bricks at the experts in music and literature—these things have always puzzled me.

In the long run, the judgment of the highbrows is far less reliable than that of the people—once it is awakened. But all that the highbrows have really been trying to do these thirty years is to get the people to take back what belongs to them.

CHAPTER XIII

POETRY, THE TRUE AND THE FALSE

§ i

NEARLY every French prose writer during the last three centuries has produced at some time or another, generally in his twenties, a volume of verse. It is no reflection upon French literature to say that this custom argues deficiency in the poetic sense. It did not prevail in the days of Ronsard or Villon. Poetry was poetry then, and prose was prose. But Malherbe and Boileau rationalized verse, and laid down rules by strict attention to which any highly intelligent person could write what passed for poetry.

That indicated a real decline in poetic impulse. The result of the Boileau convention was that such poetry as was left in France expressed itself in prose. French literature of the eighteenth century abounds in transitions from picturesque prose to verse which is frigidly prosaic.

A like phenomenon declared itself in Britain during the greater part of the eighteenth century. Most of the verse of that period was written by people who, like Johnson, Grainger, Hoole, *et hoc genus omne*, were inherently unpoetical. As the century went on, the temperature and the standard of English poetry, thanks largely to Scottish influence, rose to a level beyond the reach of cold-blooded verse-makers. Much bad English verse has been written since the days of Blake, but its badness was always in respect of technique, imagination, outlook, or sheer mentality: the very worst of it showed some trace of poetic impulse.

The temperature of French poetry rose also, but much more gradually, and never to a height that excluded the clever artificer. Even the appearance of a 100-per-cent. poet like Verlaine did not discourage fore-ordained novelists, essayists, dramatists, critics, historians, or publicists from publishing their thin little volumes of *Poèmes*, exasperating in their competent nullity, their deftly restrained simulation of the real thing. Such is the curse of a too perfect literary training.

The writing of verse may be an excellent training for the man whose *métier* is prose, but in this country most educated people have too much respect for poetry to use it in that way, or at least to publish their metrical exercises. Also, the standard of sheer poetic feeling set by our great poets is so high, the tradition of "waiting for the spark from Heaven to fall" is so firmly established, that we distrust in ourselves any motive short of irresistible impulse.

I am trying to account for the fact that an inveterate scribbler like myself, with a mind that moves in emotional and picturesque rather than in logical sequences, should have written so little verse. Apart from a blank-verse poem which I published in my teens, and which is now so rare that it is sought in vain by bibliophiles, my Collected Poems would not run to a dozen wide-margined pages; and they are so bad that I would not put my name to them. And yet I have read, carefully and with zest, a prodigious amount of poetry in English, Scots, and French, and a fair amount in German and Italian.

That, apart from natural incompetence, is probably the chief reason why I failed absolutely and completely—failed even to fail—as a poet. My imagination was intimidated and overwhelmed by the imaginations of the mighty men of old with whom I conversed night and day. I felt vicariously and in quotation. I could not write three lines without plagiarising, or remembering that what I was trying to say had been immortally expressed by some lord of language, some poet dead and gone. Even in trying to write prose I was perpetually held up and side-tracked by the intrusion of tags, epithets, and phrases from the poets. My mind could not win free. There was always a cloud of somebody else's words between me and my own thoughts or "the object".

This derivative and over-literary habit has proved fatal to not a few real poets. The outstanding example is Alexander Smith. His *Life Drama*, acclaimed at first by critics like Gilfillan, was condemned by severer judges on account of its "spasmodic" emotionalism and its rather too obvious reminiscences of Keats and Shakespeare. The harm wrought was twofold. Smith's subsequent and sounder work did not receive the attention it deserved; and it was not so good as it might have been, for Smith had been definitely discouraged.

What is the moral? Here a major point of criticism arises, affecting all the arts.

Poetry, the True and the False

The true line of progress is from a considered eclecticism to original self-expression, soundly based on the sum of previous achievement. Beethoven begins as a more virile Haydn and ends as the Shakespeare and Dante of music. Wagner begins as a Meyerbeer, but more so, and ends as the composer of the *Ring* and *Parsifal*. Each of the great artists served an apprenticeship to a predecessor, and built upon a firm technical foundation: "returns" to ancient schools, or rather to an arbitrary conception of them, as with the Pre-Raphaelites, have been artificial and in the long run unfruitful. The creator of Hamlet, Lear, and Falstaff had in his youth been an emulator of Spenser, Marlowe, and the Plautian dramatists.

Smith's imitative phase was of the wrong kind. He did not sound the full diapason of his models, but only some of their top notes. Instead of climbing the tree, he tried to jump on to the highest branches. And he aggravated his blunder by publication.

There are many poets, but there is a remarkable scarcity of good poetry. The main reason is the stupid convention that a poet should die as a poet at thirty. Musicians and artists go on creating to the end. If poets die young, it is mainly because they do not take their art seriously. They either commit the same blunder as Smith; or else, as with modernist poets, they fling all forms and precedents aside, kick away the foundation of all previous achievement from under their feet, and dance upon air and sail upon the Dogstar, clutching at passing meteors. In either case they fail to take up a sufficiency of life into their art, and condemn themselves to an unorganized subjectivism

275

that narrows and yet dissipates, and soon comes to extinction.

It needs no professor of aesthetics to tell us that whereas a prose-work is a fabric, a poem is a body, showing forth the living logic of the soul, and with an organic structure that repeats itself in every vital part. A familiar example is Shelley's *Ode to the West Wind*. "Dynamic" is of the essence of poetry, but the movement is not that of a nebula or a meteor, but of a swift beautiful body, typified by Apollo or Pegasus.

Verse sprang from the dance, and its use as a mnemonic must have been an early discovery. Its association with exalted or mystical states, and the fact that it could be remembered and handed down, gave poetry and poets a unique character: that of immortality. It was the reward and consolation of the poet that his verses might be remembered for ever. Kings and warriors patronized the bard in order that they might be sung by him and share his immortality.

This idea of immortality must have entered into the composition of every really fine poem. The poet must have been subconsciously aware that if his work would have no poetic value two centuries after his death, it had no poetic value in his own day. The attribute of immortality involved organic structure, the vital element of rhythm, and the preservative quality of beauty, which, closely analysed, is sublimated dynamic, the final earnest of an economically achieved harmony. There was no room for redundancies, clichés, periphrasis, arbitrary cacophonies, mere echoes, otiose repetitions, false rhythm, forced rhymes, logic-chopping, cerebral gymnastics, ideological theories, sighting shots, hits on wrong targets, chips from the workshop, and all that kind of thing. And for stuff of this description, immortality cannot be predicted:—

Bats in the belfry tripe on the terrace they are
    hoisting the south cone.
Six from three you cannot a 2/11 alarum clock is
    going off.
My aunt Jemima is a martyr to bunions.
Bunyan's *Pilgrim's Progress* pilgrims with bunions
    hirpling to bun-worries.
A saxophone a semitone flat the eyes of Ethiopians
    are we near Ardrossan?
The steward is singing "The Lea Rig" that summer
    night in Munich first stop Paisley.
Stimmung! Les jeux sont faits! beware of the scolopendra.

A rhythm haunted me for a whole day, and it was not until evening that the words came:—

The love that I had chosen
    Was to my heart's content;
The saut sea shall be frozen
    Before that I repent;
Repent me will I never
    Until the day I dee;
Tho' the Lowlands o' Holland
    Hae twined my love and me.

The experience is familiar to all those who love poetry but do not write it. There are poems that are held in the memory by their rhythmic ghosts. A famous example is Walther von der Vogelweide's greatest love song. Another is Bürger's *Lenore*. Where did Bürger get his stanza? Wilde's debt to Hood's *Eugene Aram* for the form of *The Ballad of Reading Gaol* is obvious. Did Hood borrow it from someone else, or did he invent it, as a composite of suggestions from the old ballads and from Coleridge, one of the greatest of "form" makers?

Scots poetry, metrically varied to a remarkable extent, is a rich field for the student of the genealogy of poetic forms. Burns's favourite stanza can be traced back to the troubadours. By older scholars, who did not know Gaelic, all our metrical forms were credited to English and French models. Dr. Sigerson, however, traced some of them to Gaelic. Montgomerie's "Hey, Now the Day Dawis", for example, is modelled exactly—metre, stanza, alliterations and all—upon a medieval Irish poem. Burns wrote some of his songs to characteristic Irish airs. The features of old Irish Gaelic poetry are better reproduced in the nonsense verses of *The Groves of Blarney* than in most Irish-English poetry down to the time of Dr. Douglas Hyde, who has done wonders in this direction. An opposite number of Dr. Hyde is needed in Scotland.

The genealogy of form can be traced also in longer and more ambitious poems, of a purely "art" character. But these things are of little interest to the more "advanced" poets of our day, who are in open rebellion against technical traditions. They are absolutely in the right in so far as they put vital, dynamic form above traditional form, and seek to enlarge the field of poetry. The first essential of a poem is that it should be spiritually and emotionally organic. But it cannot be genuinely that, cannot impress itself upon the mind as living poetry, cannot become in any sense immortal, unless it has a definite form or pattern which is ultimately governed by an idea of rhythmic beauty. The poet who breaks the old patterns commits himself to the creation of new ones more congenial to his purpose, and of a higher and a rarer beauty. He cannot be content with a mere kaleidoscope.

The poet may refuse to conform to any pattern, even to one of his own. He may insist that his impulse and his mission, suited to his period, are dynamically chaotic, and must express themselves in chaotic fashion. He may spurn Beauty as a meretricious agent of obscurantism, and maintain that qualities like rhythmic euphony have no place in an age when poetry is no longer something to be recited by minstrels, but a purely intellectual creation, a sublimated jig-saw puzzle, appealing only to the ear of the higher mind. He may do all this, and he may be right in doing it; for perhaps it is necessary that the scheme of poetry should be shattered to pieces, in order that it may be moulded nearer to the heart's desire of the coming race. But it is certain that in accentuating this chaotic, disintegrative, lawlessly subjective transition phase of poetry he is, perhaps nobly, as a kind of Forerunner crying in the wilderness, depriving his work of that total organic beauty through which alone it can take on something of immortality.

§ ii

A certain freshness still attaches, at least in Gaelic circles in Scotland, to the old controversy over James Macpherson and his *Ossian*. There are still people who believe in the substantial genuineness of Macpherson's "translations".

That question would be of comparatively little interest but for the big problem of which it forms part —namely, the immediate and tremendous world-vogue of what a German critic styled "this most magnificent of mystifications".

The publication of Macpherson's Highland "epics", from 1761 to 1763, roused a controversy that spread throughout the length and breadth of Britain, estranging friends, dividing households, and leading, in some cases, almost to bloodshed. The dispute raged for years, spread to the Continent, and is not finally settled yet.

A huge crop of "Ossianically" inspired poems, prose, rhapsodies, dramas, and romances sprang up in Britain. Within a few years, numerous translations of *Ossian* appeared in every European language. The production of an Ossianic drama in German led to a fracas among students, and formed the beginning of the *Sturm und Drang* movement that set Goethe writing the drama that set going the pen of Scott.

In nearly every book of European account, from *Werther* onward, *Ossian* was cited or imitated. Lamartine wept over him in the mountains of France. *Ossian* inspired the majestic dithyramb of Chateaubriand. Napoleon carried a translation of *Ossian* with him on his campaigns. The Ossianic wave extended outward to Poland, Russia, Scandinavia, America, distinctly influencing some of the writings of Pushkin, of Lermontov (descended from Scots Learmonths), and even of Poe.

Poetry, the True and the False

The work of the young Speyside schoolmaster formed, in fact, one of the most important headwaters of the world-phenomenon described as the Renascence of Wonder. Of that fact, a Scots delegate to an international literary congress in Poland was thrillingly reminded when an announcement of his regarding the Gaelic movement in Scotland was received with a burst of applause. When he recovered from his astonishment, he had the presence of mind to refer to Macpherson's *Ossian*.

The Ossianic rage was something quite unparalleled in the history of European literature, before or since. What was the real secret of it?

A key to the mystery was suggested by a remark made to me by "A.E", to the effect that a congenial mythology is needed for poetry.

The way had been paved for *Ossian* by the Vernacular revival (Gay, Ramsay, Lady Grizel Baillie), the growing love of natural beauty (James Thomson), and the emotional ferment and idealistic revolt initiated by Rousseau. What was still lacking was the embodiment of the vague feelings thus aroused —the congenial projection, shadowy but simple, of awakened subjectivity.

The classic mythology was hackneyed and shop-soiled, and literary people had grown tired of it. The Norse mythology was familiar only to a few scholars in Scandinavia and England. Both mythologies were too local and remote, too definite in scheme and characterization, too closely associated with certain archaic ways of life and thought. They had too much solidity and "body colour".

The unexpressed demand was for cloudland figures that would take on the colours of the atmosphere, and shape themselves to the mood of the age; Harz Mountain giants, so to speak, in which any dreamily poetic young European could at any moment behold the grandiose image of himself or herself. And the age found what it wanted in the vaguely beautiful, vaguely grand, vaguely plangent figures of Macpherson's *Ossian.*

"Ossian, that poet of the genius of ruins and battles," wrote Lamartine, "reigned paramount in the imagination of France. . . . Women sung him in plaintive romances, or in triumphal strains, at the departure, above the tombs, or on the return of their lovers. . . . I plunged into the ocean of shadow, of blood, of tears, of phantoms, of foam, of snow, of mists, of hoar frosts and of images the immensity, the dimness, and the melancholy of which harmonize so well with the lofty sadness of a heart of sixteen which expands to the first rays of the infinite. . . . I had become one of the sons of the bard, one of the heroic, amorous, or plaintive shades who fought, who loved, who wept, or who swept the fingers across the harp in the gloomy dominions of Fingal."

The world went on, licked its war-wounds, increased the number of its red corpuscles, conquered Nature, grew wealthy and strong; but still fought and loved, lost or won, laughed and feasted and wept and died; and the elemental hankerings after a topical myth-ology—a generalized poetic bodying-forth of the spirit of the age—revived. This time it was supplied, in soul-conquering, polyphonic music, by a far greater

artist than Macpherson—Richard Wagner, exploiting
the old mythology of the Teutonic races.

"Except for *Die Meistersinger*," remarks W. J. Turner,
"not one of his operas contains human beings. They
are all monsters—called, euphemistically, gods—or
they are legendary figures of an equal monstrousness.
All Wagner requires of them is that they shall rave,
fight, love, and declaim—as though they were ten feet
high with the chests of bulls and the legs and arms of
Cyclops. From the beginning to the end of the *Ring*
there is nothing but sheer vitality personified into the
figures of myth: Wotan is the power of knowledge,
Loge is cunning, Fricka is woman, Freya is joy, Brunn-
hilde is maidenhood, Siegfried is boyhood, Mime is
spite, Alberich is greed, Siegmund and Sieglinda are
merely male and female love, and so on."

That is true, but unfairly put: for, within the simple
framework of each personification, there are vast and
subtle differentiations of passion raised to the height of
spiritual beauty. Through this extraordinary spell, the
hearers identify themselves, they cannot tell how, with
those magnificent "monsters", who, like the Ossianic
figures, are both less and more than human.

Profound questionings were stirred in me when I
found myself carried away by the death-music for
Siegfried. Who was Siegfried, that our hearts should
bleed for him? Was he someone we knew who had
been killed in the war? Was he our own lost youth?
Was he the "dying god" of whom anthropologists have
so many curious things to say?

Those questions are more easily put than answered.
But the examples of *Ossian* and Wagner at least

exemplify the craving of the human soul, at certain periods, for a mythology which, while in no danger of hardening into idolatry, since its figures are merely sublimated humans, gives the poetic imagination its necessary projections, eponymous or general.

Ireland's wealth in such figures is unquestionably the main reason for her remarkable achievements in poetry and drama. Is it not curious that Scotland, the home of the original Ossian, and the focus of the great Ossianic cult of the eighteenth century, should have no familiar eponymous mythology, and should have had to concentrate her mythological impulse, not without danger of idolatry, upon Burns?

That danger, and the difficulty with which Scots poetry climbs up out of post-Burns tracks on the uplands of imagination, suggest the part that Gaelic "culture" may play in our literary future: not by producing another "magnificent mystification", but by bringing into the general national heritage the whole crock of gold with a few grains from which, artfully alloyed, Macpherson changed the imaginative currency of Europe.

§ iii

"And did you once see Shelley plain?" No—but I once saw M'Gonagall plain—and coloured.

It was in the Albion Halls in Glasgow, many years ago. The audience—by whom convened I cannot tell —included very few ladies, and most of the gentlemen were smoking thick black. The Bard of Dundee held the stage alone. He was an old man, but, with his athletic though slightly stooping figure and his dark hair, he did not look more than forty-five; and he appeared to have been shaved the night before. He wore a Highland dress of Rob Roy tartan and boy's size.

After reciting some of his own poems, to an accompaniment of whistles and cat-calls, the Bard armed himself with a most dangerous-looking broadsword, and strode up and down the platform, declaiming "Clarence's Dream" and "Give me another horse!—Bind up my wounds!" His voice rose to a howl. He thrust and slashed at imaginary foes. A shower of apples and oranges fell on the platform. Almost before they touched it, they were met by the fell edge of M'Gonagall's claymore, and cut to pieces. The Bard was beaded with perspiration and orange juice.

The audience yelled with delight; M'Gonagall yelled louder still, with a fury which I fancy was not wholly feigned. It was like a squalid travesty of the wildest scenes of *Don Quixote* and *Orlando Furioso*. I left the hall early, saddened and disgusted.

M'Gonagall's Glasgow visit was a come-down from his Edinburgh triumph, a contemporary account of which is quoted by Mr. Lowden Macartney in his introduction to the *Select Poems of M'Gonagall*. It was like Voltaire's apotheosis in Paris. When he arrived in Princes Street the moon was shining and somebody remarked that here was a theme for his Muse. With a lofty gesture he replied, "I immortalized this scene years ago." At the tea-table he informed his entertainers that Shakespeare and Burns were no more than his equals. The company consisted entirely of patricians, with titles more resounding than any to be

found in Burke or even Hare. The poet recited some
of his warlike and patriotic pieces, and finished up
with that touching—though, alas! spurious—effusion,
"The Water of Leith":—

> Oh, Water of Leith!   Oh, Water of Leith,
> Where the girls go down to wash their teeth;
> And o'er the stream there is a house right knackie,
> Of that grand old man, Professor Blackie.

Thereafter, the Order of the White Elephant was conferred upon the Bard, an illuminated address in Latin
was presented to him, and a large drawing of him, as
"The Genius of Poetry", was placed on the steps of
the throne.

William M'Gonagall (it is interesting to note that
he had the same Christian name as his great English
compeer) was in his youth a handloom weaver in
Dundee. Like Tannahill, Alexander Wilson, Watty
Watson, and many another Scots minstrel, he had
wooed the Muse at the loom; and, when times became
hard, he wooed the Press, a much stiffer job. A Dundee
weekly saw the possibilities of M'Gonagallism and
published some of his verses. Having acquired a local
vogue, he exploited it by having his poems printed on
slips of paper, and vending them himself. He was no
precursor of the Scots Renaissance; and, though of
humble origin, was strongly aristocratic in sympathy.
His well of English was the evening paper, his favourite
personages were Royalties and Generals, and his
favourite themes were of an Imperialist and even
Jingoist nature.

Poetry, the True and the False

The man that gets drunk is little else than a fool,
And is in the habit, no doubt, of advocating Home
    Rule.

He was a Conservative working-man—who never
worked—with a leaning towards Prohibition, and
Votes for Women. In his verses on the latter subject he
foreshadowed subsequent developments both in politics
and in costume:—

But the time is not far distant, I most earnestly trust,
When women will have a Parliamentary vote,
And many of them, I hope, will wear a better
    petticoat.

M'Gonagall, one fears, would have had little use for
the League of Nations. He revelled in battles; celebrated Britain's triumphs over Arabs and Egyptians,
and lamented her set-back at Majuba.

Oh! it must have been a gorgeous sight
To see Sir Garnet Wolseley in the thickest of the fight,
In the midst of shot and shell and the cannons' roar;
While the dead and the dying lay weltering in their
    gore.

Lord Wolseley good-naturedly acknowledged receipt
of the poem on Tel-el-Kebir, and "the incident", says
Mr. Macartney, "was never allowed to be forgotten ".
We are not aware whether Queen Victoria had the
felicity of perusing the poem on her attempted assassination by a madman:—

God prosper long our noble Queen,
    And long may she reign,
Maclean he tried to shoot her,
    But it was all in vain.

My Scotland

For God he turned the ball aside,
   Maclean aimed at her head,
And he felt very angry
   Because he didn't shoot her dead.

Our Poet had visions of setting the Thames on fire,
but the river proved not only uninflammable but very
cold, and he returned to Dundee. He also paid a visit
to New York, for what exact reason was never known.
Regarding the English Metropolis he notes:—

St. Paul's Cathedral is the finest building that ever I
   did see;
There's no building can surpass it in the town of
   Dundee.

New York did not please him:—

On the Sabbath day you will see many a man
Going for beer with a tin can.

     .   .   .   .   .

Then at night numbers of the people dance and sing.

     .   .   .   .   .

With regard to New York and the sights I did see,
One street in Dundee is more worth to me;
And, believe me, the morning I sailed from New York
For bonnie Dundee—my heart it felt as light as a cork.

M'Gonagall was really always a home-bird, and his
most characteristic verses are on Tayside scenes and
happenings:—

It is a very magnificent spot the Den of Fowlis,
And where oft the wintry wind it howls
Among its bare and leafless withered trees,
And with fear would almost make one's heart to
   freeze.

     .   .   .   .   .

Poetry, the True and the False

> Stately Mansion of Baldovan,
> Most beautiful to see,
> Belonging to Sir John Ogilvy,
> Ex-M.P. of Dundee.
> The scenery of Baldovan
> Is most lovely to see,
> Near by Dighty Water,
> Not far from Dundee.

Like Moses and Homer, the Bard of Dundee had a love of eloquent particularity in regard to numbers. During "The Terrific Cyclone of 1893",

> The gale swept everything before it on its way,
> No less than 250 trees and 37 tombstones were blown down at Balgray.

I have a vague recollection of a large tent near the Cowcaddens of Glasgow; a flare of lamps; and a weird odour, in which very bad meat contended with kerosene and carbolic, permeating a whole district, and taking away all relish from kippers or ham and eggs. In the tent, filling its whole length, was the Tay Whale, the capture of which inspired what some critics regard as M'Gonagall's masterpiece. When the boats went out to harpoon the monster in the Tay, it lashed its tail and splashed the water high in the air:—

> Then the water did descend on the men in the boats,
> Which wet their trousers and also their coats.

The harpooned whale dived, came up dead near Stonehaven, and was towed ashore:—

So Mr. John Wood has bought it for 226 pound,
And has brought it to Dundee all safe and sound;
Which measures 40 feet in length from the snout to
　the tail,
So I advise the people far and near to see it with-
　out fail.

Then hurrah for the mighty monster whale!
Who's got 17 feet 4 inches from tip to tip of a tail;
Which can be seen for a sixpence or a shilling,
That is to say if the people all are willing.

The mental condition of the Melancholy Dane is
not more debatable than that of M'Gonagall. Was his
madness real or feigned? I imagine that at first it had
been no more than harmless conceit; that it was a
rather deliberate pose for a time, when the poet found
it paid; and that finally he became, like the "Sobieski
Stuarts", the victim of his own inventions. He was a
decent-living old man, with a kindly dignity that,
while it need not have forbidden the genial raillery
that his pretensions and compositions provoked, ought
to have prevented the cruel baiting to which he was
subjected by coarse ignoramuses. Not many of those
who laughed at him were so kind as Mr. Lamb, of
Lamb's Hotel, who paid his passage to America, and
sent him passage-money and pocket-money for his
return voyage. M'Gonagall deserved well of his day
and generation, and Time has dealt handsomely with
him. He added to the gaiety of at least one nation,
and, as the Ossian of the ineffably absurd, he has
entered upon immortality.

CHAPTER XIV

SCOTTISH LITERATURE:
ITS FOUNDATIONS AND THE FUTURE

"THERE is no such thing as literature. There are only authors."

That is the disconcerting kind of dictum whereby the plain man as literary critic kicks the foundations from under the neatly jointed edifice of literary genealogies, influences, schools, and inter-relations, reared by the lover of evolutionary coherences and harmonies. The evolutionary aspect of literature was stressed by critics like Brunetière and Georg Brandes, for whom literary criticism was really one of the highest branches of social philosophy. Their position was derided by Sir Arthur Quiller-Couch, for whom a genius, or a work of genius, was virtually a special creation.

The extremists on one side underestimate the incalculable factor of creative genius, which is miraculous inasmuch as it produces something organically new that could not possibly be deduced or predicated from previous literature. The extremists on the other side postulate too great a miracle. They are very much of the school of Leibniz, who conceived of human beings as monads, or separate essences, as unrelated to one another as a row of watches in a shop window, but happening, by a miracle of the divine

Watchmaker, to have been so constructed and wound up that they kept approximately the same time, and thus gave the illusion of inter-relation. Where a watch went slow, that was dullness or idiocy. Where it went fast, that was genius or madness.

For myself, I fully admit the miracle of creative genius, but I utterly reject the monadic hypothesis. During the whole of my conscious life, I have been constantly and vividly aware of the organic solidarity of mankind, manifesting itself in a perpetual electric stream of vibratory influences both in time and in space. To these influences the creative genius is not less but more sensitive than other men, but he possesses the magic power of organizing them into a vital something which is different from their collective sum and which itself exercises a vibratory influence. But in doing so he consciously contributes to something which is already there, something which grew up long before he was thought of, and which transcends his own mind.

That something is literature, the imaginative sublimation of the common mind of humanity, and the only thing by which a people is really known to other peoples, or exerts a definite influence upon posterity. The Phoenicians gave Europe an alphabet, but they wrote little in it but bills of lading. Of the world-stream of literature they were unconscious, and so they contributed nothing of value to it. Phra the Phoenician connotes only tin and Tyrian purple and a little geography. In our thoughts he has no share. But Plato and Isaiah are part of our brain fibre.

When one looks back over the literary history of three thousand years, and over one's own reading, one is inclined to reverse the dictum of the plain man and declare: "There are no authors. There is only literature."

Strictly speaking, there is, for us, only one literature: Indo-Semitic-European. From that great stream all our thoughts derive; to it all our written thoughts return. But to ignore the modifications of it by race experience into what are called national literatures would be merely stupid. And the very fact of the essential oneness of what to us is literature justifies us in asserting that there may be, and indeed must be, a Scottish variety of it as well as an English, an Irish, a French, or a German variety. For what is expressed in the variant or modification is not late and adventitious conditions, political and economic, that are shared by a certain group of peoples, but immemorial distinctiveness of race and of racial and national experience. People who declare they can see nothing distinctively Scottish in modern Scottish literature are merely confessing their own lack of mental colour, and their inability to perceive in real Scottish books the inevitable expression of a particular heredity and tradition. They would be equally incapable of perceiving the essential difference between English and French literature.

By 1700, there had been almost no intermingling between English and Scots. Both nations had long separate histories behind them. Their characters were fixed. The remarkable difference in their histories is well known. Less familiar is the racial

difference which is at the root of the historical
contrast.

Britain up to the Cheviots was entirely Brythonic
for perhaps a thousand years before the coming of the
Romans. Then for nearly four centuries it was
Romanized, or rather cosmopolized, by thousands of
soldier settlers from all parts of the Roman Empire,
as far as Syria. Then came the Anglo-Saxon, Danish,
and Norman infiltrations. The final product was a
highly mixed and highly civilized people, with a
richly varied mentality that expresses itself in English
literature.

The inhabitants of Britain north of Hadrian's Wall
were Brythonic in the south, Gaelic in the west, and
Pictish in the east and north-east. They were all Celts
of some kind, with an Iberian substratum common to
all Britain; and they represented the older, more
primitive, more fiercely warlike branches of the Celtic
family. They were not to any reckonable extent
Romanized, and the only subsequent additions were
a few Angles in the south-east corner, a few Flemish
and Saxon settlers on the eastern beaches, and a fringe
of Norse in Shetland, Orkney, Caithness, the Lews,
and Skye. When the Celtic kingdom was consolidated,
most of the Teutons and Scandinavians were driven
out. The Anglo-Normans who subsequently were
invited in were relatively few in numbers. Thus the
final make-up must have been at least seventy-five
per cent. Celtic of the hard old breed, and not more
than twenty-five per cent. "foreign".

All of which accounts easily enough for the characteristics of dourness, vehemence, hardiness, fierce

logicality, and essential romanticism that distinguish
the Scot, and also for his almost insane individualism,
and his backwardness in the homelier arts of life. The
Celt reacts badly to industrialism, as witness the slums
of Glasgow and Dublin, and the singular repulsiveness
of the Lanarkshire coal-mining area.

I am certainly not contending that the final result of
racial composition and history in the Scotland of
today is finer than the product in England. I merely
assert that it is in some essentials profoundly different.
And, such as it is, the Scot cannot escape from it. He
is better not to try. His only wise plan is to work
within it and through it, and make himself the very
best kind of Scot, which means a very good kind of
European.

For the real preservative against national or provincial narrowness, as the rather lamentable history
of Scotland in the seventeenth century shows, is not
un- or anti-Scottishness, or a crude attempt at Anglifi-
cation (which means copying the things of which
England is least proud), but simply an active awareness
that a Scot, like an Englishman, a Dane, or a Czech, is
a particular modification of a European. In short, the
only safe standard for the Scot is the national and
international standard.

I do not propose to try to show how that standard
has been observed or departed from in our literature.
The Jamesian poets were strongly influenced by
Chaucer. They would not have been influenced to
such good purpose, or so well avoided merely copying
him, had they not had inherent standards of their own,
largely derived, one knows not how, from that very

My Scotland

Celticism which they had learned to despise. Their
international eclecticism is in marked contrast with
the sour inbreeding of the denationalized Scottish
mentality in the seventeenth century, when writers
were cut off both from the old Scottish culture and
contemporary European culture. In the eighteenth
century, the return, first to the old Scottish tradition,
and then to the international tradition, led up to the
triumphs of Burns and Scott. Nothing in literature is
more remarkable than the sure instinct with which
both writers took up what we now can see were the
absolutely right lines. The miracle of genius was
operating in both cases. But both had an absolutely
clear consciousness of Scottish literature.

That consciousness was lost in the half-century succeeding Scott's death. One need not go further than
that for an explanation of the poor show that all
Scottish writers except Carlyle made in that period.
They had lost the native tradition, the literary sense
of Scottishness. They floundered about in the English
scheme of things, and never caught on to anything
vital. Black made a return to Scotland—a tourist-
return—and did well on it. With Lang and Stevenson,
the consciousness of Scotland, the awareness of a
Scottish literature, came back. Scottish writers began
to get on the rails. The ministerial authors, hampered
by the curious un-Scottishness that the Church had
fostered almost since Knox, ran off on a side line with
a Sunday school picnic, and got stuck in the Kailyard.
Douglas Brown blew up the side line, and, after some
fumbling, the main line was rediscovered. It turned
out to be a mainly Highland line.

Scottish Literature

More than a century before, Ossian-Macpherson had inebriated Europe with a semi-spurious blend of Gaelic spirit. That phenomenon was repeated to some slight extent in the vogue of "Fiona Macleod", who found in Hebridean scenery, myth, and old religious poetry the media of a glamorous melancholy which was that of an exotically artistic European. But Sharp's attempt to plant out hothouse flowers in the Western Isles was countered by the genuine Gaelic studies of Irish poet-scholars, and by the authentic renderings of Gaelic life, thought, and idiom in the novels and stories of Neil Munro.

Munro's interests were mainly romantic and idyllic, and he did not deal much with contemporary Gaeldom and its human problems. But his example compelled an approach to vraisemblance in the Jacobite novels and plays that have been produced in such numbers since Stevenson's time. Further development was presaged by John Brandane's delightful comedy, *The Glen is Mine*, which was not only modern but topical. Later came George Blake's realistic plays of modern Highland life, *The Mother* and *Fledglings*.

The way was cleared for novels of an entirely new kind about the Highlands. Neil Gunn, Robert Craig, Fionn Mac Colla, L. A. G. Strong, Ian Macpherson, and James Barke are among the younger writers, most of them Gaelic-speaking, who have dealt with modern Gaelic life in a more or less naturalistic fashion, and who have faced out the actual human implications of landlordism, evictions, the sporting system, migration, Calvinism, the Gaelic ebb, and so forth. The central tragedy of the Highlands, the ruthless supplanting of crofter life by Lowland farmers and the "hungry sheep", is the theme of one of the most powerful novels yet written about the Highlands, Ian Macpherson's *Land of Our Fathers*.

John Buchan's *Montrose* has played a part in the re-orientation of Scottish history, and his excellent Scottish novels form a link between the Stevenson and Kailyard period and the era marked by the Lowland novels of Mrs. Carswell, George Blake, Dot Allan, the Muirs, Bruce Marshall, Campbell Nairne, Eric Linklater, Lewis Grassic Gibbon, and other writers. Of these novels the most notable is *Sunset Song*. Epical in conception, and lyrically racy of the soil, it is of absolutely central interest. In a dying country-side the life-impulse wildly and blindly asserts itself among a dying race. That is the sombre pedal-note that sounds beneath all the fuss and rattle and tintinnabulation of urbanized Scotland.

What is the real inwardness of this remarkable fiction series, culminating in books like *Sunset Song* and *Land of Our Fathers*, and including works so varied as *Hatter's Castle* and *Mrs. Barry*; of dramas like those of James Bridie, Gordon Daviot, Joe Corrie, and Robins Millar; of Lewis Spence's Edinburgh and Middle Scots poetry, William Jeffrey's transcendental fantasias on scenery and towns, the lyrical and other verses of Pittendrigh MacGillivray, Alexander Gray, Marion Angus, Orgill Mackenzie, William Soutar, W. D. Cocker, and many another poet, and the extraordinary progress of Hugh MacDiarmid from pure inimitable lyricism to a poetry in which traditional

Scottish Literature

moulds are broken and shivered by intense intellectual
dynamic?

To all this there was nothing corresponding in the
Scotland of twenty or thirty years ago. One cannot
account for it simply by the fortuitous arrival of genius
and talent. The 'nineties had Davidson and Douglas
Brown and the young Neil Munro; yet in the 'nineties
the stream of Scottish literature that is now broadening was barely visible.

The reason for the broadening of that stream must
be looked for in literature itself. Potential writers in
Scotland have become more conscious of European
literature and therefore of Scottish literature. The
slogans, "Back to Dunbar" and "Back to Gaelic",
have meant something that cleverly superficial people
missed.

Not all potential Scots writers would be enamoured
of the old Scots poets; only a few would follow their
tradition. Not many might write in Gaelic, or even
in a Gaelic fashion, though all would as a matter of
course learn something of Gaelic and its literature.
But the consciousness that Scottish literature went back
to Dunbar, and beyond Dunbar and the Rhymour to
the Gaelic bards of the old Celtic kingdom and the
old western Gaeldom, to illustrious primeval sources
represented linguistically by the stream of Gaelic still
flowing beside the modern main stream of Scottish
culture and waiting to enrich it, operated a subtle
change in the outlook of every cultured Scot. He
realized that the wonderful things that had come down
to him from the old Scotland, and kept Scottishness
alive in his blood, were parts of a great racial and

299

national tradition. The cataclysm of the world war helped to make him aware that the literary stream on which he was floating was not a mere tributary of English literature, navigable only for light-draught vessels, but a long, deep waterway, opening out direct upon the main oceans and channels of world literature, and affording room and depth for any type of craft.

What is loosely called the Scottish Literary Renaissance simply means that the artificial inhibitions and limitations which the Burns and Scott achievements were made to fasten upon Scots literature have been removed. A Scot, as Scot, and not as ex-Scot or Anglo-Scot, may write *A Sleeping Clergyman* or *Juan in America*; and enfranchisement in this regard had already been signalized by the cosmopolitan themes and renown of the doyen of Scottish literature, that true Scot and illustrious artist, R. B. Cunninghame Graham. Within the ambit of Scottish life, a Scots writer can postulate the complete diapason of passion and intellect, range from heaven to hell, from hell to heaven, and reveal a European universal in a Scottish particular. He can realize himself as world-citizen only by giving bravely complete expression to himself as Scot; he can become a true and complete Scot only by realizing the continuity of Scots literature with world literature.

Enough has been said on current and topical aspects of this subject, in the Press and elsewhere. What seems worth emphasizing is that the real inspiration of our modern literary movement, and of every other national movement of account in Scotland, has been Scottish literature itself, not in the narrow interpretation given to it by certain scholars who have been over-anxious to show its thematic limitations and its dependence upon English literature, but in the wider and more vital conception of it entertained by cultured and active-minded young Scots, who see in it no mere empty shell of a past and dead Scotland, but the organic principle of our nation, from which they draw their own general inspiration and to which they make their own particular contributions, not as imitators, or even as pupils, but as free inheritors of a vital tradition, capable of infinite adjustment and development, and becoming the more itself the more it is organically changed. It is from Scottish literature that they derive their "freedom of Scotland".

That is my peroration; but there are two remaining points on which something has to be said.

To stigmatize as "provincial" a movement which places the Scottish mind where the English, Danish, Serbian, or Russian mind is—at the centre of the universe—and which takes Scotland as a microcosm, is a wilful abuse of language. The provincial attitude is the one which regards Scots literature as a mere branch and feeder of English literature, restricted to "matter of Habbie Simpson", third-rate thinking, and the kind of cosy sentiment, stereotyped romanticism, and facile funniosity that appeals to people who are wrapped up in the cotton wool of bourgeois respectability. English literature itself has suffered through the parasitic adherence of provincial literatures which did not come up to its old national standard; and provincialism on an imperial scale has been fostered by the assumption, say, that the English-speaking races, stupidly described as "Anglo-Saxon", were superior to all other races in moral conduct and sensitiveness, and in inherent human worth. From that assumption the writers of Scotland, England, Ireland, Canada, South Africa, Australia, and America must once for all dissociate themselves.

Some of our younger writers appear to think that it would be well for Scotland and its literature if we simply forgot all that had been written in and about Scotland before 1920, and gave all our living writers over fifty a substantial old-age pension on condition that they never wrote another line. They adduce Finland as an example of a country which managed to build up a fine modern civilization and culture because it was unhampered by an old literature.

It is certainly better for a country to start with no literature than to be bound down by certain sections or periods of its past literature, as was, until recently, the case with Scotland. But, as a matter of fact, modern Finnish civilization, when it came into being about a century ago, was based entirely, and consciously, upon literature. Its foundation was the *Kalevala*, the epic collection of old Finnish poems, embodying ancient native myths and legends, made by Elias Lönnrot. The *Kalevala* inspired and coloured the whole imaginative and social life of the Finns, and it has formed the spiritual basis and starting-point of Finnish literature, art, and music. If a moral can be drawn for Scotland, it is that our poets, dramatists, artists, and musicians should make far more than they have done hitherto of the old Gaelic legends, mythology and folk-lore, which belong to Scotland as much as to Ireland. In any case, it is only from the basis of our literature as a whole, with prominent inclusion of its primitive Celtic origins, that we can go forward creatively into the changing future as a real literary nation.